KRUEGER'S MEN

KRUEGE

ALSO BY LAWRENCE MALKIN

The National Debt

R'S MEN

The Secret Nazi Counterfeit Plot
and the Prisoners of Block 19

Lawrence Malkin

LITTLE, BROWN AND COMPANY
New York Boston London

Little, Brown and Company
Hachette Book Group USA
1271 Avenue of the Americas, New York, NY 10020
Visit our Web site at www.HachetteBookGroupUSA.com

First Edition: September 2006

The views and opinions expressed in this book and the context in which the image of the crowd of survivors at Ebsenee (66290) is used do not necessarily reflect the views or policy of, nor imply approval or endorsement by, the United States Holocaust Memorial Museum.

Maps by Paul J. Pugliese

Library of Congress Cataloging-in-Publication Data

Malkin, Lawrence.
    Krueger's men : the secret Nazi counterfeit plot and the prisoners of Block 19 / by Lawrence Malkin — 1st ed.
        p. cm.
    Includes bibliographical references and index.
    ISBN-10: 0-316-05700-2
    ISBN-13: 978-0-316-05700-4
    1. Operation Bernhard, Germany, 1940–1945. 2. World War, 1939–1945 — Counterfeit money — Great Britain. 3. World War, 1939–1945 — Conscript labor — Poland — Oswiecim. I. Title.
D810.C85M36 2006
940.54'8743 — dc22

2006001334

10 9 8 7 6 5 4 3 2 1

Q-MART

Book design by Renato Stanisic

Printed in the United States of America

In memory of

Paul David Stark
He brought his family through the storm.

Endless money forms the sinews of war.

—MARCUS TULLIUS CICERO, 43 B.C.

[*Nervos belli; pecuniam infinitam.* Philippics, V. ii. 5]

CONTENTS

Major Characters

The Nazis

Wilhelm Canaris, chief of the Abwehr, the traditional military intelligence service.

Reinhard Heydrich, chief of the Reichssicherheitshauptamt, Hitler's security service; assassinated near Prague in 1942.

Wilhelm Hoettl, SS intelligence chief for the Balkans; based in Vienna; Operation Bernhard's Nazi laureate.

Bernhard Krueger, textile engineer by training and SS forger by assignment; chief of the operation that bore his name.

Albert Langer, cryptographer and technical director of the first, unsuccessful counterfeiting attempt known as Operation Andreas.

Alfred Naujocks, SS brawler and hit man in charge of Operation Andreas.

Arthur Nebe, chief of the Nazis' criminal police.

August Petrich, Nazi commercial printer.

Walter Schellenberg, SS chief of foreign intelligence and espionage; picked Bernhard Krueger as his chief counterfeiter.

Kurt Werner, fanatical chief of the concentration camp guards in Block 19.

Prisoners in Block 19

Adolf Burger, printer from Slovakia; author of a memoir about Operation Bernhard.

Felix Cytrin, toolmaker from Leipzig; chief of the engraving section.

Peter Edel, young artist from Berlin; his brushes and graphic tools were shipped to Sachsenhausen.

Max Groen, Dutch newsreel cameraman; organized the prisoners' cabaret evenings.

Abraham Jacobson, Dutch printing plant manager and reserve army officer; chief of the phototype section.

Avraham Krakowski, pious young accountant who wrote a memoir.

Hans Kurzweil, Viennese bookbinder; chief of the document-forging section.

Moritz Nachtstern, Norwegian stereotyper; wrote the first and most detailed memoir of the prisoners' life.

Salomon Smolianoff, master forger; the only career criminal among Krueger's men.

Oskar Stein (aka Skala), Czech businessman; bookkeeper and chief clerk.

BANKERS, MONEY-LAUNDERERS, INVESTIGATORS, AND ASSORTED RASCALS

Hans Adler, Viennese expert in tracking and indexing counterfeit currency.

Elyesa Bazna (aka Cicero), valet to the British ambassador to Turkey; Germany's most successful wartime spy.

Basil Catterns, Bank of England official unconcerned about enemy counterfeiting.

William J. "Wild Bill" Donovan, chief of the Office of Strategic Services, U.S. wartime espionage agency.

Ronald Howe, deputy commissioner of Scotland Yard; chief of liaison with foreign police and anticounterfeit organizations.

George McNally, U.S. Secret Service agent; investigated whether Operation Bernhard forged dollars.

Ivan Miassojedoff (aka Eugen Zotow), prize-winning Russian artist and counterfeiter; passed on his skills to Smolianoff.

Sir Kenneth Oswald (K.O.) Peppiatt, chief cashier of the Bank of England; during his tenure his signature appeared on every pound note, real or forged.

Friedrich Schwend (aka Dr. Wendig), chief money-launderer for the counterfeit Bernhard millions.

Georg Spitz, Schwend's money-launderer in the Netherlands.

Jaac van Harten, Schwend's money-launderer in Hungary.

David Waley, senior British Treasury official, close associate of the economist John Maynard Keynes.

Europe Under the Nazis
Maximum Extent of Hitler's
Domination, Winter 1942–43

FINLAND

Leningrad

kholm

altic

ea

Moscow

S O V I E T   U N I O N

◄ Maximum advance
of German Forces

GENERAL
VERNMENT
(POLAND)

Auschwitz

Kiev

Stalingrad

AKIA

HUNGARY

idapest

Odessa

Caspian Sea

ROMANIA

Black Sea

SERBIA

BULGARIA

BANIA

Istanbul

Ankara

T U R K E Y

IRAN

GREECE

Athens

IRAQ

anean   Sea

SYRIA

Tel Aviv

PALESTINE

TRANSJORDAN

SAUDI
ARABIA

EGYPT

KRUEGER'S MEN

Chapter 1

ATTACK THE POUND THE WORLD AROUND

The Second World War was barely two weeks old when leaders of Nazi espionage and finance gathered in a paneled conference room in Germany's Finanzministerium, at Wilhelmstrasse 61. Like that of the other overbearing buildings lodged behind pseudo-classical fronts, its architecture was proud and brooding. Most windows gracing this official avenue were topped by a heavy triangular tympanum. But the Finance Ministry had been erected in the 1870s without this classical adornment, adopting instead the Italianate style of a Medici palace. Wilhelmstrasse, Berlin's Pennsylvania Avenue, its Whitehall, gloried in the name of the kaisers of imperial Germany. The Finance Ministry stood toward its southern end. Farther down, the street was intersected by Prinz-Albrecht-Strasse, where stood a huge, pillared palace, the L-shaped headquarters of the Gestapo.

The plan on the Ministry's conference table on September 18, 1939, was simple. Why not have the Reichsbank print millions of counterfeit British banknotes, unload them on the streets and rooftops of the enemy, and then stand aside as the British economy collapsed? The idea of printing enemy currency was not especially new or even original; similar plans also rippled across the desks of no less than Franklin D. Roosevelt and Winston Churchill. A hundred and fifty years before, the British had counterfeited the currency of the French Revolution to stoke the inflation already created by the revolutionaries' own printing presses. And Frederick the Great, who had forged the unforgiving Prussian military ethos that molded the German state, had also forged money to undermine his eighteenth-century enemies. But these schemes had all been hatched in a preindustrial age. Now, given the immense resources and brutal efficiency of Adolf Hitler's war machine, it should be much easier to print English banknotes on a vast scale, in greater quantities than any counterfeit bills ever produced before.

It was not beyond calculation that the Nazi plot could devastate the economy of Britain and its empire, whose worldwide commerce was transacted through the financial nerve center of the City of London, which enriched Britain's gentry while financing its wars. Details were put forward by Arthur Nebe, chief of the SS criminal police. Nebe, a schoolteacher's son and an ambitious, opportunistic senior civil servant, habitually injected himself into the many conspiracies that lay at the heart of the Nazi movement. He was a party member even before Hitler came to power in 1933, whose principal utility was his knowledge of the criminal underworld. Inventive and sinister, he was ever at the service of his superiors. Nebe had helped Hitler win supreme command of the armed forces in 1938 by fingering War Minister Werner von Blomberg's new wife as a former prostitute, forcing the old Prussian's resignation in disgrace. Nebe was the German representative on the International Criminal Police Commission, formed after World War I principally to track counterfeiters and drug smugglers across Europe's borders and later known as Interpol, from its cable address. After the Nazis marched into Austria in 1938, they moved the commission's headquarters from Vienna to Berlin, gaining access to fifteen years of case files and suborning its original purpose of tracking counterfeiters and drug smugglers. (Nebe also helped adapt the mobile gas van, originally used in the Nazi euthanasia of mental patients, for mass murder in

Eastern Europe to soothe the sensibilities of the Reich security chief, Heinrich Himmler, who said he could not stand the sight of people being shot, even Jews.)

Nebe proposed mobilizing the extensive roster of professional counterfeiters in his police files. His immediate superior was Reinhard Heydrich, protégé of Himmler, the leader of the murderous SS, the Schutzstaffel (Defense Squadron), that began as the Nazi Party's armed militia. Heydrich was not in the least constrained by any legal scruples or even police protocol in rejecting Nebe's proposal, but he excluded the use of police files lest this discredit Germany's control over the international police organization, of which he was titular chief. Instead, he wanted to continue using the commission's European network to track down anti-Nazis and Jews who had escaped from Germany. Heydrich also hoped to extend his reach as far as the U.S. Federal Bureau of Investigation in order to obtain U.S. passport forms for possible forgery. (The FBI remained hesitantly in touch with the International Criminal Police Commission, breaking all contact only three days before Japan attacked Pearl Harbor on December 7, 1941.)

However resistant he was about using criminal files, Heydrich was enthusiastic about the counterfeit plan from the start. As cunning as he was cruel, he was an avid reader of spy stories. He liked to sign his memos with the single initial C in the mode of the English espionage thrillers fashionable between the wars. (It was and in fact remains the code letter for the chief of the British secret service.) Heydrich's days were full of dark assemblings. He ran Himmler's Reichssicherheitshauptamt (RSHA), the Reich Central Security Office. It compiled huge files on Germans suspected of disloyalty or liberal connections, and of course on Jews, whose methodical extermination Heydrich planned and initially supervised. He had his office in the Gestapo building itself, and his SS intelligence network eventually rivaled and finally took over the Abwehr, the old-line military espionage service headed by

Admiral Wilhelm Canaris, who had been first officer on the training ship on which Heydrich had sailed as a naval cadet.

Heydrich was as physically self-confident as Himmler was shy and short-sighted. He was a skier, aviator, and fencer, and succeeded at whatever he did, even at playing the violin with fierce emotion, as he had with Frau Canaris as a young officer at the Canarises' musical evenings. Heydrich's inner tensions were betrayed principally by his high, metallic voice, his harsh temper, and his nightclubbing habits in Berlin, where the women preferred his aides to the wolf-eyed officer with prodigious sexual appetites.

The only serious objection to the counterfeiting plan came from Walther Funk, a homosexual former financial journalist, fat and well fed, who served as Hitler's economics minister. Funk was the Nazis' principal liaison to German industry until the bitter end and the titular head of the Reichsbank. He refused the use of the Berlin laboratories of the central bank's print shop, warning that the counterfeiting plan was contrary to international law and that it simply would not work. He was supported by legal advice from the military high command. Funk also demanded that fake bills be barred from Germany's conquered territories. He knew that the locals would dump Nazi scrip for what they thought were real pound notes. The last thing he needed while bleeding their resources for the Reich would be an infusion of forged pounds soaking up his overvalued and suspect occupation currency.

Joseph Goebbels also found the idea grotesque — *"einen grotesken Plan,"* as he wrote in his diary — but he did not reject it out of hand. A similar plan had already been mooted privately to Goebbels by Leopold Gutterer, one of his most imaginative deputies. On September 6, Gutterer suggested dumping notes over Britain in quantities large enough to equal 30 percent of the currency in circulation. That would mean tons of paper for the overstretched Luftwaffe to carry, but it was the kind of mad scheme forever being dreamed up by Goebbels's own Propaganda Ministry, the megaphone for Hitler's Big Lies — the more often repeated, the more they stuck.

Goebbels, a blindly devoted follower who had spread the "Heil Hitler" greeting among Nazi Party members, was the only person with an advanced degree — he had a doctorate in philology — to remain in Hitler's immediate entourage throughout the war, and one of the very few with any college education at all. He confided his misgivings to his diary: "But what if the English do the same to us? I [will] let the plan be further explored." Whether Goebbels was represented at the September 18 meeting is unknown, but he clearly was well aware that a whiff of counterfeit paper might blow away the Reich's finances. They were already stacked as delicately as a house of cards because Hitler had refused to endanger his solid bourgeois support by raising taxes to rearm Germany until the day after the war actually began.

Despite the intense secrecy, word of the counterfeiting plan soon reached London. The Berlin meeting was outlined comprehensively in a letter from Michael Palairet, chief of the British legation in Athens and the very model of an English aristocrat representing his class and country. (His daughter married into the ennobled family of Britain's World War I prime minister, Herbert Asquith.) Palairet's letter to London was marked "Very Confidential" and dated November 21 — just two months after the September 18 meeting — and contained material from the notebook of a Russian émigré named Paul Chourapine. Exactly how Chourapine had come by the information was not explained, nor were his sources named. He had been tossed out of Greece by the police in October and deported to France, where he could not be further interrogated. But his report was startling in both its detail and the level of its political and financial sophistication.

During a conference of experts in monetary matters held on the 18th September of this year at the German Ministry of Finance, the following plan was discussed:

"Offensive against Sterling and Destruction of its Position as World Currency"

This plan, which was unanimously approved, contemplates in the first place the necessity of careful preparation and perfect execution of the work enabling the proposed aims to be realised in all the countries of the Near East as well as in North Africa, in the British Colonies and in South America.

It was decided to proceed with the printing in the printing works of the Reichsbank of 30 milliards [billions] of forged bank notes of £1 and of 2 milliards of various other notes. The transfer of these forged notes to foreign countries would be effected through the diplomatic bags of the Ministry of the Navy.

The consular representatives of Germany of the above-mentioned countries would be charged with the disposal of this original merchandise in the most prudent manner. They have received instructions to try to obtain at first as much profit as possible until they receive the order to distribute the bank notes at a ridiculous price and even gratuitously, the main object being to flood the money markets with an enormous quantity of forged pounds.

The plan contemplates the moment when these forged notes in spite of their perfect get-up will be discovered. This moment will be the one when the coup which is already being prepared will be executed in the largest exchanges of the world, in those of New York, Amsterdam, The Hague, Lisbon, Rome, Naples, etc. and which is to lead to the collapse of sterling or to its serious depreciation. To make the success of this coup possible, the Ministry of Propaganda is to start an accusation against the Bank of England of having itself put the forged currency into circulation with the object of ensuring the support of the "pays états" [nation-states] and of concealing from the world its own bankruptcy.

The Navy and the Air Force of the Reich will be called upon to perform certain great exploits, if possible spectacular, which should coincide with the execution of the coup explained above.

Confidence in the British currency having been destroyed, the [German] mark will be able to overrun the world market.

This document is the only known contemporaneous description of the Germans' original plan. Although the scheme was modified by the exigencies of war — and what battle plan is not? — Chourapine had captured its essence.

British diplomats shared the Athens memo with the Americans in February 1940. Herschel Johnson, the highly respected senior career diplomat at the American embassy in London, quickly passed a summary to Washington, where the State Department then warned the Treasury. Washington was watching apprehensively lest the dollar also become a counter in a game that many Americans hoped to stay out of, considering it Europe's war and the Nazis as Europe's problem.

The directors of the Bank of England, anachronistically known as "the Court," were soon alerted, along with Sir Montagu Norman, the Bank's governor. Norman ran the place with an iron hand, and the Bank's inner circle kept the information so close that for many years the staff did not know Palairet's letter had been its principal tip. Instead, they believed it had come via a dubious character dealing with the British embassy in Paris. This kind of obfuscation characterized the Bank's smug, pusillanimous behavior from then on. And indeed, for years the Bank of England was unable and, until recently, unwilling to tell the full story because its officials insisted that many of their own records had been transferred to the British secret services or lost. After the war, officials of the Bank even destroyed some records on their own.

If viewed merely as an espionage caper, the plot is one of the more benign of the Nazis' many nefarious projects endemic to such a gangster regime. But the story touches a deeper nerve and still prompts inquiries almost every month to the Bank of England, a perverse tribute to the continuing fascination with Nazi totalitarianism, which even today stimulates the darkest infantile fantasies of absolute power and stolen wealth. Allied experts later described it as "the most successful counterfeiting enterprise of all time," and Allied strategists at the highest level also realized their own vulnerability: an attack by them on the currency of a totalitarian country could not succeed. But for the Nazis, the plot proved effective in amassing loot and financing operations of marginal military utility but great propaganda value. Their best spy ended up in the movies, even though Berlin ignored his information. Their most daring commando won a place in history books, where he hardly deserved a mention. Bizarre as it was, the plot succeeded, although not in the way intended. As it ran its course, it demonstrated how easily the chaotic nature of totalitarian finance can degenerate into venal self-destruction. The British were embarrassed for half a century, but they won the war. The fundamental lesson applies today, and indeed whenever new kinds of warfare appear. In a war of choice, even the most imaginative plans for its conduct and financing can spin out of control if untested by the critical questioning essential to democracy.

A criminal subculture of counterfeiting coalesced early in the twentieth century as gold coins began giving way to printed banknotes. Between the wars, counterfeit currency circulated in the streets, shops, and back rooms of Europe. Some of the most notorious counterfeiters were failed artists like Hitler himself.

But in some countries, false bills were far less a danger than the threat posed by real ones. Every German had suffered the damage done by printing presses' spewing out billions of banknotes on the orders of the democratic Weimar Republic. Determining the first cause of that historic hyperinflation of 1923 is more than a theoretical debate of interest only to economists and their allied ideologues. Was it a deliberate move to cheapen Germany's currency in order to promote the exports that would pay Germany's punitive war debts? Was it designed to save workers' jobs? Or to enrich the great corporations and property owners by liquidating their debts? Perhaps all of these. Currencies had also collapsed in the new states of Austria, Hungary, and Poland following the demise of the Austro-Hungarian Empire in World War I. During the ensuing panic, stable currency — even when it was false — was in frantic demand. In port cities, sailors coming off ships were mobbed with offers to buy their foreign currency. With each passing minute the local scrip was worth dramatically more or less, depending on violent monetary fluctuations that undermined society and trust in authority.

In the interwar years, money therefore was rarely valued as a dependable standard of wealth as it had been throughout the rise of the bourgeoisie during the hundred-year peace that was shattered in 1914. Thereafter, no country stepped forward to serve as what economists call a hegemon, a conductor of the international orchestra, providing financial and physical security. Britain had filled that role during the Victorian age with its pound sterling and the Royal Navy, as America later would during the Cold War with the almighty dollar and the atomic bomb. But between the wars, money became a weapon. Trade could be manipulated by raising tariffs and devaluing currency to favor local products, thus seizing jobs and profits from other nations. Everybody accused everybody else, usually justifiably, of policies known as "beggar thy neighbor."

The Germans were only the first to flout the old rules with a competitive devaluation that would have been impossible under the prewar gold standard. They were followed by the French, who allowed their currency to cheapen against the dollar in the 1920s (incidentally attracting Jazz Age spenders to France and gold into French mattresses). America and Britain also engaged in a battle of wits, each trying to cheapen or strengthen its currency against the other's. The odds were stacked in favor of America, which sat on a hoard of gold earned by the wartime sale of raw materials and arms to Europe, who had borrowed from Wall Street to pay for the war.

Nevertheless, the British sought a richer pound as the lifeblood of their empire. In 1925 they went back on the gold standard, restoring the dollar value of the pound to $4.86 in order to maintain London as a financial center with a trusted currency that, in theory at least, could be exchanged for gold. As a result, British workers suffered while their counterparts in France and America thrived. In 1931, at the start of the Great Depression, the pound was finally knocked off gold and sank to $4.05. Even at that rate, British goods were too expensive. And a strong pound, easily exchanged with other currencies, made it the obvious target for counterfeiters. Why bother to print fake marks, francs, or even dollars when their value was so uncertain? British schoolboys, twisting the familiar mnemonic of volume and weight, chanted the almost mythological rhyme, "The pound's a pound, the world around." And for the wicked, the pound's stability was a magnet.

Hitler's Germany, short of gold and foreign currency even before he took power in 1933, shrewdly managed trade under a financial genius with the curious name of Hjalmar Horace Greeley Schacht. (He dropped his two American names; perhaps his parents had been influenced by Goethe's prophetic remark, *"Amerika, du hast es besser."*) Schacht's was no free-market solution. Between 1934 and 1938, Germany had concluded two-way treaties with twenty-seven countries, tying up its traditional trading partners in the Balkans, southeastern Europe, and Latin America. They essentially bartered their raw materials for whatever industrial goods Germany wanted to send them. With all foreign trade controlled by the Reich and Germany's currency kept at an artificially strong 40 U.S. cents to the mark by controls on all foreign transactions, Germany was able to pay less for imported raw materials to rearm. In exchange, it sent back goods like Agfa film and Bayer aspirin, which were hardly essential for Hitler's nascent Panzer divisions. Profits built up in the Reichsbank and were loaned to German companies, prices and wages were controlled, and full employment returned by 1937. Once the high-collared, schoolmasterish Schacht had done his job, he was dismissed in favor of the more tractable Funk.

Hitler soon realized that the construction of autobahns and financial subsidies for industry were not enough to keep Germans at work. The Moloch of modern war has an insatiable appetite for raw materials. Although German industry was the world's most technically advanced, its capacity was smaller than that of Britain's vast empire, which delivered cheap food and captive markets. On November 5, 1937, Hitler called his military chiefs into secret conclave and told them they were to be the instrument for expanding Germany's *Lebensraum*. There were too many Germans on too little land to feed themselves, and Germany, a workshop of Europe with few natural resources, could not live on international trade during a global depression. Its choice lay between participating in the liberal capitalist system (and that had failed), or conquering other countries to supply food, raw materials, and gold. Hitler had already thumbed his nose at the victors of World War I by marching into the occupied Rhineland in 1936. Next he bullied the British and French into selling out Czechoslovakia to him in 1938 for the false promise of peace, and in the same year sent his elite troops into Vienna for millions of Austrians to cheer their own conquest as a liberation. These sudden strikes took place on weekends so Hitler would catch Britain's languorous, appeasing leadership napping at house parties on their country estates.

When Britain and France actually declared war in September 1939 to support Poland's independence, a surprised Hitler is said to have exclaimed to his inner circle, "What now?" But using his pioneering tactic of the *blitzkrieg* — literally, lightning war — the Germans captured rich Polish farmland quickly, then invaded Norway to ensure passage of Swedish iron ore through the northern port of Narvik. Outflanked and overrun, Denmark gave Hitler control of the Baltic Sea. By the same swift maneuvers he would seize the colonial and trading riches of the Low Countries. Then the corrupt Third French Republic fell into his hands like an overripe fruit, after which he assumed London would sue for peace and leave the Continent to him. Riding high on these conquests, Hitler and his followers did not foresee five and a half years of total war. Quite the contrary. German military strategy depended on subduing an isolated and starving Britain into a vassal of the Thousand-Year Reich, ideally by negotiation with those who had at first tried to appease Hitler, but by force if necessary. But the British refused to cooperate. So on another summer Sunday, in June 1941, Hitler finally overreached and attacked his unprepared ally, the Soviet Union.

The Allies reckoned Hitler would run out of credit to carry on his lightning attacks and they would stall into another round of trench warfare on the Western front. This was a wild miscalculation. Most of Germany's war-making power was squeezed from its conquered territories: Belgium, Holland, and France sent millions in daily "occupation costs." Approximately $3 billion more came from German Jews, bled of their riches as they fled or were chased from Nazi Germany during the 1930s. Unlike many Jews in the United States and Britain, who became rich in finance, Jews in

Germany were prominent industrialists. Jewish scientists had been in the forefront of Germany's belated industrialization. Emil Rathenau, for example, founded AEG, the giant utility company that brought electricity to Berlin, in 1887. (His son Walther organized and ran Germany's foreign purchases of raw materials during World War I, served as a liberal foreign minister in the Weimar Republic, and was assassinated in 1922 by nationalist fanatics.) Perhaps another $6 billion was squeezed or stolen from Jews in conquered nations. Billions more, of course, would be wrung from slave labor and outright looting of wealth, especially the gold reserves in the central banks of conquered nations. Counterfeit currency would be just one more financial tactic.

For the Nazis, it was totally in character to try to undermine British finance even as they had hoped to persuade London to join in some kind of political partnership (in practice, it would have been that of a British horse with a German rider). Hitler had believed London would be open to a deal. Hadn't many highborn Tories been hoping he would turn east against the Bolsheviks, knock them out, and then, as Hitler himself hoped, arrange for the two major Aryan powers of Europe to dominate its lesser races? To him the British had seemed logical allies, and until 1937, Hitler even prohibited German espionage to operate inside Britain.

Like many Englishmen, and even influential Americans right up to Joseph P. Kennedy, the U.S. ambassador in London and father of a future president, the Germans could not imagine the historic resistance that would be inspired by Winston Churchill when he became prime minister. Like any Englishman of his class, he fully understood the political significance of the pound. Serving as chancellor of the exchequer in 1926, Churchill had been willing to provoke a general strike to restore its value and argued publicly for a strong pound "which everyone knows and can trust."

Undermining the pound was therefore a serious stratagem to the Nazi officials meeting at the Finance Ministry that 18th day of September in 1939. They had already taken on so much, with such incredible success, and now they decided they might deliver the final blow.

Chapter 2

OPERATION ANDREAS

Reinhard Heydrich had always been fascinated by counterfeiting schemes. His first and most important encounter involved the Soviet purges of 1937. The year before, Heydrich had heard through an emigré that Marshal Mikhail Tukhachevsky, a Bolshevik hero of the Russian civil war, was plotting against Stalin. Heydrich immediately decided to feed forged documents to Moscow that might help Stalin destroy the military leadership of the Reich's Soviet enemies. In April 1937, Heydrich gave orders to his forgery factory in Berlin to produce documents that would incriminate Stalin's generals. They were printed within four days with the aid of real Soviet army documents in RSHA files, documents dating from Weimar days, when the Germans had rearmed clandestinely with the help of the Bolsheviks. Supposedly attracted by the bait of these forged documents, the Russians paid Heydrich's men 3 million rubles. But the Soviet currency was marked money, and when it was cycled through German spies in the Soviet Union, they were quickly arrested. Marked money with a face value in the millions had to be destroyed personally by Walter Schellenberg, who would later become Heydrich's foreign intelligence chief.

In fact, Heydrich should have smelled a rat from the start. Stalin himself had already signaled Tukhachevsky's liquidation two months earlier in a speech that foreshadowed the Great Purge of the Bolshevik old guard. The Nazis had ignored all that, even after the fact. Heydrich nevertheless believed it was his forgeries and not Stalin's paranoia that had been instrumental in destroying the Red Army's leadership — as did his colleagues in Nazi espionage who wrote their memoirs, and even Churchill on the other side. So Heydrich, acting on the false lessons of the affair, pressed ahead with the scheme to counterfeit sterling.

Heydrich was the son of a provincial opera singer, and his enemies continually spread false rumors that he had a Jewish grandmother. His barbarity against the Jews may have been one way to demonstrate his racial purity. More likely he was simply a brutal technologist for whom human life was of no importance when ranged against the imperatives of the state. In that sense he was a principal pivot and puppet master of the Nazi regime, supplying his boss Himmler with ideas for its most heinous crimes and then managing them pitilessly. Such was the considered view of Schellenberg, who described his first, unsettling impression of Heydrich as "a tall, impressive figure with a broad, unusually high forehead, small restless eyes as crafty as an animal's and of uncanny power, a long, predatory nose, and a wide full-lipped mouth. His hands were slender and rather too long — they made one think of the legs of a spider." Heydrich had entered the Navy after World War I and rose as a communications specialist to the rank of lieutenant, only to be cashiered in 1931. Investigated by a naval court of honor about a pregnant former girlfriend, he accused her of lying about their affair. The court, insulted by his arrogance, convicted him of insubordination rather than the lesser offense of simple fornication. Heydrich was thrown onto the heap of unemployed millions in the depths of the Depression, his military background and his desperation making him a natural candidate for the SS. There his communications experience led him to code work and intelligence.

The SS was not drawn from graduates of the top class of Germany's fine technical universities but was composed largely of dropouts, brawlers, and opportunist academics with odd ideas that suited the times. Using scraps of philosophy and fake science, these professors helped cook up a dog's dinner of political thought that Hitler and his cronies hoped would make them *salonfähig,* a word normally used by those acceptable in the salons of polite German society to describe those they would exclude.

Until the rise of Hitler, Berlin had been the most modern city in Europe. Half a century before, Mark Twain compared it to Chicago for its energy and invention, and the newly unified German nation had hustled itself into the modern world, applying discoveries in electricity and chemistry that became known as the second industrial revolution. (The British powered the first with steam.) Germany led the world in preventing disease through public health. With its theories of the physical universe, Germany produced a scientific culture that built precision machinery we now would call high technology. A few hundred yards from Wilhelmstrasse, Europe's first traffic light was erected at busy Potsdamer Platz.

But Hitler ignored, perverted, and even rejected the war's genuine scientific opportunities. The jet engine, at first dismissed as unnecessary for long-range bombers, would be approved by Hitler too late to give his Messerschmitt 262 fighters a chance to reconquer the skies from the Allies. Rockets were envisioned only as last-chance weapons of vengeance, again too late to do much good beyond spreading terror when they exploded at random in London. And fortunately for the future of Western civilization, Hitler also vetoed the development of atomic weapons because he thought his enemies would be thoroughly blitzed by the time he could have his own nuclear bomb, which would be too expensive to build anyway.

Instead, the Nazis were suckers for win-the-war gimmicks of the kind that tend to attract inferior intellects and bullies. For example, the German leadership did not follow, and probably would not even have understood, the intense debate within Britain about how to pay for the war. The great economist John Maynard Keynes's widely read pamphlet on the subject advocated carefully calculated tax increases, low interest rates, and forced saving to avoid the inflation that had doubled Britain's prices during World War I. Keynes also opposed rationing as an infringement on the liberty for which the war was being fought. But Hitler was more attracted by the blade of the sword than its handle, even after the postwar inflation that had impoverished the German bourgeoisie. Germany was rationing goods, but the shops offered little except shortages. Because there was no money to tax away, the Nazi solution to paying for the war was to steal it or print it, and they did both.

It was only fitting that an important participant in this fantastic scheme to bring down British finance was the man who fired the first shots of World War II, Alfred Naujocks, an SS major who served as Heydrich's errand boy as well as the whipping boy for his mistakes. While still an engineering student in the Baltic naval port of Kiel, Naujocks became an energetic Nazi Party brawler; his body carried many scars, and his nose had been smashed out of shape by the Communists. Heydrich had been the boss of the storm troopers in Kiel, so when the ambitious Naujocks arrived in Berlin, he became the point man in what we would now call the dirty tricks department of Heydrich's security service. That department was as bad as anything the "low, dishonest decade" of the 1930s produced, to apply the famous phrase of the English poet W. H. Auden, who himself frequented the Berlin demimonde in the Weimar years. Naujocks organized the assassination of an anti-Nazi broadcaster in Prague and in October 1939 served as the muscle man in the kidnapping of two British secret service officers at the Dutch border. (He expropriated their luxury sedan, which he loved to drive at high speed.) In the greatest exploit of his career, Naujocks gave Hitler his flimsy excuse to invade Poland, killing concentration camp prisoners dressed in Polish uniforms to make it appear that they had attacked a German radio station near the Polish border. When his life story was later written up, Naujocks blessed the bombastic title, *The Man Who Started the War.* Amoral, thuggish, and partly educated, he was the kind of enterprising hit man who is indispensable to any gangster enterprise, the Nazi Party included. Heydrich and Naujocks were emblematic of a society that had gone off the rails, exalting racism and even death. All members of the SS wore a belt-buckle badge inscribed, "Meine Ehre heisst Treue" — My honor is [my] loyalty. Not even religion or ideology was implied, only loyalty to Hitler and fealty to orders from above.

Heydrich had made Naujocks commander of the security service's technical section, which also put him nominally in charge of a brothel known as Salon Kitty at Giesebrechtstrasse 11, just off the Kurfürstendamm, then as now Berlin's fashionable avenue of shops and restaurants. The place was under the daily supervision of Arthur Nebe's criminal police and catered to diplomats, providing girls who were multilingual employees of the SS. The customers' conversations were recorded for any useful intelligence, and their passports seized in order to be forged while their pants were, literally, down.

Naujocks's technical command put him in charge of the Nazis' first counterfeiting factory. Its headquarters were located at Delbrückstrasse 6A in a leafy residential neighborhood known eponymously as Grünewald, in the Charlottenburg district just west of downtown Berlin and less than a mile from Salon Kitty. Set in a large garden, the grand stone mansion, with rooms lined in wooden wainscot, was a former SS training center that now turned out incriminating documents like the ones in the Tukhachevsky affair — false passports, identity cards, miniature cameras, portable radio transmitters, and much of the other paraphernalia essential to any secret service.* Naujocks was not technically qualified to supervise a meticulous operation for the duplication of British currency, although readers of the inspired account of his exploits are led to believe that he devised it and supervised it closely. What he really did was to cut red tape with great speed since his operations were known to have Hitler's backing.

Arthur Nebe, the police chief who presented the first detailed plan, had ultimately walked out on the operation because Heydrich would not permit him to use the forgers in his confiscated Interpol files. Operational control was given to Dr. Albert Langer, Naujocks's technical director. Langer, a physicist and mathematician by training, had served in Austria's code-breaking service between the wars, first for the military, then in the political police. Hitler incorporated Austria into the Reich in 1938, and Langer joined the Nazi Party on May 1 of that year, the very first day he was eligible for membership. Naujocks brought him to Berlin to build a code-breaking machine, or so Langer hoped. Instead, he was put to work the following year building the counterfeiting operation from scratch, probably because he was the type of slightly loopy intellectual favored by the Nazis. Among his papers at his death were not only his account of the counterfeiting operation but a treatise on the role of mental processes in curing cancer and another on the symbolism of Freemasonry. One of his assignments in 1939 was to write an article on English symbolism —

---

*This former den of thieves was torn down in the 1980s and, in another bit of the irony that burnishes almost every turn of this tale, was replaced by an agreeable three-story condominium that sits next to a private Jewish primary school at Delbrückstrasse 8. It caters to the children of prosperous Russians who migrated after the fall of the Berlin Wall. The school is guarded against neo-Nazi skinheads and kidnappers by a polite German policeman patrolling outside its high fence, and inside by an aggressively rude Israeli security man who excludes all unknown visitors.

from King Arthur's Round Table to the "Astral-Magic meaning of the Union Jack etc., etc." Langer, a fragile, thin, bespectacled man who walked with a cane, had only a tenuous grip on reality, but because he was surrounded by so many others with similar obsessions, he fit right in.

Initially "not even a pencil or eraser was available, to say nothing of shops or machines," Langer wrote in the only official account that survives from anyone who actually worked full-time at Delbrückstrasse. "Naujocks didn't have the slightest idea about the technical process." But whenever a machine or material was needed and they could not find or develop it themselves, Naujocks could be depended on to obtain it on their relatively tight budget of 2 million reichsmarks (then officially worth about $800,000, or at least $8 million to $10 million in today's money).

Langer was supposed to have a scientist's knowledge of counterfeiting, but the jump from theory to practice was not easy. At first studying secretly at home with the help of his wife, Langer went through the technical literature of engraving, papermaking, and other skills a forger needs. Then he visited factories and workshops for practical knowledge. This preliminary study took him about a fortnight. As a mathematician and code-breaker, he was confident that he already knew enough about arranging serial numbers to make his manufactured bills plausible when presented at banks. But the numbers were the easy part. His team obtained samples of sterling from the police because the Reichsbank had only a few thousand five- and ten-pound notes in its reserves and needed every one of them for foreign purchases of war materiel. Langer and his craftsmen studied the British paper under a microscope and cut out the notes' unprinted surfaces to mash up the blank segments for analysis. They discovered the paper was made of a combination of linen and ramie, a lustrous fiber spun from a tough Asian nettle. The Germans grew plenty of flax to make linen, and they found the ramie plant growing in Hungary. They used calf's-foot glue to stiffen the mash so it could be pressed into paper sheets, following as best they could the old-fashioned manufacturing traditions of the British. These traditions argued for handmade paper, an idea that was hotly disputed by the Nazis because it would slow production. Langer at first proposed handmade sheets large enough to print four bills at once; the alternative was rolling out the paper by machine, which would produce more notes, but at greater risk of detection. With time short, Langer adapted a Dutch machine that shot shredded paper through a sieve. It also left a watermark, a feature of every pound note. He knew that the British crinkled the paper next to their ears to test whether notes were genuine. Once he was satisfied that he had manufactured paper of the requisite thickness, transparency, texture, and consistency, he enlisted testers whose hearing had been sharpened by blindness.

Although the bills now had their own certified British accent, the paper still did not look exactly like British stock. Under the ultraviolet light of a quartz lamp, the standard bank test for suspicious currency in those days, the color of the German paper tilted toward the pink side of the spectrum instead of the British original, which lay somewhere between violet and lilac. Langer concluded that the problem was in the water. Most of the paper was produced to his specifications at the government's Spechthausen factory at Eberswalde, fifty miles from Berlin, and a small amount from the private firm of Hahnemühle, farther west in Dassel, near Hannover. The British paper, Langer knew, had been manufactured since 1725 exclusively at the Portal family factory at Laverstoke in Hampshire.* Langer used a chemical cocktail to duplicate

---

*A wrinkle in this story has been repeated so often it has become part of the mythology: Naujocks and Langer realized — or perhaps learned from spies — that the Portal factory economized with used rags or even mailbags, so Delbrückstrasse supposedly solved its problem by distributing rags to factories for use as machine wipes, had them returned to be washed, and then put them into the stewpot to produce the proper tint. This is not confirmed in any archive.

the water as best he could, thus adjusting the color of the paper to pass his ultraviolet test.

More problematic was the British watermark, which varied in accordance with the alphanumeric combinations designating each issue of notes during the previous twenty years, the serial number of each individual bill, and the name of the man serving as chief cashier of the Bank of England. But when Langer attempted to figure out the precise relationship of these variables, he failed. Duplicating the blurry British watermarks was also no easy matter. The British sieves had been softened by years of use, while the new German copies left more distinct impressions. It took Langer more than a hundred trials to produce a watermark he found indistinguishable from the British.

The Britannia seal in the upper-left-hand corner, a line drawing of a demure young lady sitting on a throne and surrounded by a classical oval design, proved a similar challenge. The vignette, as numismatists call it, was based on an 1855 drawing by Daniel Maclise, a noted British painter of Victorian times. He gave his subject a girl's classical innocence, some of which was lost when the Bank's engravers balanced a crown above her head. At first Langer thought it would be simple to photograph a copy on a zinc plate and etch the lines in acid. He had two cameras, an extendable one with bellows that he had bought and another manufactured by Paul Drews, one of the German precision-engineering firms that were then the envy of the world. The cameraman was a professional named Artur Rau, who photographed five-, ten-, and twenty-pound bills many times over. "But it didn't work," Langer recalled. "Hundreds of original notes . . . were photographed and enlarged (to three times their size) . . . In each printing none of them looked alike . . . The first medallions looked in their original size very good; but in the enlargement! The young girl's face looked like an old woman's. It was as if it were hexed."

After weeks of trials, Langer found an experienced engraver in his late sixties named Walter Ziedrich, who made what looked like an exact copy after six attempts. In the photo studio and the etching, engraving, and galvanizing rooms at Delbrückstrasse, copper plates were prepared and mounted on steel to prevent the delicate lines from blurring in the softer metal. Paper was delivered to the ground floor for printing on a flatbed press, then dried and "aged" by machines so the counterfeit banknotes could be bundled and sent for use. Once the presses got rolling, the shop was put under a foreman named August Petrich, a Nazi Party veteran who ran his own printing business. The civilian technicians at Delbrückstrasse arrived in neat work clothes, some even wearing ties. They proudly posed for photographs of themselves engraving and inking the plates, running the presses, and looking dedicated to the German war effort.

Naujocks thought the notes were to be dropped on Britain just before the expected invasion. But Hermann Goering, the chief of the Luftwaffe, knew very little of the plan, which was actually more grandiose in scope. Its code name, if nothing else, supports that view: *Andreas-Angelegenheit*. This translates literally as the "Andrew Affair" but is more usually referred to as Operation Andreas or Operation Andrew. The reference is to the X-shaped cross of Scotland's St. Andrew in the British flag, which is overlaid by the cross of England's St. George. Langer thought that the latter "canceled" the former, obviously not realizing they were meant to join symbolically as Great Britain's Union Jack. (He ignored the third cross, of Ireland's St. Patrick.) Although the German original of Langer's report has not been found, a hurried English translation in 1945 stated: "We wanted to strike through the worth of the pound, thus make its value to nothing." He explained the basic idea as follows: "Through the production of banknotes a business system [economy] can be ruined, especially if the falsification were so good that it was impossible to differentiate between the counterfeit and the original." The counterfeiters, he wrote, believed they could help end the war with fewer casualties "through the collapse of Britain's business." There is no doubt he was right, at least in theory. If enough counterfeits were circulated to make all pound notes suspect — and it would have taken millions — the British people would have reverted to some primitive form of barter. Even the Bank of England realized that.

It is unthinkable that such a bold plan would have been launched without Hitler's approval. Langer confirmed that "the Fuehrer personally gave [the] orders." Others have taken it even further than that, into a realm that is too entertaining to ignore but probably too good to be true. According to the former SS officer Wilhelm Hoettl, Heydrich put the plan in writing and sent it to Hitler. The dictator, Hoettl reported in his 1955 memoir, "minuted in his scratchy hand in the margin of Heydrich's proposal: 'Dollars no. We are not at war with the U.S.A.' and scrawled his name." This story has been picked up by most authors, but there is no evidence for it anywhere else. Although Hitler's observation accords with his strategy of surrounding and isolating the United States instead of attacking it from across the sea, writing it down would have been totally out of character — as Hoettl himself admitted. Historians are still searching for Hitler's written order for the liquidation of European Jewry — also supposedly issued to Heydrich. They will probably never find it. Hitler rarely put any orders on paper; he simply told his adjutants what he wanted, and the orders often got garbled because they were not always clear to begin with. In most cases it was hardly necessary for him to have written anything. His ranting against the Jews, for instance, had been in print since 1925 in *Mein Kampf;* the book was literally the nation's bible — at weddings, instead of a family Bible, every couple in Germany got a copy — the royalties for which were the basis of Hitler's fortune. All around him were waiting to execute his every whim. If they were not certain of Hitler's precise command, an educated guess was usually possible.

Thus, when in January 1942 Heydrich held the infamous conference at Wannsee, the Berlin suburb where the Reich Security Service maintained a guesthouse, his purpose was not to approve the final solution to the Jewish problem, for which he probably needed only a few terrible words; it was instead to coordinate the complex and murderous work of fractious, turf-protecting bureaucracies in carrying out a *Fuehrerbefehl* (leader's order) and there was only one leader in Nazi Germany. The Finance Ministry conference that had set Operation Andreas in motion in the opening days of the war was another such interagency meeting, through which bureaucracies of all nations put directives in motion. In approving the orders for the counterfeiting operation, just as at Wannsee, only Hitler's fingerprints are lost to history.

Hoettl later disparaged his own memoir as mere journalism and said that while the background and "some details . . . are based on actual events," it had a strong "literary make-up." He had a good ear for a quote even if he had to put it in someone else's mouth. The fact is that the first time he ever heard of Operation Andreas was in September 1940, a year after it was given the go-ahead and Alfred Naujocks was already on the way out.

Wilhelm Hoettl was a failed Austrian academic who had parlayed his historian's knowledge of the Balkans into a job as SS chief of intelligence in Vienna. Through the war and afterward, he was an incorrigible peddler of information to whatever naive secret service would buy it. A 1952 entry in his CIA file bespeaks collective exasperation. One Simon Graham wrote on U.S. Army stationery: "His reports normally consist of a fine cobweb of fact, heavily padded with lies, deceit, conjecture and other false types of information. This organization will have absolutely nothing to do with Dr. Hoettl or any members of his entourage. He is persona non grata to the American, French and British elements in Austria." But this type of rascal was naturally attracted to Operation Andreas's honeypot of money and probably helped contribute to its failure.

At this point mythology again muddies the trail. Some accounts include the dramatic story of a young German soldier sent in civilian clothes for a wild week in neutral Zurich, where food was more plentiful than in wartime Berlin. He was carrying a false Swiss passport and a packet of pound notes manufactured at Delbrückstrasse. The Germans tipped off the watchful Swiss about the false passport, hoping they would run a check on the currency. To Delbrückstrasse's delight, the counterfeits passed. A story in the London *Evening Standard* of January 7, 1941, reported that the Bank of England was consulting with Scotland Yard after the paper's Geneva correspondent discovered that "the Swiss police are trying to track down a gang of forgers of British notes." The Swiss were as slow to react as the British. The Swiss Bankers Association did not issue a warning against sterling counterfeits for almost two years. A Bank of England official blithely told the *Standard* that the Bank had not seen any such counterfeits or even heard about them. Two months later the Bank was still nodding, its own guarded account reporting: "By 1 March 1941 a trial parcel had been accepted at a Swiss bank as genuine with, apparently, confirmation obtained from the Bank of England that the numbers etc. tallied with notes still outstanding in the Bank's registers." Hardly an eyebrow cocked at the Bank.

All of this should have given the green light for the presses to roll at Delbrückstrasse, but in fact Operation Andreas was already foundering. Naujocks had begun falling out of favor with

Heydrich almost a year before. Early in April 1940, Naujocks and his boss, the genial chief of SS foreign intelligence Heinz Jost, were called into Heydrich's office and asked to produce false Norwegian notes as quickly as possible. Naujocks said that would take at least four months. As Jost described the scene, Heydrich, "as usual, lost his temper, insulted Naujocks and told him he could go to hell with all his alchemist's humbug if he couldn't produce the notes within a week." Naujocks was gone in six months. He would have been shipped to a frontline SS regiment except that anyone who knew so many state secrets was barred from combat duty to forestall the risk of capture and interrogation. As for Heydrich, Hitler made him "Reich Protector" of Bohemia and Moravia, the western half of Czechoslovakia, in September 1941. Heydrich adopted carrot-and-stick policies of increasing the rations of Czech workers and farmers while putting down the middle-class resistance with such brutality that he became known as "the Butcher of Prague." The Czechoslovak government-in-exile parachuted in two agents from London, who assassinated him in May 1942. The following month, the population of Lidice was liquidated and the town leveled in retaliation.

Albert Langer, meanwhile, soldiered on, although to little effect. One Communist author reported the Delbrückstrasse factory was diverted to counterfeiting rubles after Hitler invaded the Soviet Union. Langer, who left around 1942 with back problems, claimed that during his tenure his factory produced 200,000 five-pound notes and 200,000 ten-pound notes, or about £3 million in false notes. They were mixed with real notes and sent for appraisal to banks and other institutions, none of which, he insisted, "could distinguish between them." Langer may have been exaggerating the quality of his product, or the bank tellers may have been nearsighted or simply lazy, but he had no doubt that his real problem lay in a lack of leadership: "It became more and more unorganized. Personal betterment came before everything else, and in all probability treason too." It is almost an axiom of secret espionage that such slush funds are skimmed by those in control of the money, and Operation Andreas ran true to type. Noted Langer: "Thievery was present but it was the high SS functionaries and not the workers."

But the fundamental fault had been there from the start. A civilian print worker who had been drafted to serve in Operation Andreas reported that he had six different SS bosses after Naujocks left. And Artur Rau, the photographer, believed the work was farmed out to private firms, including August Petrich's own print shop. Everywhere in Nazi Germany, ideology, personal loyalty, and deadly office politics were the order of the day. This struggle for preferment was only natural in a society where only one voice counted. Anyone who could win Hitler's ear won his favor, and it did not pay, to say the least, to raise uncomfortable questions with his favorites about his decisions or theirs. A few months after the Nazi surrender, a graphic account appeared in a Frankfurt newspaper quoting the unnamed print worker explaining why Operation Andreas failed.

One would now assume that the men who wanted to finance puppet governments with counterfeit money, carry out sabotage and win wars, would at least have selected the right experts for this work. But the fact was that here too, where the most exact technical knowledge is indispensable, National Socialist [Nazi] Party people had more say than technicians. The failure of SD [Sicherheitsdienst — Security Service] Division VI F [4] showed in the continual change of directors. If the technicians suggested something that did not suit the SS members, the work was first done according to the plans of the SS men. Not until things could no longer continue did the technicians receive a hearing. Thus Dr. Langer, who surrounded himself with a scientific nimbus and engaged in the identifying of numbers, serials, borders, dates, and signatures of documents, was soon dismissed.

Operation Andreas languished for about a year until Himmler himself formally revived it in July 1942, drawing on an extraordinary pool of skilled workers who were most unlikely to skim the money or question the orders of their commander.

Chapter 3

WHITEHALL AND THE OLD LADY

In the most celebrated of all wartime memoirs, there is no mention of a Nazi counterfeiting plot, perhaps because it does sound rather like a child's game in the midst of a battle to the death. Less than a week after the Wilhelmstrasse meeting approved the Nazi plan, and certainly without any knowledge of it at that moment, Britain's First Lord of the Admiralty wrote a confidential letter on stationery adorned with the traditional anchor and crown. The First Lord was the civilian politician responsible for the Royal Navy and maintained his office and private apartments in Admiralty Arch. This grand piece of imperial architecture abuts Whitehall and bridges the Mall linking Buckingham Palace with Trafalgar Square, which memorializes the Navy's greatest victory over an earlier European dictator. The letter was carried a few hundred yards down Whitehall to the office of Sir John Simon, the chancellor of the exchequer in the cabinet of Prime Minister Neville Chamberlain.

Private   24 September [1939]

My dear John,

I hear from many quarters a plan for scattering forged notes of marks in bundles or tempting little packets in Germany from our aeroplanes, like Pitt spread his assignats. I cannot fully think out the consequences of this but I should think it would be just as good as leaflets. I should very much like to know how it strikes you.

Yours sincerely,
Winston S. Churchill

The Right Honourable Sir John Simon G.C.S.I., G.C.V.O., O.B.E., K.C., M.P.

Churchill, whose curiosity and inventiveness were rarely equaled by politicians of the twentieth or any other century, had just returned to the government in the beloved office he held during the World War of 1914–18. Simon quickly passed Churchill's letter to David Waley, principal assistant secretary in the British Treasury, after scrawling a request on it: *"Mr. Waley for obsvns, pl. JS 28/9."* Waley, who ranked near the top of the civil service meritocracy that formed Britain's highly efficient permanent government, was the same man who two months later would receive the secret memo from Athens detailing Germany's counterfeiting plot.

Those who recall the daily challenges of financing the war during that critical period still cherish the close comradeship of those arduous days. They mastered the intense intellectual challenge with the help of their unpaid adviser, John Maynard Keynes, or Maynard as he was known to all, a tall, elegant conversationalist and polemicist equally familiar in the banks of the City of London and the world of British ballet. This attention to wartime finance should come as no surprise in the country that literally invented the study of political economy. Before Keynes revolutionized economic thought about tradeoffs, it was a series of indisputable propositions: the Iron Law of Wages, Say's Law that supply creates its own demand, the Law of Comparative Advantage, and so on. They were like medieval notions of a static universe before Newton's discovery of the laws of motion.

The Treasury was led mainly by first-class scholars who knew and understood this intellectual history. Many had begun their careers as tax officials, which meant they had a feel for the attitude of the public toward the demands of the state. This practical experience was good training for the administration of the sacrifices demanded for the nation's survival, and they felt themselves to be, above all, practical men. But, as Keynes wrote at the conclusion of his masterpiece, *The General Theory of Employment, Interest and Money,* "practical men, who regard themselves as quite exempt from intellectual influences, are usually the slaves of some defunct economist." He converted them by applying his talent for argument and administration to countering the terrible forces of depression and war.

David Waley, born Sigismund David Schloss, was a member of a distinguished German-Jewish financial family long settled in England. He graduated from Balliol, Oxford's most intellectual college and a principal supplier of brainpower to the British elite. Waley adopted his mother's name during the anti-German hysteria of World War I, just as the British royal family changed its name from Battenberg to Windsor and its nonroyal members anglicized their names to Mountbatten. Waley had served in that war as a frontline officer and was decorated for bravery with the Military Cross. He had never felt the need to conceal his background as he made his career at the Treasury, where his colleagues called him Siggie. When Waley later received the Athens memo, he would seek a reaction from a quite different institution, the Bank of England, a clubby hub of finance that the Treasury regarded as decidedly inferior.

In those days the Bank of England was an official hybrid, owned by its member banks in the way that stock exchanges are still owned by brokerage firms. The Bank recruited young men of good family who had to be nominated by one of the Bank's directors. Few went to university, and they were known mainly for being trustworthy and dependable, especially if they could count pound notes without making mistakes. The Bank had the important responsibility of not only printing Britain's pound notes but also regulating their supply to protect the nation's currency against inflation. Its legendary caution and discretion, its top-hatted doormen guarding its entrance at the crossroads of London's financial center, lend credence to its nickname "The Old Lady of Threadneedle Street." Situated along what was once a medieval lane named for the artisans who worked there, the Old Lady symbolizes Britain's financial district like a huge, sleepy Edwardian elephant. Its original structure was dressed up with dome and pillars by Sir Herbert Baker, close colleague of Sir Edwin Lutyens in designing and building New Delhi, the model par excellence of an imperial outpost. The public buildings of Lutyens and his disciples were to architecture what the romantic nationalism of Sir Edward Elgar's compositions were to music. The Bank's dome is topped by a gilded statue of the globe-girdling Ariel, the magical Shakespearean messenger who (in the majestic words of the Bank's own guide to its museum) "is the symbol of the dynamic spirit of the Bank carrying credit and trust over the world."

As Churchill reminded Simon in his letter, this was not the first time the English had thought of counterfeiting enemy currency. In 1794 Prime Minister William Pitt approved counterfeiting huge amounts of French assignats, which were originally printed as promissory notes against property of the nobility seized by the revolutionaries and traded inside the country as money. Napoleon retaliated by counterfeiting British pounds and filtering them through neutral ports. It was but one episode in the long history of official forgery that continues to this day. In 1470, when the Duke of Milan warred on the great commercial empire of Venice, he counterfeited its money to undermine its bankers. Frederick the Great of Prussia counterfeited the currency of his enemies, and the British also flooded the rebellious American colonies with counterfeit notes during the Revolution. During the American Civil War, confidence men made a killing on each side by crossing to the other with counterfeit Union or Confederate bills. Reds and Whites counterfeited each other's currency during the Russian civil war of 1918–1921. When the Soviet Union was starved for foreign currency a decade later during its first Five-Year Plan, Stalin ordered $10 million worth of bogus U.S. hundred-dollar bills printed, partly to finance his secret service abroad. His financial agent in the United States was caught, convicted, and sentenced in 1934 to fifteen years in jail, although the full story did not come out until a Soviet general defected five years later. These tactics can be traced to the ancient world, when the Greek city-states forged enemy silver coins in base metals. They persist today in the rogue nation North Korea, which has been printing bogus American hundred-dollar bills since the 1970s on a press purchased from a Swiss company.

Churchill himself received a polite put-down from Simon in less than a fortnight. Addressing his Admiralty colleague in his own hand on October 4, 1939, the nation's chief financial officer informed "My dear Winston" that the Treasury had carefully examined his idea, "and I am bound to say that, on balance, I think the Noes have it."

John Simon was an intelligent but indecisive lawyer who sometimes made marginal comments on his official papers in Latin verse. (When Churchill succeeded Chamberlain, Simon was kicked upstairs to be lord chancellor, the head of the judiciary.) Simon enclosed a closely argued memorandum based on the thinking of Ralph Hawtrey, the Treasury's chief economist. First of all, Hawtrey warned, dropping counterfeit reichsmarks would discredit Britain politically in the eyes of neutral nations. On a practical level, the memo continued, "the difficulty with forged currency always is to introduce it into circulation." Further, in a totalitarian society anyone trying to spend such a windfall would come under immediate suspicion, so most of the notes would be turned in, and the operation would therefore offer little hope of debasing the enemy's currency. If the Germans nevertheless decided to retaliate by dropping counterfeit pounds, "we could then cry quits, except the discredit would apply to us." The Treasury mandarins played their own version of three-dimensional chess with the idea for half a year, but Hawtrey seems to have made the decisive move in a memo to his Treasury colleague David Waley in April 1940: "It strikes me that this is a game at which two can play, and we're probably not the best at it."

Churchill's suggestion had not been the only one. Bright ideas had begun streaming into Whitehall as soon as war was declared on September 3, 1939. The first to reach the Treasury was prompted by news of leaflet raids over Germany. On September 6, Robert Chapman, a retired colonel, wrote his MP from his home in rural Sunderland with a proposal to scatter large amounts of counterfeit marks in low denominations "to cause consternation and help to get the [German] people into a state of unsettlement and fear." He conceded that the Germans might retaliate but remained confident that it would be far more difficult for the Germans to duplicate the high-quality paper of British banknotes. Chapman's letter landed on Waley's desk, and he circulated it in the department. One Treasury man, quivering with such outrage that his signature is deemed illegible by the official archivist, commented, "War may be war, but I should have thought we should not indulge in this sort of business." The following day, a noncommittal reply was dispatched to Colonel Chapman assuring him that "all suggestions from any quarter are always welcome." Across the Treasury's file copy in a neat hand, another official harrumphed: "Ingenious but not British."

Indeed. In Brussels, a friend of the British ambassador coyly signing his letter "A Belgian 'neutral,'" urged his British friends to wage the war against Hitler "with imagination." He proposed an airborne mechanism, complete with automatic timer, to scatter packets of counterfeit reichsmarks at one-mile intervals. Not surprisingly, Britain's Ministry of Economic Warfare weighed in with its own proposal, and so did the chief of the secret service, Stewart Menzies, an elderly and not particularly competent superspy whose network was riddled with Soviet agents. For more than a year, other complex schemes to undermine German currency arrived from patriotic worthies in the best neighborhoods of London and retired officers like Colonel Chapman tending their estates in the shires.

Other suggestions carried aggressive titles like "Means of Overcoming the Hun." That particular letter was sent in May 1941 by a Royal Air Force pilot on behalf of his wing commander, H. B. Maund, obviously flush with the aerial victory in the previous autumn's Battle of Britain. Maund felt confident enough to suggest that Britain's credit was good enough for the nation to borrow an astonishing $3.5 billion in gold from the United States and issue currency in shiny new coins instead of printing pound notes. Maund argued that this would prevent the Germans from dropping their own printed counterfeits. All these brainstorms received a polite brushoff, although one Treasury official privately gave the wing commander more credit than "the present prime minister" — Churchill — for his foresight in devising an ingenious if financially implausible scheme to forestall German retaliation.

The barrage of suggestions not only tried official patience but created its own form of internecine warfare. With the German war machine unable to loot Russia as profitably as the richer and more pliable nations of occupied Europe, the propaganda people at the British Foreign Office sought permission to discredit

German currency by dropping forged bills, some with lewd messages. Waley was still opposed because "we should look rather silly when we were found out." He passed the suggestion to Keynes, with whom he worked closely as a specialist in international finance. Keynes had a greater understanding than any purely public servant of how the activities of the Treasury and the Bank interacted with the real world of finance, and of the importance of the fine balance between economic liberty and social justice. From his days as a young Treasury official, he also understood how government worked, and to him, counterfeiting must have seemed like a reversion to precisely the type of the moral barbarism against which Britain was fighting. He gave the idea the back of his hand: "Mr. Waley: I agree with your comments. The proposal to introduce forged currency has been made at least a hundred times before and always rejected for good and sufficient reasons. JMK 28.5.42."

Right through the war, the Treasury doubted the British could successfully pull such a trick on the Germans, while realizing that Britain's less tightly controlled society remained vulnerable to enemy counterfeits. Some limited experimentation took place. From time to time, Britain's secret "black propaganda" units dropped forged German ration books to disrupt the official food distribution system. In 1943 Radio Berlin reported one of these air-drops and warned that anyone caught using fake ration cards could be executed for sabotaging the war effort. Similar penalties could be imposed for holding foreign currency without official permission, so the British knew that the Nazis would retaliate mercilessly against their own people for passing counterfeit foreign bills. They were the defense mechanisms of the totalitarian state; no British government could countenance such draconian punishments against its own people, even in wartime.

*   *   *

The Treasury's David Waley had the wit to put himself in the Germans' place as soon as he had seen the Athens memo outlining the German counterfeit plan. He thought the British might forestall the scheme by publicly announcing they knew all about the plot to undermine sterling and would simply refuse to honor any pound notes held abroad. "Perhaps it is a fairy story," he wrote Basil Catterns, deputy governor of the Bank of England, "but it certainly seems a good idea from the German point of view."

Waley was gently tweaking Catterns, because the Treasury had warned him of such plots before the war and had been rebuffed. In May 1939, as war loomed, Sir Frederick Phillips had attempted to arouse the Bank of England from its torpid superiority. Phillips, a laconic, pipe-smoking Treasury mandarin who "could be silent in several languages," was a brilliant mathematician who consulted with his economists and had long been at odds with the Bank's hard-money policies. During World War I, the Bank had actually printed up excellent counterfeits of *German* money with the full knowledge of the British government. They were delivered regularly by taxi to the head of naval intelligence, probably for use by spies in Germany. But when it came to fakes, Catterns of the Bank had a short memory. Replying to Phillips, he insisted it would hardly be worth the expense and trouble of printing a special reserve of pounds to defend against "a danger which does not seem very likely to materialise," and in any case, "[W]e do not believe that notes could be put out which would not be distinguishable from our own issue."

The Treasury took a while to digest this pompous claim before parrying with its own politely skeptical and canny analysis on June 5. Maybe the Bank could spot a fake, Phillips replied, but would an ordinary Englishman be able to tell the difference between a good counterfeit and a real pound note? And once the rumors started flying, "the average man . . . would begin to suspect all notes." What would the Bank do then? Publicize the scheme or try to hush it up? What if the Germans dropped the bills in installments, printing up new versions to keep up with the Bank each time it issued a new design? And, finally, who would compensate the trusting but unfortunate souls who got stuck with the air-dropped fakes?

The Bank retreated to ponder Phillips's uncomfortable questions and came back on June 9 with its solution: It would print a small reserve stock embedded with a special metal thread in a cellulose strip. The Bank had been experimenting with this for several years but hesitated to stick the strip on a new issue of notes for fear of public embarrassment if the device failed. Phillips nevertheless told the Bank to print 300 million pounds' worth of notes as a secret reserve to replace slightly more than half of all notes in circulation. New bills, fetchingly lithographed in mauve and rose, were finally issued in May 1940 in denominations of one pound as well as a half-pound, or 10 shillings. The only catch was that the Germans, already working on their counterfeits, had wisely decided to get more punch out of each pound by forging mainly black-and-white fivers, more or less the median weekly wage for an English workingman (and nowadays merely the price of a round of drinks at a pub). Thanks to a typical British muddle, Nazi plans for a financial blitzkrieg were pointing straight at the biggest gap in the enemy's defense, the five-pound note.

Five-pound notes were imposing certificates measuring eight by five inches, with flowing script. The intricate drawing of Britannia on a throne, the date which was also impressed in the watermark, a serial number for each bill, a system of letters and numbers denoting successive issues — all these, the Bank was certain, made its system virtually inscrutable because each note had to match the Bank's own records or it would be rejected as a forgery. Further, each new issue was designed with security markings so subtle — a broken line, an off-center dot — that counterfeiters were meant to mistake them for misprints and correct them, thus falsifying the note. Out of tradition and prudence, shopkeepers insisted that their customers sign the notes on the back with name and address as if they were being endorsed like a check. The face of the notes bore the bold signature of the Bank's chief cashier, Sir Kenneth Oswald Peppiatt — K. O. Peppiatt — who, like the Treasury's Waley, was a World War I officer decorated with the Military Cross. A racing enthusiast and bridge player, he was a man of tall and imposing bearing, easily displaying his supreme self-confidence whenever cornered by extracting a cigarette from the gold case in his waistcoat pocket, tapping it on the metal, and posing even the most uncomfortable question without raising his voice. Peppiatt was certain no one could get the better of him or his banknotes.

If Phillips, Waley, and Keynes represented the English social conscience of what the playwright George Bernard Shaw once called Heartbreak House, Peppiatt was a doyen of Shaw's equally symbolic but opposing Horseback Hall. He reported to Sir Montagu (later Lord) Norman, governor of the Bank from 1920 to 1944, whose staff basked in his personal arrogance — a reflection of the institution's independence of elected governments. Norman never doubted that he alone was the rightful guardian of the nation's currency. Keynes, also later ennobled and long a denizen of Heartbreak House in his role of financial eminence to the writers and artists of that corner of upper Bohemia which gathered in London's Bloomsbury, was considered by his social equals, and probably by himself, as the cleverest man in England. Not surprisingly, he disdained Norman as "always absolutely charming, always absolutely wrong." No wonder the Bank was the first institution to be nationalized when the Labor government came to power at the end of the war and placed it under the governorship of Thomas Catto, a Scottish self-made banker and Keynes's close wartime associate.

In marked contrast to the mindset of Germany, this dichotomy between brains and character marks all of English life and helps explain why the English would shy away from counterfeit currency as a weapon of war while Germany embraced it. Ideas flicker across the English horizon like summer lightning, from Shakespeare to Francis Crick, but they are generally distrusted even though they eventually turn out to be world-changing. Because of the emphasis on character, breeding plays perhaps an excessive role, but Britain is saved from stagnation by the openness of its aristocracy to new talent. Its great prime ministers come from all classes — Gladstone, Disraeli, Lloyd George, Churchill, Attlee, Thatcher. All had to think on their feet under fire in the House of Commons and dispose of their opponents with wit rather than Nietzschean will. For example, Disraeli's classic put-down: "There sit the leaders of the opposition like the coast of Chile — a line of extinct volcanoes."

But the Germans are the great philosophical system-builders of Europe, along with the French, the latter tending to emphasize logic rather than heavy Teutonic ideas about duty, will, and power — *Macht,* as the Germans call it. There is little history of tolerant argument in Germany and a strong component of Martin Luther's obedience to divine will. (Even that founder of Protestant individuality thought in lockstep terms of "the priesthood of all believers.") The deep play of imagination does poke into German literature and philosophy during occasional romantic outbursts, but in general, the debasement of human standards, first money and later life itself, was within bounds permitted for the benefit of the *Volk.* Long before its rhetorical capture by Hitler and Goebbels, this word commingled ideas of race, nation, and state. There is no equivalent in English.

＊　　＊　　＊

Even when the Bank of England issued the low-denomination counterfeit-proof notes in 1940, the British government decided not to warn the public of the real reason, lest a counterfeiting scare cast doubt on Britain's currency. In 1940 a reporter for the *News of the World,* the most widely circulated paper in the country, telephoned Sir John Simon for the exchequer's comment on what he had been hearing from various sources, including an unimpeachable High Court judge: that the British government already knew Germany was going to dump huge amounts of counterfeit pounds on Britain. The chancellor recounted the conversation coolly in an internal memo: "I said I did not wish to make any request to the News of the World or any other paper, but that as I was asked whether it was in the best interests of the country to publish such a yarn, I should be disposed to say that it would be better not." The article never appeared, and both the Treasury and the Bank did their best to kill any other newspaper stories.

Ignorance of counterfeiting plots was cultivated externally and, unfortunately, internally. At the Bank, Peppiatt refused the offer of the French police to lead him to an informer who claimed to know about a "factory" producing five- and ten-pound counterfeits. The chief cashier told British authorities to divert the French to the Metropolitan Police at Scotland Yard and to keep the French treasury out of it entirely. He did not trust or even like foreigners and easily fell into patronizing them, one reason he could not imagine them clever enough to match any piece of paper with *his* signature on it.

In fact, Peppiatt had already passed up what could have been his best source of intelligence about German counterfeits, even though it had been offered to him with the endorsement of Scotland Yard. In May 1938, Sir Norman Kendal, assistant commissioner of the Metropolitan Police and a lawyer who previously had helped command the Yard's detective force, forwarded a plea from Vienna for help in finding refuge for Hans Adler, a special adviser to the International Criminal Police Commission. Adler, descended from Jews, edited a standard European numismatic handbook and an internationally recognized review, *Counterfeits and Forgeries*. He had rich knowledge and extensive files. Adler had already lost his job, and his life was threatened as the Nazis began integrating Austria into Germany and applying their notorious racial laws. Although Adler had been on first-name terms for years with the master craftsmen at the Bank's printing plant, Peppiatt callously dismissed his plea in a brief note to Kendal: "I have made many enquiries, but fear I must report that we cannot be of help. I suppose there is no possibility of [Adler's] carrying on his work in London?" Kendal tried again early in 1939, reporting to Peppiatt that "the wretched Hans Adler has been hounded out of Austria and later hounded out of Italy" and finally given shelter in Holland. Saved by the kindness of strangers, Adler survived the Nazi occupation and returned to work for the ICPC's counterfeit division when it was reconstituted after the war under Dutch control. But his unique expertise was unavailable to the Bank and to Scotland Yard when they most needed it.

The Bank's strategy was the gradual withdrawal of all notes worth ten pounds or more, under the guise of restricting large bills to complicate life for black-marketers who dealt mainly in cash. The Bank's own printing plant on Old Street, located since 1920 in what was once St. Luke's mental hospital, was evacuated from the City of London in 1940 because of air raids and as part of this antiforgery plan stopped printing large bills altogether in 1943. The only other defense was mounted on August 20, 1940, when the Bank banned the repatriation of its own banknotes — between £10 million and £20 million held abroad. Such an import barrier was virtually unprecedented in modern war; nations generally try to hold their money close rather than allowing bills en-cashable in their own banks to float freely around the world. Like most unprecedented decisions, this one would have unforeseen consequences. The fake Nazi bills eventually went flying in all directions, surprising even those who had conceived the scheme.

Chapter 4

NOBEL PRIZE–WINNING IDEAS

None of America's important novelists of the Depression was more politically committed than John Steinbeck, the author of the saga of the great Dust Bowl migration, *The Grapes of Wrath,* and *In Dubious Battle,* a novel about courageous union workers that would be inconceivable among today's navel-gazing fiction. Steinbeck was a devoted New Deal Democrat as early as June 1940 and had already been received in the Oval Office by Franklin D. Roosevelt with a proposal for a radio and motion picture propaganda office "to get this side of the world together." Even though the idea had the backing of the Librarian of Congress, the poet Archibald MacLeish, it lay dormant. But the president was always looking for ways to stand alongside the embattled British in that dark year and simultaneously to prepare the ground for America's inevitable entry into the war. So when Steinbeck wrote again on August 13 that he had a distinguished scientist in hand with an idea for a secret weapon, Roosevelt was all ears. After all, hadn't some of the nation's leading physicists brought him a letter just a year earlier from Albert Einstein proposing the ultimate secret weapon?

Steinbeck, of course, knew nothing of plans for the Manhattan Project to develop an atomic bomb and therefore could not have known how open Roosevelt might be to the urging of the future Nobel Prize winner that "our weapons and tactics would have

to come not only from military minds but from the laboratories."*
The letter continued:

> Perhaps you have heard of Dr. Melvin Knisely, who has
> the chair of Anatomy at the University of Chicago. Sev-
> eral weeks ago Life Magazine carried a series of pictures
> of his new light which permits microscopic study of cap-
> illary circulation of the blood for the first time. He is a re-
> markable scientist and an old friend of mine. Discussing
> with him the problem of the growing Nazi power and pos-
> sibilities for defense against it, he put forth an analysis
> and a psychological weapon which seem to me so simple
> and so effective, that I think it should be considered and
> very soon. I would take it to someone less busy than you if
> I knew one with imagination and resiliency enough to see
> its possibilities.
>
> What I ask of you is this — Will you see Dr. Knisely
> and me within a week or ten days — see us privately and
> listen to this plan? Within half an hour you will know that
> we have an easily available weapon more devastating than
> many battleships or you will not like it at all. Afterwards —
> if you agree — we will discuss it with any one you may
> designate on the National Defense Council.
>
> Please forgive this informality, but frankly, I don't know
> anyone else in authority whom I can address informally.

That was certainly starting at the top, and next to the last sentence
some anonymous aide scribbled in the margin, "Very nice!" James
Rowe, a valued White House assistant, forwarded the letter to his
boss, attaching a note saying the novelist had a "high reputation

---

*Steinbeck received the prize in 1962 for literature, sharing the platform at Stockholm with Francis
Crick, James Watson, and Maurice Wilkins, who shared the science prize for deciphering the ge-
netic code.

as an amateur scientist . . . certainly he is not a crackpot." Rowe nevertheless reckoned that the president would send Steinbeck to some subordinate. But the combination of naked flattery and scientific intrigue proved irresistible. The novelist and the anatomy professor were invited to Washington at their own expense for a twenty-minute meeting with Roosevelt.

Just before lunch on September 12, Knisely outlined with high seriousness his plan to scatter large numbers of high-quality counterfeit German marks across Hitler's Reich. No official account of the White House meeting was kept, so only Steinbeck's highly dramatized version survives. With his novelist's eye for detail, he recalled that as they made their terse presentation, Roosevelt's face was in shadow, with the sun glinting on his forehead "as far down as his closed eyes. His cigarette in the long holder stuck straight up in the air, with curls of blue drifting in the sun-streaks." The tale continued:

> Suddenly the President opened his eyes and banged his chair forward. He was laughing. "This is strictly illegal," he said, his eyes shining. Then he added in a low voice, "And we can do it."
>
> "Why, for the cost of one destroyer we could send Italy spinning. For the cost of a cruiser, we could have Hitler on a hot stove lid."

What happened next is fully recorded in official archives. Roosevelt picked up the telephone and was put through to Henry Morgenthau Jr., his wealthy secretary of the treasury and Hudson River Valley neighbor. They were personally so close that when the Morgenthaus came to dinner, the Roosevelt grandchildren addressed them as Uncle Henry and Aunt Elinor. Like the president, Morgenthau was a landowner, but unlike him he was an honored member of New York City's German-Jewish aristocracy, which guarded its reputation for probity and propriety against the inevitable slurs of the time. Roosevelt told Steinbeck and Knisely he was sending them right next door to the Treasury; Morgenthau was then to report back. It was not for nothing that Roosevelt was the most celebrated political animal in Washington, so it is hard to believe that FDR did not have a good idea of what would happen next. As the two visitors unveiled their secret weapon for the second time that afternoon, the atmosphere in Morgenthau's imposing Victorian office, furnished in polished wood and leather, grew "cold and then freezing," in Steinbeck's words. Morgenthau, tall, bald, and obviously shocked, peered ominously through his pince-nez at his visitors.

Also at the meeting was Herbert G. Gaston, a former editor of the *New York World* who had come to Washington with Morgenthau in 1933 and been promoted the year before to assistant secretary in charge of the Treasury's law enforcement agencies. That included the Secret Service, which defended the president against assassins and the dollar against counterfeiters. In a memo to Morgenthau that served as minutes of the meeting, Gaston noted that the secretary had summoned him right after receiving "the most extraordinary telephone call from the President [who] . . . said Steinbeck had proposed what seemed to him a grand idea — it was to counterfeit German currency in large quantities and arrange to have it introduced into Germany. You [Morgenthau] asked the President to have them come over and see you. You remarked to me that you didn't think you ought to let these people leave with the idea that the Government would countenance such a scheme."

It made no difference to Morgenthau that Knisely had studied in Germany and argued that he understood German psychology, that he was certain counterfeits on a large scale would sow great confusion and undermine German finance, or that Knisely went into detail about how best to analyze and manufacture replicas of

German reichsmarks that would defy detection. When Morgenthau raised moral and legal objections, Steinbeck replied that they were trumped by the fact that the Nazi war effort was mass murder and must be stopped. The arguments and counterarguments lasted just under half an hour, although on a higher moral plane than the practical wartime discussions that had engaged the British at greater length the year before.

Steinbeck was told flat out by Morgenthau, "It's against the law, and I will have nothing to do with it." The secretary dismissed the plan as something he would have expected from the Germans, adding that the United States was not at war with Germany anyway. (Morgenthau would have been truly shocked to learn that a similar argument against counterfeiting American dollars had been attributed to Hitler.) Gaston chimed in that counterfeiting German currency would be just as much an act of war as sending a fleet across the English Channel, and he would prefer that to having British planes dump fake bills on the foe.

In any case, Morgenthau said, the British ambassador would be calling on him later in the afternoon. Steinbeck, obviously expecting support, said he would be pleased to have the plan put to Lord Lothian.

Unbeknownst to the plebeian native of the dusty California farming town of Salinas, Lothian was an even larger landowner than Roosevelt and Morgenthau together — 28,000 acres as he recorded in his *Who's Who* entry. But he was also a cool and experienced public servant, could be blunt when the occasion called for it, and knew America well from his position as interwar secretary of the trusts administering the Rhodes scholarships. Morgenthau and Lothian went to see Roosevelt, and by late in the day the ambassador had forwarded to Morgenthau an unsigned memorandum prepared by Gerald Pinsent, the British Treasury's man at the embassy. It was brief, and its salient arguments, totally new to Washington, were probably heightened by Pinsent as he realized that two Americans even as worldly and widely traveled as Steinbeck and Knisely seemed to have no conception of life under the totalitarian regimes of Europe.

MEMORANDUM

The suggestion that counterfeit Reichsmark notes should be dropped from aeroplanes over Germany was exhaustively considered by the British Government some time ago. At that time it was thought that this would be regarded by the world at large as a particularly odious and dishonest method of warfare, and if this argument has to any extent lost its force since then there are other arguments which seem decisive.

The fact that such notes were being dropped would certainly be known without delay to the German authorities. In a country ruled the way Germany is ruled, it would not be difficult for the authorities to organize collection by Party or official organisations of the notes dropped, and to frighten the population so that they would not dare to collect these notes and retain and use them themselves. Precautions have probably been taken already by the German Government.

Even insofar as the population were able to retain and use such notes the effect would probably be disproportionately small. In Germany nearly all goods are either rationed or are simply not obtainable; the holders of these counterfeit notes would not be able to spend them to more than a limited extent and it is probable that they would flow to a considerable extent into savings bank accounts, etc. The German government could increase their borrowing accordingly from these banks, and decrease their borrowing on the markets.

To overcome these objections in such a way as to cause a substantially increased demand for goods which would endanger the German price control, or as to create distrust among the population in the currency, would require a scattering of notes on such a large scale as might be beyond the capacity of the Royal Air Force if it is not to limit its attacks on military objectives to an undesirable degree.

Lastly, if Great Britain started this method of warfare and Germany retaliated in kind, it is not improbable that the effect on Great Britain, where we have not the same totalitarian methods of government, might be greater than the effect on Germany.

12th September, 1940

Morgenthau quickly wrote to thank Lothian: "Mr. John Steinbeck put the proposal up to me. I told him I was absolutely opposed to it as I thought it was crooked and I am delighted to learn that the British government agrees with me." In a letter to Archibald MacLeish, Steinbeck was contemptuous: "A friend and I took a deadly little plan to Washington and the President liked it but the money men didn't. That is, Lothian and Morgenthau. It would have worked, too, and would work most particularly in Italy." This tribune of the oppressed had devised a way to use the capitalists' own weapons against the fascists, and the capitalists had rebuffed him.

The rejection still rankled years later when Steinbeck's memory dimmed in retelling the story: he mixed up Lord Lothian with his successor Lord Halifax and dismissed him as a "spluttering" moneybags. Steinbeck also wrote: "Much later, when I sat with the President, he said ruefully, 'Killing is all right, and you could attack religion with some impunity, but you [Steinbeck] were threatening something dearer than life to many people.'" The author would later encounter the president when he helped draft the passages on minority rights in FDR's 1944 re-election platform. It would have been characteristic of Roosevelt to utter some sort of emollient remark like this in lieu of thanks, although whether

Steinbeck would have remembered it with precision is another matter. Roosevelt's remark nevertheless passed into the record through a *Collier's* magazine article Steinbeck wrote twelve years later, where he recycled the idea for use against the Soviet Union — whose leaders hardly believed in money at all! — and wondered why the United States would not dare try it out. (He was wrong. In 1950, the newly organized Central Intelligence Agency had the idea on its secret list of things to think about for the next war.)

While all this was going on, public alarm was sounded about the threat of counterfeit American currency. The U.S. Secret Service, breaking with the tradition embedded in its name, intensified its nationwide "Know Your Money" campaign to inform the public how to recognize fake bills. Anticounterfeiting educational films were prepared in 1940, and when America entered the war the Treasury Department staged exhibits of counterfeit bills, starting in New York's Rockefeller Center and moving across the country. These inspired an article in *Life* magazine giving the Treasury view that "sometime soon Germany and Japan may try to panic this country by passing out great quantities of counterfeit money." A front-page article in the *New York Times* of January 25, 1940, reported the Secret Service's suspicions that the Nazis were counterfeiting dollars and circulating them in Italy, Egypt, and the Balkans. This sent the German chargé d'affaires, Hans Thomsen, to the State Department the very next day to object that his government was doing no such thing. Because the United States and Germany were not yet at war, diplomats tried to mollify Thomsen.

Officials clipped the newspapers for stories on counterfeits and paid particular attention to a report by the Turkish ambassador that counterfeit dollars were being used by the Nazis to buy oil in Romania. This report, almost certainly false, was spread throughout the State Department. Although counterfeit dollars were reported in wide circulation throughout Europe, it was assumed by American officials that they probably did not originate as wartime weapons, but through an underground network of what a *New York Times* reporter called "black bourses." These usually unscrupulous money changers had been feeding for some years on refugees, exiles, and others hunted by the totalitarian regimes of the era. The fleeing buyers had little recourse after they discovered they had been stung, and likewise every incentive to pass on what was in effect hot money.

At almost the same time, early in April 1940, Herschel Johnson's London memorandum about a real plot to counterfeit British pounds was passed to the U.S. Treasury and virtually ignored. Johnson, a career diplomat from an old Southern political family, was so highly regarded by the British that he was remembered into the twenty-first century by the Churchill biographer and British statesman Roy Jenkins. Nevertheless, the American embassy was told curtly by State Department officials that they were "cognizant of such stories as have appeared in the press, but have been unable to substantiate them" — because no one had tried to pass counterfeit pounds in Washington! Among those initialing that inane memo was the State Department's senior economic official, Adolf A. Berle, who had joined the New Deal in 1933 from Columbia University as one of the professors in what became known as Roosevelt's idea-spinning brain trust.

Then, over New Year's of 1941, came a sign that some sort of forgery operation really was happening in Germany. As many as two dozen members of a gang were arrested in neutral Turkey for passing counterfeits in denominations of one, five, and ten pounds. The gang included a Chilean diplomat and a number of attractive women with false passports, leading the Turkish police to order all foreign nannies — most of them German — to leave the country after questioning.

The police reported that as much as £150,000 worth of false notes originating in Germany and Italy had been circulated in Bulgaria, Romania, and Yugoslavia. Moreover, they remarked on the superior quality of the German notes, a sign that they may have been products of Operation Andreas. The Turks made it clear they believed this was part of a Nazi plot to undermine the pound. The Bank of England took note of the roundup and clipped the story from the London *Evening Standard* for its files. A week later another story in the same newspaper reported that counterfeits in denominations as high as £100 were circulating in Switzerland. The Bank of England clipped that story, too, assured the newspaper that none of the counterfeits had made their way to England, and then called Scotland Yard.

The American imagination was proceeding on similar lines, and the same arguments were rehashed. Early in 1941 the *New York Times* ran a typically tut-tutting editorial about the increase in the number of reichsmarks in circulation, with the consequent danger of inflation (as if that were the worst crime then being committed in Germany!). On January 25 a reader named Henry D. Steinmetz wrote that it might not be a bad idea for the British to throw a little fuel on the fire, print up "a few score billions of excellent counterfeit mark notes" and dump them on Germany to undermine its economic morale. He was put down five days later by another reader, Manfred A. Isserman, who pointed out that the RAF had already dropped forged ration cards on Germany, and the damage done by dropping counterfeit money would be minimal because rationing made money less important; moreover, the Germans might retaliate and harm Britain's much freer economy.

Letters also arrived in Washington from personages high and humble as soon as war broke out. Two weeks after Pearl Harbor, Private N. E. Cortright of the Weather Squadron at Langley Field, Virginia, sent a handwritten plan to shower "exact duplicates of

the enemies [*sic*] paper money," enumerating nine potential bene-
fits in economic disruption and weakened resistance. His superiors commended his "patriotism and sincerity" and saw to it that
his letter was forwarded up the chain of command, where it eventually reached Lieutenant Colonel Robert A. Solborg in the in-
fant office of the Coordinator of Information, predecessor of the
Office of Strategic Services (OSS), America's wartime espionage
agency. (Like all spy shops in those days, it masqueraded behind
an inoffensive name.) Solborg commented dryly in a handwritten
note that "Mr. Morgenthau said we are not in the counterfeiting
business." He kept the letter on file anyway.

On January 6, 1942, Colonel (later General) William Donovan, who had been named chief of the espionage services, was forwarded a letter from a "very able Colorado publisher" by that
state's Senator Edwin C. Johnson, a member of the Military Affairs Committee. Once again, the letter writer thought he had a
brilliantly original idea: flood Germany with fake marks. Donovan replied on the basis of advice from his economic section chief,
Emile DesPres, deploying many of the familiar arguments against
its effectiveness: tight German control, rationing rather than lack
of money as the cause of scarcity, and finally the risks of retaliation. These were elaborated in a letter to the president from
Donovan's deputy, G. Edward Buxton, who warned: "Distribution
is a major problem as dropping from planes is inefficient, and success seems to depend on a widespread underground penetration
of the country by agents. The program seems promising if done
on a large scale at a moment of crisis in Germany or Japan. In occupied countries it might produce more distress to the conquered
than to the conquerors."

In a slight twist only a month later, the irrepressible Donovan — he was not known as Wild Bill for nothing — asked Roosevelt for permission to drop fake lire over Italy to undermine
Benito Mussolini's tottering Fascist government. But unlike the

Nazis, Donovan saw the plan more as propaganda than as outright economic warfare against a resolute enemy, proposing to deliver the counterfeits with great fanfare so the Italians would "look at their money and decide for themselves which is good and which is bad." He appended a brief, staff-written history of counterfeit money as a weapon of war: the Reds and Whites in the Russian civil war, the Hungarian government's counterfeiting of French francs during the 1920s, and of course the scheme used by Pitt against the French revolutionaries cited by Churchill. Unlike Churchill, however, Donovan's researcher was careful to note in his opening summary that Pitt's was the only authenticated scheme to inflate an enemy's currency and disrupt his economy, but it was still "generally regarded as having failed."

Donovan had already recruited a Boston industrialist, Stanley P. Lovell, as his director of research and development. Lovell's first job was to manufacture false passports, ration books, and other documents essential to all secret agents operating behind enemy lines. The original proposal for a secret forgery factory seems to have come from a young New York lawyer actively prosecuting organized crime, whence the idea may well have sprung. America's supreme commander in the Pacific, General Douglas MacArthur, requested 10 million counterfeit pesos in Japanese occupation currency. The assignment went to Lovell. His team was headed by a master printer named Willis Reddick, a reserve officer from Springfield, Illinois, to which he added a member of the Kimberly-Clark paper family and the president of the Papermakers' Institute. Lovell prudently decided he needed Treasury approval, which, as he wrote in his memoirs, was "vital to us if we weren't to be closed up and arrested as soon as we started work." After all, the United States was a solemn signatory to anticounterfeiting treaties, and the Treasury held the dollar's reputation in its hands as well.

Lovell quickly got through to Morgenthau, who agreed to ask Roosevelt. The Treasury secretary instructed Lovell: "You come over here tomorrow at eleven o'clock. If I say, 'The President has a cold and I was unable to see him on your problem,' that means he allows you to go ahead full speed. If I say, 'I took that matter up with the President and he refuses authorization,' that means exactly what I say." The next day, Lovell presented himself at Morganthau's huge office to discover him accompanied by some of his senior deputies among at least ten potential witnesses. As Lovell entered, Morgenthau swung around and introduced him clearly as "Dr. Lovell of the OSS." In an exquisite minuet of bureaucratic deniability, Morgenthau continued: "Now, on that matter you asked me about, I was unable to see the President for approval because he has a cold. Do you understand that, Dr. Lovell?" The newly anointed chief forger replied: "Yes, I do, Mr. Secretary, and thank you."

Lovell was hardly elated: "I suddenly realized how utterly exposed I was. If anything misfired, if our forgeries and duplicates were to be discovered by some newspaper columnist, and a wave of criticism be loosed against such 'un-American' activity, then Secretary Morgenthau had more than a dozen witnesses to say he had not taken up my problem with President Roosevelt. If anything went wrong there was but one sacrificial goat . . . me." Lovell had no need to worry. With White House help, the nation was successfully scoured for currency paper made of kudsu and mitsumata, fibers then grown only in Japan. (Kudsu later infiltrated the American South, where its spelling morphed into *kudzu* and it became a botanical pest.) Bills were printed and circulated via the Philippine underground to undermine the occupation pesos. MacArthur's request for counterfeit currency was the only one known to have been put in writing during World War II. Not even Morgenthau could persuade his own friend and boss, President Roosevelt, to protect him with a signed order. Later, the general's compliments were passed to Donovan, and in turn to Lovell. But the counterfeit coup of 10 million pesos ultimately mattered little except to Morgenthau's conscience and MacArthur's ego, both as inflated as the currency of the Occupied Philippines. The Japanese themselves were already printing 1 million occupation pesos a month, drowning MacArthur's forged American contribution to the occupation currency, which totaled about 100 million pesos — and was rising.

But Germany remained the prize target for America's amateur spies. The U.S. Treasury's Secret Service, already forewarned, more wisely asked the OSS to stay on the lookout for counterfeit dollars. Miles Copeland, an OSS and later a CIA operative who retired to England after the war, recalled later to Murray Teigh Bloom, the leading American author on the subject, that "everyone in the OSS had the same idea: let's counterfeit German notes," and the idea was still kicking around long after it had been discredited. (Copeland, who believed that this great brainstorm had been blocked by a mysterious German-American bankers' cartel, became in retirement a public purveyor of hare-brained excuses on behalf of American intelligence, or so he was regarded by journalists serving in London during the 1960s and 1970s.) Willis Reddick, the master printer, could feel the wartime pressure mounting on his boss Lovell. Even as late as 1944, an Army Air Force major sent Donovan a carefully reasoned plan for Allied bombers to drop forged reichsmarks along with their high explosives, to promote German inflation. As Reddick later told Bloom:

> I went down to the Bureau of Engraving. I said we were
> exploring the idea of flooding Germany with counterfeit
> Deutschmarks [sic] and what did they think. They thought
> I was crazy. But they did some figuring, how many millions
> of notes we'd have to do to make any kind of impression in
> a country the size of Germany. It was hopeless. When you
> got right down to it, even if they could turn out the notes on
> the Bureau's presses — of course they'd have to stop making

U.S. notes — the delivery problem was impossible. We'd have to be sending bombers day and night all over Germany and letting them hurl out bales of money. And then all the Germans would have to do is issue a new series of notes and our stuff would be dead. It wouldn't be cheap, either. Just making the notes would run $10 million.

Such logic was out of fashion in Germany. The Nazis had not forgotten their dream of an easy victory through financial sabotage, and they finally found the perfect field commander for their counterfeit war.

Chapter 5

THE COUNTERFEIT CHAIN OF COMMAND

Bernhard Krueger, an obscure SS officer, was by his own un-contradicted boast "the greatest counterfeiter the world has ever known." But he also conceded that he would be a mere footnote to history, and indeed he even looked like one. No Aryan demigod, Krueger stood 5 feet 8 inches. His receding hair was not blond but dark, his deceptively innocent doe eyes brown, not blue. The Allied file card on him for postwar Nazi hunters described him as slightly bowlegged. When jailed after the war, Krueger peered into the camera for his mug shot with a smirk on his thick, slightly sensual lips, as if he was both relieved and proud finally to have been noticed and unmasked. Anticounterfeiting police in Britain, France, and the United States expressed their grudging admiration for both the quality and the quantity of the pound notes produced under his supervision. "I do not say this with any particular conceit . . . I followed orders, as any soldier must. But, I must admit that I was proud of our final product. We did make beautiful banknotes." This was no doubt the highlight of his life. Forty years later, he said with undiminished satisfaction: "It was technical perfection."

Where others had failed, Krueger succeeded by bending or breaking the most barbarous Nazi rules to protect his workers. But mostly, he was the right man for the job. Born November 26,

1904, he was the son of a telegraph inspector from whom he inherited a methodical nature and a technical bent. Unlike his predecessor Albert Langer, who had to bone up on printing techniques in a fortnight, Krueger was trained as a mechanic and engineer at the technical college in Chemnitz. The city, in the far southeast of Germany, stood on the medieval salt route to Prague, but more significantly, it was on the banks of the river Elbe, which gave it a bleaching monopoly in the Middle Ages. This turned Chemnitz into a textile manufacturing center with a long history. After the industrial revolution, it also became an engineering center, producing some of Germany's renowned machine tools, as well as the nation's first railroad locomotive. Thus Krueger was steeped in the German traditions of precise and meticulous craftsmanship that would produce Leica cameras, Mercedes automobiles, and even today, printing presses and mechanical looms that are world renowned. He certainly never would have fallen for one of Goering's mad ideas such as saving steel by constructing locomotives out of concrete.

By profession an engineer of complex textile machinery, Krueger was familiar with factory life at three different Chemnitz companies. He had also worked in Poland and France during the 1920s. But in the economic crisis of 1929, he lost his job at the B. Ascher company and immediately applied to join the Nazi Party. Two years later he was accepted as a member, inducted into the SS, and immediately assigned to the technical section, setting up communications networks and listening stations to monitor foreign broadcasts. This brought him into the ambit of intelligence. His industry and efficiency earned him rapid promotion to master sergeant within three years and an officer's commission in four.

Krueger appeared in occupied France in September 1940 as a Hauptsturmfuehrer, the SS equivalent of an army captain. By November, he was forwarding packets of French identity cards and other forms to Alfred Naujocks in Berlin. But Krueger's principal task was to obtain and forge passports and other identity papers of enemy and neutral nations including the United States; these were often obtained from drunken or drugged sailors. (Some of the best work, indistinguishable from the originals except by experts with special examining tools, fell into Allied hands after the war and was deposited in the U.S. National Archives.) Krueger moved in high circles as well as low. He was authorized to visit the former French foreign office on the Quai d'Orsay and consulates of conquered Western European countries. The visiting card of Pierre Laval, the most notorious of the French politicians who collaborated with the Nazis, was later found among Krueger's papers.

Krueger's talents had obviously been noticed by his superiors, because Langer invited him to a meeting in May 1941, when Operation Andreas was on the skids. In July, Krueger had been put in charge of the SS foreign intelligence service's own forgery department creating foreign passports and identity papers for Nazi agents abroad. It was designated Section VIF4 in that highly structured Nazi way, giving the appearance of order and legitimacy.* In the autumn of that year he visited military intelligence posts in unoccupied France, recruiting agents, searching archives, and possibly trying to set up a network to smuggle the Andreas counterfeits into neutral countries.

On May 8, 1942, Krueger was summoned "on an urgent matter" to the office of Walter Schellenberg, the chief of SS foreign intelligence, and given the most challenging assignment of his life.

---

*The designation works out as follows: VI refers to the foreign intelligence section of Himmler's RSHA (Reich Central Security Office); other sections were the Gestapo and similar internal security agencies. F refers to the group: A was Administrative, B Western Europe, C Russia, and so on. F was Technical Support. Each group was divided into desks, and Desk 4, headed by Krueger, was responsible for forgeries and photography.

He suspected something special and probably sinister as he was being driven to Schellenberg's office on Berkaer Strasse in Charlottenburg. He thought of spiders spinning their webs in the sun's early-morning rays to trap their prey, a sight which, he recalled, had always aroused the suspicions of his superstitious mother.

At thirty-two, Schellenberg was six years younger than Krueger and like him had been driven into the Nazi Party by hard times. The seventh child of a Saarbrücken piano manufacturer whose business had slumped, he switched his studies from medicine to law because it offered the possibility of a steady career in government service. In 1933, the year Hitler came to power, Schellenberg applied for a government grant to do his apprenticeship in a law office and was advised that membership in the Party would advance his career. He enrolled in the SS because he felt it was composed of "the better type of people." Schellenberg was soon mingling with them as a young agent in the industrial Ruhr district on Germany's western edge, where foreign economic intelligence flowed in from the overseas branches of German industrial companies. He quickly became SS chief Reinhard Heydrich's favorite and a regular fencing partner, catapulted to his office and rank from master sergeant to brigadier general in four years as a reward for ingenuity and courage. Among his exploits were kidnapping two British intelligence officers in 1939 at Venlo just across the Dutch border with Germany and pumping them for information about their secret organization. He tried to lure the Duke of Windsor from Portugal to Germany in 1940 to be held in reserve as a puppet king of England for Hitler's occupation, but the British spirited the duke away just in time to become governor of the Bahamas for the duration. Schellenberg also supervised a remarkably savvy Gestapo handbook for the prospective occupiers. Its arrest wish-list of 2,820 individuals indicated a surprising understanding of the British establishment, for it included not only the obvious political leaders but influential financiers, academics, and even artists, from Noël Coward to Virgina Woolf.

Schellenberg had taken over SS foreign espionage from the easygoing Heinz Jost on the day Hitler's armies invaded Russia. In the chain of command, he was only two levels below Himmler, who had the formal title of Reichsfuehrer SS and reported only to Hitler. Schellenberg, an activist bubbling with plots, stood 5 feet 9 inches in his dashing black SS uniform, his pasty face nicked with dueling scars. He walked with a brisk gait but maintained a low-pressure demeanor. That sociable manner was deceptive. Schellenberg had a headquarters staff of five hundred operating around the clock, three shifts a day. He was the perfect spy chief, usually skeptical of raw information and silent about his successes. Not only did he present a rare combination of daring and administrative ability, he knew how to use technology and was proud of it: forgery of all sorts, miniature cameras and secret inks, communications and wiretapping. He was particularly proud of his ingeniously catalogued file of half a million cards on individual agents, contacts, and cases, readily accessed via an electrically powered system. He passed along the German post office's transcript of a radiotelephone conversation between Churchill and Roosevelt. He even claimed he tapped the undersea Atlantic cable for convoy schedules to guide the U-boat wolf packs.

Schellenberg's office, although deeply carpeted and luxuriously furnished, was both a communications hub and a fortress. He had a direct telephone line to Hitler's chancery and many less important places (including his own home). Hidden microphones were embedded in the walls, lamps, and his desk. The windows were covered with a wire mesh connected to an alarm system triggered by photoelectric cells scanning the office. Two buttons controlled a warning siren and, if that did not summon the guards in time, two machine guns built into the desk were trained on all visitors as they advanced toward him.

There had been many challenges to the German production of counterfeit notes, one of which had been guaranteeing secrecy as well as technical reliability. Drawing staff from the trained civilian labor pool had not been particularly successful. But there was one group that might fit the task perfectly. As Krueger entered Schellenberg's lair, the senior officer addressed him politely and without ceremony in his controlled tenor. "Please sit down, Krueger. I have asked you to come to me to transmit an important order from the Reichsfuehrer SS [Himmler], which I received personally from him late last night. This order directs that the necessary measures be taken immediately for the fabrication of English pound notes. Production must begin in the shortest possible time. To this end, the Reichsfuehrer SS has ordered a secret printing press to be set up in KZ [Concentration Camp] Sachsenhausen. The workforce is to be taken from the reservoir of prisoners of Jewish descent."

Schellenberg had already informed the Sachsenhausen camp commandant that Krueger would be arriving the following day. Then he told the SS captain, who was sitting across the mahogany desk with increasing and perhaps evident discomfort, that he had been chosen because he was already working successfully as a forger. Schellenberg continued: "Krueger, seize this task with both hands; it will demand everything you have. You have my full confidence." And as a sign of his trust, Schellenberg announced that it would be named Operation Bernhard, after Krueger. This kind of eponymous honor was routine in Nazi Germany, where power was the only organizing principle. It elevated such operations to the personal fiefdoms that became a driving force in Hitler's administration.

The use of a name also fixed responsibility. Krueger realized he was being handed a poisoned chalice, but it would also be suicide to refuse. "Brigadefuehrer! You have presented me with a very difficult task, which I cannot reject. It is an order behind which stands the Reichsfuehrer SS himself. Remembering the soundless demise of Operation Andreas which was begun with so much hope, I really do not know whether another attempt will end in failure like the first. It depends as much on the skills of the prisoners as on the abilities of the leaders."

Krueger thought once again about that early-morning spider and exacted one concession. Fully aware of the quarreling SS leadership and bureaucratic chaos that had defeated his predecessor, Krueger insisted, "Please allow me, Brigadefuehrer, to ask for complete freedom in all technical organizational matters. You know that many cooks spoil the broth. Since I am to be held responsible for the operation of this project, I need a clear answer to this." Schellenberg replied: "Krueger, all decisions are in your hands alone, no one else's."

Far from being elated, Krueger spent a sleepless night. Skeptical from the start, he was immediately struck by the "cold calculation" of Himmler's order to use Jewish prisoners. He saw Reinhard Heydrich's hand behind it, even though Heydrich was in Prague (and would be mortally wounded by assassins late that very month). Predictably, neither Schellenberg nor Krueger had received a written order, and the latter knew he never would see one. But he also realized immediately that, successful or not, at the conclusion of the operation bearing his name the Jews would be slaughtered and thus "the mouths of the prisoners were to be sealed forever."

This, he also knew, presented him with his own unique prisoners' dilemma, far more subtle than the technical problems of producing passable counterfeits. He would have the unquestioned power of life and death over the Jewish printers, engravers, photographers, accountants, and other specialists in his charge. How would he obtain the best results from these skilled and intelligent men? By promises or threats? By good treatment or bad? His experience in industry told him that disgruntled workers could slow down and even sabotage production. And these Jews would know it, too — that the longer they could keep Operation Bernhard going, the longer their lives might last. After the war, Krueger reflected on his task:

> In order to achieve my purpose, I could not stand there and say: "I trust you, trust me!" Impossible. They would not have believed a word, me with the [German] bird on my sleeve and the [SS] Death's Head on my cap. At most, they would have thought me a complete idiot.
>
> There are situations where a human being may not reveal his principles or his thoughts without endangering himself. This danger was always acute in associating with prisoners. For my purposes, tolerance was the only way to obtain their human understanding without endangering discipline. If I could succeed in winning their trust, then Operation Bernhard would certainly succeed. That was my motto, my key to success, but also my secret.

While these postwar thoughts were necessarily overlaid by his justifications for the searing experience, Krueger's wartime behavior confirms that he was not trying to turn himself into a humanitarian after the fact, and that he had to tread a very fine line that brought him to "the narrow gate between duty and crime." Krueger was certainly not an Oskar Schindler (or at least the popular conception of this confidence man and entrepreneur who saved his Jewish employees while working them hard in his factory). There is no record or remembrance of him trying to lift the death sentence hanging over his prisoners. But he was not an Adolf Eichmann, either. Bernhard Krueger was an SS officer. His orders were to print money, not to save souls. What kind of a person he really was no one can say with certainty, since all civilized standards of moral judgment, from the Ten Commandments to the Prussian penal code, were suspended throughout the Third Reich. Only the raw imperative of survival prevailed, and the goal of virtually everyone's life was simply to hold on to it. In such a moral vacuum, uncertainty is the dominant condition of life, and irony the only possible optic through which to view ordinary people like Krueger — to say nothing of the prisoners caught in the maelstrom.

Once his course was set, there was much to organize. First Krueger negotiated with his SS group leader, not quite successfully, to obtain guards with temperaments that were stable enough to follow his lead in handling the special prisoners he would later choose. He visited Sachsenhausen, located about twenty miles north of Berlin near the town of Oranienburg, to view the barracks set aside for housing the men and machinery of Operation Bernhard. Then, several days later, he visited Delbrückstrasse 6A, which stood only a few blocks from Schellenberg's office, to inspect the abandoned rooms that were filled with the detritus of Operation Andreas and held its late-model printing presses, soon to be shipped to Sachsenhausen for the successor operation bearing his own name.

He found the heavy machinery carefully covered with tent canvas, and a film of fine dust on the tables used to dry the counterfeit Bank of England notes. He pulled the shrouds from the largest hulk and found a steam press, still carefully greased. To the left stood two presses for stamping alphanumeric serial numbers on the newly printed notes. Next to the entry stood a large, bulky safe, which he hoped would contain technical data and other records to advance his own operation. He swung open the heavy steel door. On top was a deep shelf filled with packages of bundled notes in orderly piles. Below, in some disarray, were wire gauzes for making watermarks. Some spelled out "Bank of England." A few had been handled carelessly and bent out of alignment. Other devices contained only groups of numbers and letters. Krueger also found five copper plates for printing notes of £5, £10, £20, £50, and £100. They seemed to be in good condition, so he moved them to an upper shelf.

Then he extracted one of the counterfeit notes from its package. "'Bank of England — the Sum of Ten Pounds,' it read in a very pleasant, curvaceous, fine-lined, chiseled script," Krueger recorded. "By the smoke of a cigarette, I examined the false note carefully, held it against the light to look at the watermark. Holding the paper with my fingertips, I tore it a bit. Since I had no way to compare it with an original note, I folded the Andreas note and shoved it back into the bundle, reconstituting the complete amount of notes."

When he examined page after page of documents, he mainly found long lists of useless numbers on pages initialed by Albert Langer. What he most hoped to find were orders or records explaining why Andreas had been shut down; he wanted to avoid his predecessor's mistakes. But he found no such papers. "I was convinced there had been none and could not have been . . . Everything emerged from oral orders, like those I had received a few days earlier."

It was years before scholars discovered the only written evidence of any order from the Nazi leadership for Operation Bernhard, and even that was oblique. In Himmler's personal daybook, his entry for July 16, 1942, reads: *"Pfundnoten zunächst Verwendung genehmigt"* — Pound notes authorized for use for the time being. The entry does not stipulate what use was to be made of the notes, where they came from, or even whether they were real. But it seems certain that the feared chief of all Nazi security services was referring not just to the production of counterfeit notes that he had again set in motion, but to a grander strategic plan to finance the secret schemes of the SS. The unique place of the SS in the Nazi system helps explain why the abortive plan to print counterfeit pounds was revived.

From the moment Heinrich Himmler took command of Hitler's bodyguard of 280 men in 1929, this timorous, bespectacled, yet heartlessly cold individual began building it into a paramilitary police force. Its mission was the detection and ruthless repression of uprisings in the rear echelons, animated by the stab-in-the-back myth that Germany had lost World War I because domestic upheavals forced the frontline fighters to surrender when they were supposedly on the brink of victory. With Hitler in power, Himmler single-mindedly pursued his goal of building the SS into an *über*-state within the Nazi state. SS men were not just the Hollywood caricature of the sadistic brute — although they certainly were that — but something as unparalleled in history as Nazism itself: a political army. It was not to be like the Red Army, which was a military arm of the state with political commissars, but a disciplined party force pledged to defend Hitler's blood-ideology and not just Germany's territory.

Far from the propaganda picture that has passed into history of a flawlessly organized war machine that ran Panzer divisions and death camps with equal efficiency, we may take it from Hitler's most exhaustive biographer, Ian Kershaw, that virtually all power centers in the regime were ceaselessly engaged in bureaucratic empire-building, Himmler's no less than any of the others'. Hermann Goering's four-year economic plan ran counter to Walther Funk's financial ukases. The aristocratic military command was also at daggers drawn with the Nazi Party, whose members the Prussian generals rightly regarded as scum. So were their rival intelligence services. Working at cross-purposes was the norm.

Himmler's security services were also chronically short of money. Interior Minister Wilhelm Frick, Himmler's sworn enemy from the 1920s, kept him so strapped for cash that before the war, SS recruits had to buy their own uniforms. Many of his opponents within the Nazi Party feared that one day Himmler or his henchmen might, with only the flick of a finger, use their unchallengeable powers of arrest and detention on their political rivals. But he deftly slipped his enemies' financial leash. He loved imaginative but untried projects and had started out in life as a breeder of prize chickens (the enterprise failed). As Reichsfuehrer SS, Himmler put his organization into business for itself. By 1939 the SS was running four companies: one used concentration camp labor to manufacture bread-making machinery and cutlery; another managed forests and farms; a third produced SS uniforms at the Ravensbrück women's concentration camp; and the largest turned out brick and granite for the grand reconstruction Hitler was planning for Berlin. (According to Albert Speer, Hitler's architect and later his minister of war production, the bricks were useless because the SS employed a new process that failed, and the granite cracked because the slave laborers were ill-trained and badly led.) Cash was also donated by forty wealthy businessmen styling themselves Himmler's *Freundeskreis* (Circle of Friends). On August 27, 1943, for example, the list of donors included the three major German banks, steelworks such as Flick, Rheinmetall, and Siemens Electric. The biggest corporations each had given 100,000 reichsmarks. They neither sought nor received an accounting of their monthly contributions, although Himmler personally checked on their attendance at regular monthly meetings.

So ambitious was Himmler for power that the money went into his organization and not his own pocket; his personal cash shortage remained chronic. In 1942 he had to beg for a loan of 80,000 marks in Party funds to buy a house for his pregnant mistress and secretary, Hedwig Potthast. Meanwhile, the SS acquired more than forty businesses. The profits equipped, trained, and fielded thirty-eight divisions operating as shock troops, sometimes independent of the military high command. SS funds also underwrote the plan to murder Europe's Jews, which was codenamed *Aktion Reinhard* in memory of Heydrich and actually diverted resources from the war effort.

But there was one particularly weak link in the financial structure of the SS. Aside from stolen gold, most of which passed through a special Reichsbank account, none of these enterprises earned the foreign currency that is essential to the reach of any espionage service if it is to find useful information. Looted gold from the central banks of conquered Europe would soon run out, and most of the wealthy Jews of France, Belgium, Holland, and Czechoslovakia were being squeezed as dry as their German brothers. In the East, almost all Jews were as poor as their own governments. By the start of 1944, when the SS death camps were in full and monstrous operation, wedding rings pulled from the fingers of Jews, gold and diamond jewelry ripped from their necks, and gold crowns yanked from the mouths of their murdered bodies yielded only 178 million reichsmarks ($70 million at the wartime rate of exchange). That had to be deposited in a special Reichsbank account, and even Himmler suspected that millions more had been stolen by his own men.

Precisely who had the idea of reviving the operation to counterfeit English pound notes is not certain — such things rarely are — but all evidence points to Schellenberg. He ran the SS foreign intelligence service in direct competition to the Abwehr, the espionage arm of the German military which also regarded itself as a state within a state; the Abwehr was headed by Heydrich's old mentor and then rival, Admiral Wilhelm Canaris. Heydrich took

Schellenberg to lunch with Canaris the day before he gave his protégé command of SS foreign intelligence. The junior guest was eventually to swallow the senior when the Abwehr was absorbed by the SS.

Schellenberg's memoirs devote a chapter to the achievements of his cadre of technicians, but Operation Bernhard is dismissed in less than two pages. Perhaps he feared a postwar demand for restitution; but more likely, he was still bitter about the restraints placed on his schemes by his masters. Toward the end, he wrote vindictively in his memoirs, many of the counterfeits were "wasted as a result of unrealistic fantasies and brain waves of the [Nazi] leaders."

Secrecy was essential to the revived counterfeiting operation lest the British discover its significance (they were aware of the plan, but not the size of it). Equally important, Himmler and Schellenberg had to hide any expansion of the SS espionage service, first from the German economic ministries but above all from the Abwehr. Military intelligence already had its own expert forgery staff of twenty engravers and graphics specialists. Schellenberg had to develop his own shop if the forgers and their product were to remain under his control and not be dumped on the British Isles. By 1942 it would have been treason, or at the very least a grave affront to Goering, for anyone to say that the Reichsmarschall could not mass enough planes to send paper banknotes fluttering down over England, and no one was willing to take that chance. But it was the truth and Schellenberg knew it: Goering's Luftwaffe was not even able to resupply German troops fighting for their lives at Stalingrad during the winter of 1942–43, when they were surrounded and lost the decisive battle of the war. Schellenberg could therefore safely insist that the pound notes were being printed to scatter over England — the perfect cover for the scheme to finance his own nascent foreign intelligence service.

Keeping secrets was easy in wartime Germany. Basic Order No. 1 of January 11, 1940, stipulated that "No one, no office, no officer, may learn of something to be kept secret if he does not have to have knowledge of it for official reasons." When Krueger's money factory at Sachsenhausen was up and running, he was supposed to deliver the best notes in person to Schellenberg's office in Berlin. It is doubtful he was told what Schellenberg intended to do with the money, but that was not his concern. His task, no more and no less, was to get presses rolling as soon as possible. To accomplish this he had to contact high-quality German manufacturers of paper and ink while recruiting and training a workforce of experienced prisoners.

The following directive soon went out from Germany's main concentration camp administration, signed by Lieutenant Colonel Hermann Dörner. He was the chief of the RSHA technical division, successor to the erratic and often uncontrollable Alfred Naujocks, and he operated in a very different style indeed. Dörner, age fifty-three, was of medium height, with a strong neck and roundish face topped by thinning blond hair, and conducted himself in a stately manner befitting his rank.

Business Administration Main HQ
Oranienburg, 20 July 1942
Group D-Concentration Camp
D II/1   Ma. Hag.

Subject: Report on Jewish prisoners
To: commanders of KL Buchenwald, Ravensbrück, and Sachsenhausen

You must inform me immediately about all Jewish prisoners who are from the graphic arts. Specialists in paper, or any other skilled worker (e.g., hairdresser).

These Jewish prisoners may be of foreign nationality, but they must have a knowledge of German. Send me names and nationality by 3 August 1942.

Chief of Office D2

Dörner

by order SS Obersturmfuehrer

To ensure a wide choice, two more appeals were circulated, one on Dörner's deadline day of August 3, and the next on August 11. The Nazis could not have imagined who and what they would find among the Jews.

Chapter 6

INGATHERING OF THE EXILES

*A*ufstehen!" In the darkest hour before the dawn, that daily wake-up call ended the restless sleep of every prisoner in every freezing, louse-infested hut across the constellation of Nazi concentration camps during the dozen years of Hitler's Reich. Whether weary, ill, or even dying, each miserable inmate had to tumble instantly from a wooden bunk and run, not walk, to the camp's central square, there to stand silent, motionless, and utterly vulnerable for the ceremony of roll call in the *Appellplatz*. The humiliating ritual was designed to demonstrate the absolute power of the SS over their prisoners' very existence. Some prisoners keeled over and breathed their last, robbing the SS of their prey as they paced wordlessly up, down, and across the mute rows, sometimes doubling back to review those who thought they had been passed over this time, weeding out the weakest with a death sentence through a curt nod or one horrifying word, *Raus!* Out!

All prisoners had already passed through the dehumanizing initiation of being stripped of their last few miserable possessions, every stitch of their clothing, and their dignity by having their head and pubic hair shaved. Finally, they had been stripped of their very identity by being given a number by which they were always addressed. "Naked, alone, and unknown," in the words of Primo Levi, the great laureate of Auschwitz, each prisoner would be issued a striped uniform and hat that were no proof whatever against any weather. Their wooden clodhoppers blistered instead of protecting their feet, or froze them with a mixture of ice and sand that no one dared move to shake off as they stood, motionless and fearful.

Avraham Krakowski, a pious young Polish accountant, survived a typical roll call shortly after he was immured in Auschwitz. The prisoner serving as block warden barked at his charges to remove their caps. Immediately, they did, and the warden reported: "Six hundred and fifty-five prisoners. Ten dead!" The SS man reviewed the rows, counting the living and also counting the dead. Krakowski recalled: "We were the lucky ones. The count checked out. The *Appell* was finally over. If it had not checked out, we would have been made to stand, as later we often were, an entire day without food in the rain or the freezing weather."

So it went every day among those few who survived after their train pulled alongside the platform at Auschwitz, the epicenter of this industrialized genocide. They ran a gauntlet of snarling dogs and guards who flicked them along with whips. At the end of that infamous ramp, SS doctors plucked almost all the camp's 1.5 million victims to be gassed and cremated immediately. The few survivors knew that it would only be a matter of time before they, too, went "up the chimney," in the unforgiving slang of the camps.

There were forty-five separate installations spread out around Auschwitz, of which the three principal ones were the eponymous camp headquarters, where Polish and other political prisoners were interrogated, tortured, and executed; the gas chambers and crematorium, which were linked to the huge holding and slave labor camp at adjoining Birkenau; and nearby Monowitz, the IG Farben synthetic-rubber plant where Primo Levi labored during the final winter of the war, and which never produced a single tire.

But it is still necessary to distinguish, as indeed the German language itself does, between the *Vernichtungslager* — extermination camps whose names are etched in modern memory as Auschwitz, Majdanek, Treblinka — and the more numerous slave labor camps such as Ravensbrück in Germany, Natzweiler in Alsace, and Mauthausen in Austria. Treblinka, for example, was a pure death factory, occupying less than a square mile of Polish farmland, where 900,000 Jews were murdered, 99 percent of them within two hours of their arrival. "Keep in mind," said Franz Suchomel, an SS sergeant at what was supposed to be a model camp, "Treblinka was a primitive but efficient production line of death." But at Mauthausen, prisoners were systematically worked to death, carrying rocks up from the place where Vienna used to quarry its paving stones. Contributing to the torture were 186 steps of deliberately uneven heights and dimensions.

The prisoners were not exclusively Jews. Within days of Hitler's coming to power in 1933, thousands of the Nazis' political opponents were "concentrated" in cellars, makeshift lockups, and local jails, where they were kicked or beaten to a pulp, or worse. As Prussian interior minister, Goering demanded a bureaucratic structure for political terror. A punishment camp for Communists and Social Democrats was established in a disused brewery in the town of Oranienburg. Dachau was established near Munich, Buchenwald near Weimar. The Oranienburg camp soon grew into the much larger Sachsenhausen, a camp with special status and history. It was built in 1936 by its own inmates, the first one conceived after Himmler took full control of the police throughout Germany and therefore seen as a model of the SS goal of total subjugation. Sachsenhausen was set on a flat, sandy plain at the edge of the town, for whose inhabitants it soon became a principal source of employment. The headquarters and inspectorate of the entire concentration camp system also established itself there, along with Gestapo interrogation and torture chambers that were moved from increasingly crowded premises in Berlin. It was at

Sachsenhausen that the prisoners for Operation Bernhard were to be assembled.

In 1942, with Germany's military supplies exhausted by the unexpected ferocity of the first winter campaign in Russia, all concentration camps came under the SS Economic Administration, the *Wirtschaftsverwaltungshauptamt,* one of those comically ponderous German titles that help conceal their diabolical purpose.* The WVHA's boss was SS veteran Oswald Pohl, who once had to beg for funds from the Party and was determined never to do so again. He opposed Heydrich's uncompromising Wannsee plan for the "final" extermination of the Jews, simply because he needed their hands in his SS enterprises. Heydrich had himself figured on working Jews to exhaustion before gassing them but then realized that natural selection might produce a race of Jewish *Übermenschen,* which was, of course, unthinkable. Therefore the essential dispute inside the SS focused on the speed at which to work the Jews to death. Himmler at first favored whipping them to maximum effort because he could always find replacements in the vast pool of both Jews and non-Jews in the conquered territories, especially among the *Untermenschen* in Eastern Europe. Then he decreed that the prisoners' output be raised "by reasonable (if necessary, improved) food and clothing; prisoners must be encouraged to take interest in the economic enterprise concerned; cooperative prisoners should be held up as an example to the listless majority." The greatest success proved to be the textile factory producing uniforms at Ravensbrück, which reached 40 percent of civilian productivity, unusually high for a slave labor camp.

---

*Fritz Lang's classic film *Metropolis* (1927) portends such camps in its dystopian vision of a sleek, modern city with underground workers organized as mere numbers, performing assembly-line tasks clocked by a machine without a human in sight, and run aboveground by a pitiless and tyrannical megalomaniac prepared to bring the whole operation down on his head rather than surrender power to anyone else. Germans thus imagined all this while it was brewing: regimented, dehumanizing technology and spies following even the boss's family.

Another slave labor group produced a fuselage rejected as substandard for Heinkel aircraft, then went right on turning out ten more so their German managers could dodge the draft.

With Teutonic precision, the SS performed gruesome calculations on their slave laborers, reckoning that the average worker lasted nine months. With a daily attrition rate of about 1 percent, each prisoner would yield profits of 1,631 reichsmarks, on top of which the SS could also count on "the proceeds from the rational utilization of cadavers: gold from teeth, clothing, valuables, and cash . . . plus proceeds from utilization of bones and ashes." The camp administration meticulously deducted the cost of incineration at two reichsmarks per corpse. The principal profit, of course, came not from rendering the dead bodies but from renting out the live ones to the great industrial combines; those donations by Himmler's "Friends" were in fact thinly disguised kickbacks. At Dora-Mittelbau near Nordhausen, thousands of prisoners dug tunnels in the rock in 1943 to prepare underground storage facilities for the V-2 missiles that would rain down on London a year later. They lived and slept in the choking dust without water or ventilation. During the first six months, almost 3,000 of 17,000 prisoners died. "Never mind the human victims," said SS Brigade-fuehrer Hans Kammler, the commander of the operation. "The work must proceed and be finished in the shortest possible time."

At Sachsenhausen it was more difficult to turn human beings into machines because they were assigned to more exacting tasks, such as repairing shoes and watches and recycling captured equipment into raw materials. There were more than 3,000 in this *Kommando Speer,* the largest single unit among the camp's 10,000 to 15,000 prisoners. It was named after the technocrat Albert Speer, Hitler's chief of war production, who had complained that mere extermination wasted economic resources. As in all SS operations, corruption was endemic; in 1941 the commandant of land-locked Sachsenhausen had the prisoners build him a yacht, an offense for which he was transferred to Norway. His successor, a more practical man, used the prisoners to conduct grueling tests on experimental shoe soles. Around a track with separate lanes covered in gravel, cinders, sand, concrete, and the like, about 150 prisoners circled daily for a run of about 25 miles to determine the durability of different materials, their backs sometimes weighed down by 33-pound packs of sand or their feet pinched by shoes that were two sizes too small. Such consumer research was relatively harmless compared to the experiments in noise measurements conducted on pistol silencers by Arthur Nebe's criminal police, which reputedly included shots into the skulls of prisoners.

Although Sachsenhausen was not an extermination camp as such, there was virtually no check on violence. Eighteen thousand Russian prisoners were executed there in 1941 with bullets in the back of the neck. A thousand prisoners were whipped for infractions as minor as a blink of an eye at roll call, every victim ordered to count out each stroke of the lash in his own voice as it flayed open the skin on his back. Others were hung from poles by wire wound around their wrists to be punished or to simply expire. Tens of thousands would die of exhaustion, illness, or execution, especially in the panic of the Nazi defeat.

Outside the camp's main wall stood small individual stone huts for prisoners held as possible bargaining chips, including the two British intelligence officers captured by Walter Schellenberg at the Dutch border. The inner camp was laid out in a semicircular grid of 56 barracks inside a triangle enclosing 18 acres of the camp's total of 44. This triangle was delineated by a wall rising almost 9 feet and studded by nine watchtowers armed with machine guns. The barracks measured 200 by 40 feet. With slightly peaked roofs, these blocks — or so they were called, like prison blocks — hugged the ground and were separated by wide spaces to enhance visibility from the principal control tower at the base of the triangle. Just beneath it, in the form of an inner semicircle with a radius of about 350 feet, was the *Appellplatz*, ringed by the notorious running track. On the other side of the triangle's base, surrounded by a wall of its own, was the camp headquarters. To the right stood a tight rectangle of half a dozen rows of wooden blocks, known as the Small Camp. These were built in 1938 to house Jews rounded up after the *Kristallnacht* pogrom.

In mid-1942, the barred windows of Block No. 19 were painted over, and the building itself, the last one in the first row closest to headquarters, was enmeshed in a barbed-wire netting to await its troop of specialists and their machines. Of course, the camp was also enclosed by the standard barbed-wire fence electrified to 1,000 watts, a standing invitation to suicide for those nimble enough to reach it ahead of the main guard force, who would either be racing to catch them or shooting at them so they could torture them to death instead.

Before Krueger could recruit his Jewish workforce, suitable guards for Block 19 had to be assigned by the SS command. Many guards were wounded veterans, some missing an arm or leg. Krueger had been promoted to Sturmbannfuehrer — major — and his first choice to run the four-man guard room was a ramrod-tall SS-Hauptscharfuehrer, Sergeant Major Kurt Werner, whom Krueger knew as conscientious and incorruptible. Unfortunately, Werner could not be spared, and Krueger had to settle, at least temporarily, for two Oberscharfuehrer — quartermaster sergeants — named Herbert Marock and Heinz Weber. Both had blemished records as cutups, and Krueger shrewdly deemed them unreliable lightweights. The SS general in charge of personnel obviously felt the way to keep Marock and Weber on their toes was to shout at them as they stood apprehensively at attention. He warned them that they must measure up to their challenging but as yet undefined new assignment, or "you will only need to change your jackets." Whether he meant jackets worn by frontline troops or prisoners was not clear, but either way, he meant to instill fear. This was virtually the only tool in the SS disciplinary arsenal, but it was not Krueger's chosen incentive.

Next Krueger summoned August Petrich, the master printer for Operation Andreas. Having no idea what Krueger wanted, Petrich had closed his print shop for the day. At first he thought that reviving the mad counterfeiting scheme was a joke. Krueger admitted he had almost thought so, too: "Imagine, graphic artists, engravers, repro-photographers, and so on from Jewish inmates. I find it a unique story. Almost like an April Fool's joke. Are there really artisans among Jews? I thought they were traders, brokers, capable stock market and business men, experienced doctors and lawyers, and here and there also a police chief." Krueger informed the equally skeptical printer that it would be his job to train the Jews to use the machinery. In short, at Himmler's orders he was to teach printing and engraving within six months instead of the usual German craftsman's three-year apprenticeship. Petrich replied: "Let's not kid ourselves. It is a very difficult task we have to undertake, and it will cost us a good many gray hairs. It may yet turn out all right, it may not. The prisoners are the principal players."

And so they journeyed to Sachsenhausen. Krueger paused to consider the inherent contradiction of the Nazis' universal camp motto wrought in iron letters over the stone gate: *Arbeit Macht Frei* — Work Brings Freedom. He knew this was a lie, indeed that life would turn out precisely the opposite for those he would choose from the eighty candidates the camp commandant put on display for him at a roll call in Block 19.

As Krueger approached, he heard the command "Hats off!" and saw eighty pairs of hands being held stiffly against the trouser seams of the blue-and-white-striped uniforms. He had never before come so close to the wretched truth of Nazi rule. The tension and fear were evident in the prisoners' faces as he inspected the men slowly, Petrich at his side.

"How old are you?"

"Sixty years."

"Your profession?"

"Paper expert."

"Where do you come from?"

"Eichenberg in Bohemia."

"Why are you here?"

"I am a Jew."

"Step forward."

And so Krueger began the methodical work of selecting the men on whom the future of Operation Bernhard depended. They had no idea what they were being selected for at this roll call, but they immediately noticed something different: Krueger addressed them by the formal and polite German *Sie,* instead of the familiar and demeaning *du* reserved for children, servants, Jews under the Nazis, and indeed all other concentration camp inmates except recalcitrant German pastors and prominent politicians from occupied countries held hostage there.

Down the line he walked, selecting a professional engraver in precious metals, a banker, a paper salesman, even a Polish doctor to help maintain his workforce. Contrary to Krueger's expectations, he found four men from the building trades — two carpenters, an electrician, and a mason — several specialists in the graphic arts, and four printers.

"Where did you work?" Krueger asked one printer.

"At various Berlin firms."

"Do you want to join the others?"

"Yes, sir, Herr Sturmbannfuehrer."

"Join the others."

He finally picked thirty-nine inmates instead of his planned thirty, mainly middle-aged men, about half from various graphic trades, including a well-known Berlin fashion photographer, Norbert Levi. There was even a tall, slightly grotesque drifter, a half-Jewish *Mischling* who looked like a clown and agreed to Krueger's suggestion that he was a joker by nature; such a person would help keep up morale. When Krueger reported the results, the commandant said: "Four printers! Excellent! I hope they can print what you want." Still, no one in the camp, not even the commandant, had the least idea what was happening, and neither Krueger nor Petrich told them. Petrich doubted he could succeed with printers who had no experience working with high-quality inks and who had probably ground out "cheap lottery tickets, store advertisements, calendars, business stationery, calling cards for teenagers." Krueger reproached him: "Think, be patient, do your duty and have a strong will." The optimistic SS engineer said he knew Jews from civilian life who had fought bravely for Germany in World War I, so why couldn't these Jews become good printers? Moreover, he continued, "The prisoners are most likely not dissatisfied with the opportunity of landing in a secret printing plant and will work doubly hard to remain in it. Operation Andreas was easier. They just drafted the required experts out of their positions without asking the owners of their companies whether they liked it or not." He did not need to remind Petrich of the fiasco that followed.

The SS guard Marock insisted from the start that Krueger was too soft on his charges, especially since they were Jews. "Prisoners should be handled firmly. They are used to it," the SS quartermaster sergeant told Krueger. What none of the others seemed to realize was that the usual Nazi ways would not work here. Krueger was not just looking for craftsmen and specialists, but individuals of intelligence and dexterity whom he could train and organize for the various interlocking tasks of engraving, printing, sorting, and counting that were essential to the success of the operation bearing his name. Hairdressers, for example, were not chosen for their skills or ancestry, but for their nimble fingers.

The prisoners' recollections of Krueger's selections later at Auschwitz match the tenor and some of the details of his own account. At Auschwitz-Birkenau, Moritz Nachtstern, an anarchist stereotyper who had worked in the print shop of *Dagbladet*, Oslo's largest newspaper, was told one evening late in 1942 that he and six other printers had been picked out on the basis of the occupations listed on their prisoners' cards. Presumably the cards were part of the Hollerith classification system the Germans had adapted from a joint venture with the International Business Machines Corporation of the United States. As with all products of that great company, however, the information disclosed by the system was only as good as what had been disclosed to it, a condition later known in the information industry as GIGO: garbage in, garbage out. Nachtstern had been listed as a printer rather than a stereotyper because the clerk had found the name of his occupation too difficult to spell. "Printer" is a generic term often used loosely. Used precisely, it refers to a worker who runs a printing press. A stereotyper is a specialist who makes an impression from the original type and casts the metal plates that are used on the press. The distinction matters mainly inside the print shop or in union negotiations, but in this case Nachtstern correctly sensed it might be a matter of life and death.

When Nachtstern and his comrades arrived a couple of weeks later at Block 19, they found that "not even a cat could have gotten through that barbed-wire netting unscathed." Krueger, wearing civilian clothes, met them in the small exercise yard outside the barracks.

"Good day, gentlemen. I think you'll like it here. What's your trade?"

That first question was addressed to Fritz Schnapper, a German who had arrived with Nachtstern.

"Printer," he replied, confounded by Krueger's polite demeanor and formal usage.

"Excellent, sir," Krueger replied, turning to Nachtstern, who announced his trade truthfully but not without apprehension.

"Ah, stereotyper. Splendid, sir," mused the Nazi official. "I shall have good use for you."

Krueger patted a relieved Nachtstern on the shoulder and walked off with a friendly nod.

Around the same time, Avraham Krakowski found himself before Krueger in a line of a hundred prisoners placed in rows of five abreast. He watched Krueger pick Mordka Tuchmajer, a printer from Poland, who asked for his brother to go along so they could stay together, even though his brother was a furniture varnisher. The brother was named David Marjanka, also a Pole, and may or may not have been related to Tuchmajer, who was seven years younger. Nevertheless, Krueger amiably replied, "All right, put his number down, too." As the line shortened, and men from printing and allied trades were selected, Krakowski reckoned he had been called by mistake. After twenty-five men were picked, Krueger ordered: "Enough!" But then he impulsively decided he needed a few more, and for some unknown reason, which Krakowski attributed to no less than divine intervention, Krueger spotted him.

"You over there, come on up here. I'd like to talk to you."

Krakowski stood before him.

"How old are you?"

"Twenty-five."

"What kind of work do you do?"

"I'm an accountant."

"Let me see your hands."

Although roughened by forced labor, they remained soft enough to convince Krueger.

"Take down his number, too."

Krakowski became the thirty-first and last choice; of those thirty-one, nineteen had been selected earlier that morning for the gas chamber.

Adolf Burger, a Slovak, was deeply suspicious when all photographers, retouchers, chemists, and typographers like him were ordered to report. He knew that whenever a call went out for specialists, they ended up with the hardest jobs. But once his number was read out at roll call, he had no choice. Hesitantly he entered the camp director's office, where an SS officer scanned his personnel card.

"Prisoner Burger?"

"Yes, sir."

"Trade, typographer?"

"Yes, sir."

The raw voice turned friendly and, wonder of wonders, the officer put out his hand.

"You are going to Berlin, Herr Burger." Suddenly he had been transformed back into a human being. "We need specialists such as yourself. You will work under excellent conditions, and things will go well for you. I cannot give you any further information; you will be told everything else upon your arrival. I wish you good luck."

Max Groen and his boyhood friend Dries Bosboom had been picked up in their native Amsterdam for breaking curfew and were shipped to Auschwitz, where they were among only 38 of their transport of 1,150 souls to survive. One day Dries was asked a curious question by an SS corporal. Had he worked in the graphics industry? Yes, he was a lithographer by trade. At that precise moment the gong sounded for a selection, but before it could begin the corporal stuck his head in the barracks and asked if anyone else had worked in graphics. *"Jawohl, ich!"* shouted Max. He was a newsreel cameraman, but what difference did that make? Dries whispered to Max that he must say he was a litho-photographer, because he could handle a camera, and not a photo-lithographer, because that skill took years to learn.

In the office the two Dutch Jews were called before an author-itative SS major whom they found suspiciously well mannered. The major did not give his name and asked a number of questions as if he were interviewing them for a job. When he reached Groen, he asked about his skills in photo retouching. Groen had ab-solutely no idea what to say. At that moment, he recalled a trashy romance novel on his mother's kitchen table with two words re-ferring to some obscure reproduction process about which he knew nothing.

"American retouching," Groen blurted out.

The officer nodded knowledgeably. "Ah, you mean positive re-touching."

In the blink of an eye, Groen's life had been spared by Krue-ger, for of course it was he. Max and Dries were put on a train to Berlin with sixty others in a third-class carriage with windows and wooden seats. The mere fact that it was not a boxcar made the ride a luxury.

Not until they reached Sachsenhausen did any of the prisoners know why they were there. Groen, quick and wily, needed little time to discover the purpose of the secret print shop through the classic prison "jungle tom-tom" whose beats he could read so well. He also learned of the fatal sword of Damocles that hung over all their heads. Moritz Nachtstern discovered the purpose of the place from Marock shortly after his interview with Krueger. The boastful sergeant picked up a counterfeit five-pound note in

Block 19 and preened before the new prisoners: "We have beaten England in the military field. Now, with the notes, we shall also ruin their economy. They have dropped counterfeit bread-ration coupons over Germany from the air. We shall reply with these notes, until inflation is over them like a storm."

The idea that a team of printers, graphic artists, and accountants, all bearing the Nazi equivalent of the mark of Cain, would be employed in what might otherwise be a vast criminal enterprise and then disposed of as casually as a herd of cattle, at first seemed no crime at all in the murderous context of a concentration camp. To the prisoners themselves it seemed a blessing, or at least an opportunity to mitigate the harshness of their treatment. Krueger clearly thought of it as his duty as a soldier, albeit an onerous challenge that might endanger himself as well as the prisoners if he failed, but he was cool enough never to offer a hint of that as he faced his workers for the first time at Sachsenhausen. Mostly, he hoped that the shock and relief of their sudden reversal of fortune would win them over and turn them into motivated, industrious workers. He addressed them in order to introduce Petrich and the two guardroom sergeants and to alert them that he and they alike were working under Himmler's special orders. He continued:

Those of you who have long and involuntarily been out of professional life because of your incarceration have an advantage, because you will be working with modern, complicated machinery and will first have to learn the techniques under the supervision and guidance of Master Printer Petrich. You will begin with simple printing tasks.

Always remain aware of the proper performance of your tasks. I put the greatest value on smooth cooperation. Practice this within and outside your community. The perspectives of your camp service are different from before. SS Unterscharfuehrers Marock and Weber are responsible for supervising your work. You are always to turn [first] to them. Both are obligated to treat you correctly and are answerable for order in Block 19.

Work begins daily at 7 o'clock and ends at 4 o'clock. Lunchtime is from 12 to 1 p.m. There is no work on Sunday. If you have complaints, whatever their nature, tell me. I am also available for personal questions.

As of today, you are freed from participation in camp roll call. Did you understand me?

The prisoners replied to this blessed reprieve with a rousing yes.

Chapter 7

THE COUNTERFEITERS OF BLOCK 19

O ver a period of about two years, from the autumn of 1942 to the autumn of 1944, Krueger made these selections, starting with the vanguard of prisoners in Block 19 until he had assembled a crew of just over 140 prisoners from fifteen nations and representing fifty-five trades or professions, mainly Jews but some *Mischlinge*. Some Jews volunteered, gambling between the hope of lighter work and the risk of the unknown that was the essence of life and death in a concentration camp. Almost all were skilled craftsmen or professionals. Some simply faked their connections with the printing trade. One of those was Richard Luka, a Czech civil engineer who had spent four years in Buchenwald and said he would have applied "even if they had been looking for sword-swallowers." The first to be picked was more typical: Felix Cytrin, forty-eight, a toolmaker and engraver in Leipzig until his arrest. With a high forehead and hooded eyes, he was intelligent and methodical by nature, made suspicious by prison experience. He soon was named chief of the engraving section and worked on the plates with his four assistants. The plates were made by government engravers, probably drawn from the Reichsbank but doing wartime duty at the German military espionage center deep in a nearby forest at Friedenthal Castle, whose secrets were protected by antiaircraft guns.

Petrich came from Berlin to supervise the engraving at Friedenthal and teach the prisoners at Sachsenhausen how to use the machinery, but he soon proved superfluous. Krueger's story was that the prisoners preferred working without Petrich's domineering daily supervision and actually did better on their own. Petrich remained at Friedenthal, where civilian technicians photographed genuine pound notes, enlarging them sixfold to discern the details and then reducing the photos to etch them on metal. Cytrin and his men then carefully retouched the Friedenthal plates and "vastly improved" them, in Krueger's own complimentary words. The SS major demanded nothing less than perfection, and the prisoners were both pleased and relieved to follow his orders to the letter. The more carefully they worked, the longer they could stretch out the operation and their own lives.

Despite their technical skills, the first prisoners were ordered to perform clerical drudgery for three weeks as Block 19 was readied for them. Cytrin recalled: "We sat from morning to night counting strips of paper. We were practicing counting banknotes. We counted and counted until we were going mad. A Gestapo-pig was in charge, and he was ten times worse than [the SS sergeants] Marock and Weber put together. He waved his revolver and hollered like a stuck pig every time we even lifted our eyes from the strips of paper."

This enforced familiarization with the paper was not just make-work. Matching the Bank of England's paper was Krueger's first and most difficult production problem. The long fibers in a printed sheet of British notes left a slightly ragged edge as they were removed from the mold and torn into two individual bills, leaving them with what are known as deckle edges. To speed production, the Germans had decided to print four bills on one larger sheet of paper. The properties of the principal ingredients of papers differ widely, depending on the soil and climate where the cotton, flax, and ramie are grown and the water in which they are pulped. Suc-

THE COUNTERFEITERS OF BLOCK 19

cessfully replicating and cutting fine paper is as difficult as making and bottling fine wine. Even if the raw materials come from different shipments, genuine notes of different issues nevertheless emit only infinitesimally different fluorescent tones when examined under the ultraviolet light of a quartz lamp, which was then the principal tool for detecting any counterfeit bill. Industrialized Germany had also lost the art of making paper by hand, and there is a telltale difference between the fibers of machine-made and handmade paper. The former run in one direction, while the fibers of handmade paper, lifted in one mass from a pulping vat and then pressed dry, have no bias in any direction. This paper will usually remain flat when immersed in water, while machine-made paper will curl.

Krueger tested more than a hundred sample batches before he felt confident he could match the strong, thin British paper, with the familiar and distinctive sheen and crackle. He abandoned the Spechthausen factory that had ill served Operation Andreas and turned to Schleicher & Schuell, manufacturers of cigarette papers and coffee filters. It helped that the water in their Hahnemühle plant near Hannover bubbled through meadows in a clear trout stream carrying "few suspended particulates" as Krueger carefully noted. Clear streams also supplied the Portal plant in England's rural Hampshire, and Krueger finally claimed 95 to 97 percent of Hahnemühle's production was good enough to serve his purposes.

The washbasins and toilets in the center of Block 19 conveniently separated the workshop from the sleeping quarters, each section about a hundred feet long. The prisoners slept on individual cots, not on standard wooden concentration camp tiers with three or four inmates to a shelf and each man's feet in another man's face. They also were assigned personal lockers and exchanged their striped uniforms for used civilian clothing painted with a broad red stripe on the trouser legs and a red cross on the jacket. In many cases the clothes had been worn shiny, but they were warmer and more comfortable than prison rags. The prisoners were also allowed to grow their hair and thus retain some of their individuality.

New arrivals were issued a towel and soap, a food dish, and a knife, fork, and spoon. They ate at wooden tables, and their rations were black bread and soup that, like all food in Germany, deteriorated throughout the war into a foul brew of grass, tomato leaves, and potatoes. It was called spinach soup, although the closest thing to spinach was the sand that got in their teeth. But they also received a small cigarette ration of Zora ten-packs made of yellow tobacco from Yugoslavia, and sometimes they were served jam and even margarine. A majority of the German and Czech prisoners were only part-Jewish and had non-Jewish wives or relatives who were allowed to send them food parcels supplementing their diet. Krakowski recalled arriving early in 1944 to "a bowl of the most delicious hot oatmeal, cooked in milk and sugar, and afterwards, hot coffee with cream and sugar, as much as we wanted" — although it proved too much for this emaciated prisoner from Auschwitz. But they were fed potato-and-sauerkraut soup on Sundays, which were, wonder of wonders, rest days to play chess, cards, Ping-Pong, and listen to the state-run radio, from which they could obliquely plot the course of the war. Every week they were led out to the showers, where sadistic guards switched the water from scalding hot to freezing cold without warning.

But the men in Block 19 were kept in a semblance of health. So this would be neither a work camp nor a death camp, but halfway between: a death camp with a difference. Like all Jews under Nazi dominion, death was to be their eventual fate, only for them it would be more certain or less, depending on unpredictable events. This is not as unusual as it sounds. Virtually every survivor tells a story in which utter chance plays the determining role.*

Once the machinery arrived from Delbrückstrasse and was installed on December 2, 1942, the gates of Block 19 slammed shut. It became a world unto itself, with its own doctor, a Pole named Boris Rojzen; a barber; repairmen; and its own diesel-powered generator to keep the presses rolling in an emergency. One new group was greeted by the chief printer, Arthur Levin from Berlin: "Friends, from here there is no exit. Only an accident can deliver us from this life, and we have to trust in this accident." When a fire broke out on the barrack's roof, Krueger's prisoners had to save their own lives by forming a bucket brigade; machine gunners outside the wire mesh prevented anyone from fleeing with the secrets of Operation Bernhard or firemen from entering to discover them. The prisoners had been warned repeatedly that death was the penalty for disclosing anything about Operation Bernhard. When the stereotyper Moritz Nachtstern was taken to a physician, he was asked what they did in Block 19. With an armed guard at his elbow, the prisoner replied, "Shovel sand."

Gradually the workshop expanded into a factory occupying Blocks 18 and 19, which were knitted together by a new barbed-wire mesh of double thickness. One prisoner likened it to being inside a mousetrap. The buildings were separated by a narrow strip for exercise and recreation with four Ping-Pong tables. Inside were the most modern printing machines, a book bindery, a photo laboratory, an engraving workshop, and a countinghouse. In addition to the counterfeit pounds, the prisoners forged passports

---

*The author's wife was only one of three to survive out of her Jewish kindergarten class of twenty-two. One night in 1942, German trucks sealed off the street where her family lived in Antwerp. Troops started at one end, systematically rousting out the inhabitants house by house. The trucks were filled up with doomed Jews by the time the Nazis reached No. 18 and were driven away. Her family lived at No. 22. The next day she, her parents, and her baby brother went into hiding. Just a few weeks before, her father, the pillar of the family who eventually saw them through the war, had been walking across town. He encountered an ordinary German soldier who hissed, "Run, Jew, the Gestapo is here." That anonymous act of grace, for which the soldier risked much and could expect no reward on this earth, helped save four lives.

and identification documents. Visas, date markings, and rubber stamps were available from an inventory of 68,000 representing government bureaus, banks, and other institutions in scores of countries, all stolen or copied from original documents.

Trial and error played a part in Krueger's method. A spot of water dropped unintentionally on a test bill led to the solution of one problem, a drop of household cleanser another. Nor was Krueger above seeking help from the prisoners themselves. Artur Springer, a fifty-five-year-old Czech businessman, had been nursed back to health in a prison hospital to join the vanguard, an extraordinary effort to save any prisoner, especially a Jew. It soon became obvious why: upon arrival Springer had remarked to his fellow-prisoners that he knew "a little bit about paper." Shortly after his recovery, Krueger appeared in the barracks, welcomed "Herr Springer" with great courtesy, and allowed the newcomer to precede him through the door of the sleeping quarters to tour the printing plant.

During its manufacture at the Hahnemühle factory, the paper for the counterfeit bills had to be watermarked with wavy lines, the batch code of each issue, and the denomination spelled out as 5, 10, and so on. The principles of watermarking are simple: As pulp emerges from the vat, it is almost 99 percent water, which is pressed out by successive rollers or screens, one of which squeezes out slightly less water in an embedded pattern that can be seen when the sheet is held up to the light. Since the watermark is a security feature, it has to be impressed with tolerances to the millimeter and coordinated just as closely with the images printed on the bill. "It took unending patience to discover how the watermark effect was created, its intaglio impress, and its striking dark and light transparencies," Krueger wrote. Given such demanding specifications, paper production could be erratic. In the early days, there were sometimes no deliveries for several weeks; the prisoners would begin to think that Operation Bernhard had been suspended and they were done for. "It was a nerve-wracking period," Nachtstern recalled. "Had they discontinued the plant, the road to the crematorium wouldn't have been long for us."

The delays arose because Krueger kept trying to achieve a total match but never quite succeeded, and he knew it. He later wrote: "It was never possible to eliminate entirely the difference between the soft-blue fluorescence of the British and the bluish-gray of the B[ernhard]-notes under the quartz lamp. But given the deceptively close visual identity, the odds were against anyone resorting to a quartz lamp . . . From a psychological view, it was unthinkable to wage war against the English pound with a quartz lamp. Chemical additives did not eliminate the fluorescent discrepancy but markedly weakened it."

Setting aside the problem of paper, an old-fashioned five-pound note appears deceptively easy to counterfeit. Apart from the engraved lines of the Britannia vignette, the bill seems merely to spell out the Bank's classic promise to pay the bearer a specific sum, with the promise and date arrayed in elegant calligraphy, all guaranteed by the bold signature of the Bank's chief cashier. The bills had no crosshatched or geometric patterns, known as a guilloche, which are difficult to duplicate and so complex that they now are engraved by computer. There was, however, a code or "cypher" of a few numbers and letters identifying each batch.

Right into the war, the Bank of England had maintained a complex, cross-referenced process of authentication for each bill it issued. It was the job of the technicians at the Note Issue Office to number, disburse, and keep track of all pound notes. The senior officials as well as the technicians at the Bank believed their system to be virtually inscrutable. All notes of five pounds or more were given a place and date — for example: London, August 8, 1938 — and no more than 100,000 bills were printed with that date, often less. Each batch was assigned an alphanumeric code that appeared in small letters — say, $2\frac{B}{58}$ — its cypher. And each bill had its own serial number indicating its sequence within that batch. There were enough alphanumeric batch numbers to last forty years, at which point the cycle would start again. But there was no risk of duplication because by then the Office of Chief Cashier, whose bold signature was printed on each bill, would certainly be occupied by someone else.

The functionaries of the Note Issue Office believed this would trip up counterfeiters, but with typical British insularity, they overlooked one thing: the pound sterling, as the Germans well knew, was an international currency. Forgers abroad simply had to duplicate a bill that was easy to fake, and then copy the batch and serial numbers straight from a real one. As long as the counterfeit bill did not actually reach Threadneedle Street for inspection (and foreign banks only cabled the dates, numbers, and letters for verification), counterfeits could be blithely passed from hand to hand.

Producing a duplicate on a plain press seemed simple to any printing specialist, and matching up the identifying codes only slightly more complex. The least trouble was presented by the ink used by the Bank of England. It was known as Frankfort black because its pigment was made from the charcoal of German grapevines boiled in linseed oil. Schmidt Brothers of Berlin produced it, and Krueger improved it to imitate ink's normal spread into banknote paper over the years.

Since the black-and-white notes first made their appearance in the 1830s, the Bank had erected its own secret hurdles against counterfeiting. During the Weimar Republic, the Reichsbank recognized this and asked for samples, which were supplied with great reluctance by London and heavily stamped SPECIMEN. It was only after many different pound notes from the Germans' regular stock were enlarged and projected onto screens in Friedenthal and Sachsenhausen that sharp-eyed engravers in both places, working on different bills in tandem and literally comparing notes, realized how many security marks had been deliberately designed to pose inconspicuously as minor printing flaws.

Before the war, most freelance counterfeiting gangs ignored these marks at their peril, underwriting the Bank's smug certainty that its specialists would quickly recognize any fakes and confiscate them. Over the years, the Bank's engravers had carved as many as 150 different security marks, varying them as they changed plates for new issues after press runs of 100,000. The Britannia medallion itself always had three secret marks: a group of five dots on the back of her right hand, a shading line down the length of her spear that stopped slightly short of the base of its handle, and a hairline break across the shading lines in the upper-right section of foliage surrounding the figure. On some issues, the shield was irregularly curved and the sea variously shaded. The prisoners came to call the engraving "Bloody Britannia" and missed some of these details, but not many, as they learned to become master counterfeiters, spotting and duplicating the purposely malformed text letters, the tiny nicks in the large letters of the elaborately carved blocks that denoted the value of each bill in words rather than numbers, and the almost invisible dots they called "fly-specks." They soon learned to look for a tiny, off-center dot just above the i in the signature of chief cashier Peppiatt. Furthermore, one p in his name had a little swallowtail; if the plate had been too heavily inked, it would blur or blot out.

One morning in 1943 Krueger arrived with proof of their success. He pulled a sterling note out of his pocket and smiled as he waved it in the air. "Look at this, gentlemen. This note has been circulating in English banks and accepted as genuine. Congratulations on excellent work. I'm proud of you, gentlemen. Now we can really go to town. We are going to expand the plant." As a reward, he ordered loudspeakers to pipe in German radio, but their spirits were already high with the news that the operation was succeeding and growing larger. They had won a further reprieve from the gas chamber, and a jubilant Krueger had won their grudging respect. "One would think he had already been appointed Governor of the Bank of England," said Max Bober, a Berlin printer and barracks wit.

As new recruits arrived, most of the men went on twelve-hour shifts starting at 6 a.m. and 6 p.m. so production could continue around the clock. It reached its peak in midsummer 1943, when more than 100 workers produced an average of about 650,000 notes a month, until about mid-1944. Six flatbed presses, including four of the latest Monopol Type 4 models with special registering apparatus and manufactured under special wartime priority, spewed out five-, ten-, twenty-, and fifty-pound notes. (Krueger stopped there because he knew that hundred-pound notes would always be examined closely, probably too closely.) Each press had two pressmen. The walls of the room were lined with wooden crates full of blank paper awaiting watermark inspection, and the tables were piled high with half-finished notes whose massive presence some prisoners found overwhelming. The room was sectioned into areas for cutting, aging, and sorting — *Reisserei, Altmacherei,* and *Sortirei.* The printed sheets were laid on a drying rack, then torn into four individual bills with a steel ruler and stacked in bundles of one thousand. Then the sides were roughed up with metal rasps to imitate the deckle edge.

A double line of prisoners with intentionally dirty hands aged the bills artificially by rubbing, folding, and puncturing them, writing English words on them with English ink, and stamping the names of English banks on the reverse side to manufacture a life history for each bill. At first little notches were also torn away along the side at specific levels for different denominations to mimic a method used by bank tellers to speed counting the bills, but that was discontinued after Krueger realized this was not English but Continental practice. Finally the bills were placed in a press to smooth them out before they were inspected and classi-fied according to the quality of the counterfeit, perhaps the pris-oners' most important and demanding task.

Each note was placed on a wooden box containing two harsh electric bulbs covered by a translucent glass pane. A real pound note was sometimes placed on the light box next to the counter-feit for comparison, flaws and all. Each man had to perform a meticulous inspection of five hundred bills a day, thus allowing an average of slightly less than two minutes for each one. The in-spectors were initially on seven-hour shifts to forestall eyestrain, but as the pace of production intensified, they worked ten hours a day. It was a grueling test of nerve and eyesight, since each prisoner-inspector was held accountable for missing any flaws, which could be literally the size of pinpricks. Paradoxically, that served the counterfeiters well because these tiny blemishes could be obliterated with the prick of a pin. Such scars were normally inflicted on genuine notes by British bank tellers, who for genera-tions had bundled up notes with straight pins. It was particularly useful for obscuring blemishes in Bloody Britannia; usually her glance was clear, but if it was not, a note could be upgraded with a pinhole by stabbing her in the eye.

One day a nearsighted SS sergeant named Apfelbaum who normally delivered paper from the factory was standing in as a guard. Apfelbaum had the habit of warning the prisoners that nothing escaped his sharp eye. Curious, he wandered past the in-spection station of Isaak Glanzer, a Czech veteran of Block 19. Glanzer began boasting that the counterfeits were superior to the real thing because of the prisoners' keen ability to spot flaws. "We have to see that the lady [Britannia] is properly centered in her oval. As we say in the trade, the lines in the watermark must not swim, or sit too high on the note, either. The Bank of England can permit that, but not us," he lectured the guard, going on about the secret dots as he pointed to the fiver on his light box.

"The Bank of England issues notes much worse than this. As a whole, sir, counterfeit notes are much more perfect than the genuine." Fortunately, an air raid siren interrupted Glanzer before the sergeant had time to realize how preposterous were his boasts and slap him down.

Moritz Nachtstern had learned all the peculiarities of the bills in the engraving room and was transferred to the inspection room to teach the newcomers. "Do you notice that cut in the letter *f* and those three dots?" he asked a recruit, pointing precisely to some of the deliberate faults that the Bank believed to be utterly unknown to outsiders. "Those are the things you've got to watch for when you sort. You have to watch carefully how this watermark is placed. This note is perfect. Study it. Put the notes with faults in a separate bundle. Turn the good ones over to the foreman."

Sometimes tiny splinters of wood or fiber were embedded in the paper and had to be scraped away carefully with small knives. The success or failure of this surgery determined whether a note passed inspection as a perfect specimen. Oskar Stein, who ran the countinghouse as office manager and head bookkeeper, advised his charges: "Don't hesitate to use the knife. Even if you ruin a few bills, it won't matter because we have plenty of the stuff. When in doubt, always place the note in a lower category."

Stein, formerly a Prague businessman who went by the Czech name of Skala, counted and indexed the notes in a ledger as if they were real; his is the most reliable record of almost 9 million separate notes with a face value of £132 million that were ultimately produced by Operation Bernhard. Stein maintained four separate categories that provide an important key to the shifting priorities of the enterprise. The most perfect notes were placed in the first category, to be sent to German spies in foreign countries or delivered to them to pay their contacts and sources. These were of such high quality that they could be safely used in England, although they rarely, if ever, were. The second grade was almost indistinguishable from the first by Allied and even some British experts because of only minor errors. A third category had more serious flaws, but flaws that nevertheless might be found in real pound notes. They were sent to foreign and especially neutral countries where the Nazis bought raw materials for their war machine. The fourth class was at first piled into a strongroom to be flown over England later and released; hence they were called *Abwurf*, the German word for "air-drop" — in full, *Abwurf aus der Luft*. But as that founding idea receded with the huge Luftwaffe losses, the SS passed these notes, too. (They were later declared "good enough to fool anyone but an expert" by the chief American investigator, himself a Secret Service agent.) Last came the spoiled notes — *Ausschuss* (rejects) — that were either returned to the paper factory for pulping or burned at the camp. Felix Tragholz, a Block 19 prisoner from Vienna who took care of incinerating the paper, was supplied with a filter for the smoke-stack, lest even a charred scrap be found and give the game away.

By the late spring of 1944, Krueger had stopped mentioning the plan to ruin the British economy, instead stressing secrecy above all: "You are collectively responsible for seeing to it that no one shall ever find out what is contained in those boxes and what is being done here . . . Your assignment is nothing more and nothing less than the manufacture of enemy bank notes." But when the printer Adolf Burger arrived in 1944, he recalled, Krueger did not bother to conceal the principal purpose of his operation: "We must pay our agents well and respect their wishes to be paid in dollars or British pounds. They shall have them. They will never realize that they are being paid in counterfeit pounds; they believe the money is genuine."

Every Saturday, Krueger picked up the week's output from the camp and drove it to SS foreign espionage headquarters in Berlin; by 1944 production was so heavy that his briefcase would hold only the first-class notes. Some of the rest were shipped directly to

German commercial attachés in Norway and Denmark (over-ruling economics minister Walther Funk's prohibition against distribution in occupied countries) and to neutral nations such as Spain, Portugal, Turkey, and Switzerland. The fakes were sent in pale green linen envelopes, their four flaps folded over into a packet 9½ by 11½ inches and sealed with wax. Although they were addressed by the prisoners and marked SECRET in red letters, Himmler himself was named on the envelope as the sender.

Krueger certainly did not go unrewarded. Exactly how much money he skimmed will never be known, but the prisoners always gave him twenty first-class notes from each new series "for his personal use." This type of corruption, only a shadow of what was to happen to the huge Operation Bernhard output, was endemic throughout the SS. Auschwitz was a plum SS assignment not just because it was a noncombatant post but because it offered opportunities for enrichment by theft from the hundreds of thousands of arrivals carrying gold watches, jewelry, pound notes or dollar bills, and diamonds sewn into their clothing. These valuables were catalogued and sent to Berlin, but the loot was skimmed so widely that the guards' lockers were searched, and some were disciplined by transfer to frontline duty. For the prisoners with the gruesome job of sorting the clothes, the prize was food the victims had carried with them. In the sardonic humor of the camps, the area where goods were sorted was known to guards and prisoners alike as "Canada" — a place rich in natural resources.

With Krueger's money factory humming, the counterfeiters' main concern was simply to stay alive as long as they could and survive the always latent SS sadism. The elderly Artur Springer was caught dozing over his inspection box one hot summer day. Sergeant Weber crept up behind him, fired his pistol to awaken and frighten him, then stuffed him into a full field uniform with gas mask and helmet, forcing him to work in that stifling getup for two hours.

Outside, Weber's comrade Marock zoomed in circles on a noisy motorcycle, spitting pebbles against the side of the barracks.

Such behavior was typical of the two petty tyrants, who enjoyed taunting their charges and, more often than not, extorted items from their food parcels. Sven Hoffgaard, a *Mischling* Danish bank teller, realized he had been diverted to Operation Bernhard by the guards so they could loot his Red Cross parcels. Marock slapped around a hunchback from Poland named Leib Italiener when he arrived because the sergeant thought the new prisoner was lying about his incongruous name. Italiener took a while coming to terms with the total incongruity of the place itself, wondering whether it was some front for the anti-Nazi underground and fearing he would never be equal to the task. He decided he could live through it somehow, taking things philosophically: "Time is only a concept. Life is the only real thing."

Generally the prisoners were let off with beatings or punitive physical exercise for infractions that would have meant instant execution at other camps. The one fatal exception was tampering with the pound notes. A wrinkled little man named Hermann Gütig, a drifter from Frankfurt and a camp clown who was roundly hated for puffing up his own authority as a minor block assistant, burned about two dozen bills after he was demoted, most likely to take revenge on the section where the ashes were found. His crime was soon discovered. He was beaten and whipped by the guards into confessing, whereupon he was hanged. Throughout Operation Bernhard, four prisoners with serious communicable diseases are believed to have been summarily dispatched in order to protect the project from an epidemic. One prisoner, a young teacher from Poland named Izaak Sukenik, was blessed with an intelligent curiosity and a gentle manner, but cursed by an advanced case of tuberculosis. Lying on his bed, he would say, "I would love to live through the end of this, just the end. I would like to know that my life had not been in vain." For a while he was protected by Dr. Rojzen, who switched test vials of phlegm in the barracks under the nose of an oblivious SS guard. But one day Sukenik spat up blood during a punishment exercise and was X-rayed; he knew that meant his death, which he faced with great courage.

For any prisoner, a visit to the doctor or dentist was both an ordeal and a risk: an ordeal because prisoners were not permitted anesthetic lest they unconsciously spill their secret; a risk because they never knew whether a medical injection was intended to cure them or kill them. In the prison parlance of Block 19, any shot in the arm could turn out to be a *Himmelfahrtspritze,* an injection to a heavenly journey.

In the end, Marock and Weber proved more dispensable than the prisoners themselves. On leave in Berlin, where they bedded the lonely wives of officers at the front, they made the foolish mistake of boasting about their work. Two Gestapo agents in civilian clothes appeared at the camp, roughed them up, and stripped them of their insignia before taking them away. Krueger reported that they had "shown themselves unworthy of the confidence placed in them." Marock was shot, Weber sentenced either to fifteen years in prison or to duty on the Russian front. The prisoners' first reaction to their tormentors' fate was not personal relief, not even classic German schadenfreude, but anxiety that such a gross violation of secrecy might bring Operation Bernhard to a halt. Krueger assured them it would not.

The prisoners viewed virtually every event, even the good news of the D-Day landings, through the single prism of whether it might induce Himmler to shut down the operation that was prolonging their lives. Incentives to stretch out the work became stronger as the tide of battle turned and liberation seemed possible. The lenient treatment may also have encouraged the few active saboteurs, but no one talked much about such things lest they be overheard. Chief engraver Felix Cytrin's dogged pursuit of perfection was his preferred form of rebellion: adhering closely to Krueger's orders in the engraving shop and at the inspection section — to print and pass only the very best notes. Counting-house manager Oskar Stein found fault with the paper deliveries for minor imperfections. Prisoners in the print shop also performed small acts of sabotage, fouling the rollers to stop the presses temporarily, chipping at the printed letters, or damaging the engraved plates. Abraham Jacobson, who had managed a printing plant before he was arrested as a Dutch underground leader, said his fellow-prisoners were seized by a spirit of resistance, but not to the point of refusing to work. "We agreed, however, to sabotage the orders as much as possible because by doing so we would lengthen our own lives," Jacobson said. "If the process were shut down, for whatever reason, we knew absolutely for sure that it would be our end."

During working hours, the prisoners' minds were too fully engaged to think of their bleak future, but after they left the hurly-burly of the print shop or the intense concentration of the inspection tables, they were enveloped by a melancholy that was difficult if not impossible to shake. Some diverted themselves with newspapers and magazines; others played practical jokes. Max Bober commandeered the public address system (the guards were in on the prank) and, declaring, "This is England," announced that the Bank of England knew all about Sachsenhausen and two of the principal counterfeiters, Leo Krebs and Hans Kurzweil. When the two section chiefs heard their names, they paled, and even the guards joined in the laughter at their expense.

The lugubrious Cytrin declared such stunts were "a mere pretense to drive us completely crazy." He was certain that one day Berlin would decide it had enough pound notes, and that would be the end of them. Bober's view was more sanguine: "That won't happen so soon, so you can rest easy. It's a long way to Tipperary, as it goes in the song. Plenty can happen before Hitler gets to that stage." Cytrin could only hope that "if a collapse happens quickly, maybe we here in this block will have a chance, too."

If not a constant visitor, death was always a presence. Max Groen, the Dutch newsreel cameraman, thought of Krueger without rancor as "the big chief, a very nice man, softly spoken, but in the back of my mind, I knew that even with his nice undertone, he would send me to the gallows if necessary." But life was a presence, too, by the mere chance of their continued survival, even if by a thread. The prisoners confronted an exquisite dilemma in short, emotional bursts, and the debate engaged them all, each in his own way. Avraham Krakowski, reproached for not extinguishing his light box lest he violate a prohibition of the Jewish Sabbath, stabbed his knife into a stack of bills out of frustration and anger but also a profound declaration of faith. Krakowski and Isaak Glanzer, another observant Jew, discussed the Torah and prayed together. Glanzer told his younger companion that "we will need divine mercy to get out of here alive. So let's stick together."

They did.

Nachtstern, surprising himself with his frankness, asked Springer one day whether he thought they would ever leave the camp alive. Springer looked equally surprised at the question and replied, "You don't think, Mr. Nachtstern, that the Germans will let you go back to Norway and tell about what happened in this block? No, only a miracle can save us. But anything may happen in this crazy world. For you young folks' sake I hope the miracle will happen. As for myself I don't expect much more in this life. I'm too old to start anew, sick and penniless as I am."

Nachtstern was depressed by the exchange until Glanzer, Richard Luka, and Fritz Schnapper called him over for a hand of cards. They joked that theirs was a very exclusive club, and since Schnapper was the oldest, he should be elected president. Glanzer extended the gallows humor: "We can also safely make him a member for life." Schnapper growled in Yiddish: *"Kish mir im tuchus"* — Kiss my ass.

A few months later, Dr. Rojzen, like most good doctors a man of some equanimity, succeeded in taking the edge off a similar, occasionally despairing exchange. "Luck or miracle, what's the difference?" he concluded. "What counts is that I had already given up when I was saved. It's the same with all the others who came here with me. We have a pretty good chance to survive, as I see it. Remember, we are the geese who lay the golden eggs. Don't worry, they won't get rid of us until the very end. Before that happens, a lot of things may come to pass."

They did.

Chapter 8

"THE MOST DANGEROUS EVER SEEN"

To inspect the bound ledgers of the Bank of England's trans- actions is to enter a lost world. Until World War I, some clerks, shabby in top hats and tailcoats, still used quill pens. Even when they modernized with steel nibs, copperplate script re- mained the norm, elegantly recording the exchange of notes in and out, true and false. From the slump of the early 1930s until the early 1940s, barely a dozen large counterfeit notes had reached Threadneedle Street instead of being stopped in commercial banks by tellers who were trained to spot them. In April 1941, new forg- eries started appearing. They had been skillfully photographed and then printed by lithography, but were easily detected by their limp paper. Relatively few of these Type Z forgeries (as the Bank designated them) passed through the Note Office in the following months, and they caused little alarm. They were traced to the oc- cupied territories of Belgium and France; the neutral transfer point of Switzerland; and to Palestine, then under British rule, having probably originated in occasional distributions by Opera- tion Andreas.

Then on September 21, 1942, just as Operation Bernhard was gearing up, nine forged ten-pound notes were accepted by banks in Tangiers, a colonial city of international rogues and smugglers at the northern tip of Morocco, just across the straits from Gibraltar. They were forwarded to London for credit and zipped right past the Bank of England's own inspectors before the Bank's Note Office bounced them. They were similar to but far more expert than the Type Z forgeries; the batch and serial numbers showed that real notes with those designations had already been cashed at the Bank by someone else. Craftsmen at the Bank's St. Luke's printing works studied them and declared them counterfeit. The new fakes were designated Type BB, and the deputy chief of the Note Issue Office reported they were "the most dangerous seen for many years." Someone above him in the Issue Department, which supervised the offices handling the notes, upped the ante and wrote in the margin that *BB is the most dangerous ever seen.* Confirmation came from viewing the paper under a quartz lamp, which terrified Bank officials had sent one of their number rushing out to buy: the reproduction and printing were so close to perfect that flaws appeared only when a microscope was trained on the bills. According to the Bank's own war history: "After prolonged microscopic examination of many specimens only one small consistent irregularity in the printing was found in this type (in the reproduction of the hair falling to the right side of the face of Britannia)."

A flood of counterfeits soon followed. In January 1943, the Bank's clerks wrote their litany in stately copperplate. "On 19th January 1943 a forged £5 note was discovered in the Sorting Office . . ." "On 21st January 1943 a forged £10 note numbered 20.740 and dated 19 April 1938 was presented by Nat. Pro. [The National Provincial Bank] Bishopsgate in their charge received No. 154 and paid. The forgery was not discovered until . . ." "On 27th January 1943 a forged £5 note numbered $^{B}_{2}14$ 12.783 dated 5 May 1938 was detected in the sorting office." "On 27th January 1943 a forged £10 note $_{1}^{K}34$ 17.644 dated 19 April 1934 was detected by Miss Strong . . ." And so on. The Bank quietly stopped issuing all notes over five pounds, ostensibly to prepare for postwar controls on the international use of sterling. The real reasons were discreetly hidden. The chancellor of the exchequer, Kingsley Wood, gave a brief reply in writing to a prearranged question in Parliament about forged notes, reporting that the number circulating in the country was both decreasing and insignificant. Even in the Bank's own archives, extracts from the minutes of its senior management committee are completely silent on forgeries of any kind, from Sir Kenneth Peppiatt's presentation of a memorandum on one-pound forgeries on January 10, 1940, until his first damage assessment after the war, more than five years later. The Bank had taken it virtually as an article of faith that its notes could not be counterfeited, just as Germany was certain that its Enigma machine made its codes unbreakable. Both, of course, were wrong. Although the British level of hubris reached only that of David Low's famously pompous cartoon character, Colonel Blimp; the Germans' misjudgment proved fatal. Once the flood of Bernhard notes became so great that it started lapping at English shores, the Old Lady actually got a look at her illegitimate German progeny. Like any well-bred matron facing scandal, she slammed the front door and kept a stiff upper lip.

Wood was narrowly correct in his statement to Parliament that forged pounds were causing few problems in Britain. But the war raged in the rest of Europe, and by this point enough Bernhard forgeries were circulating to buy large amounts of gold, other valuables, and scarce raw materials, or to be used in SS espionage operations. Inside Sachsenhausen, the exact number and sum of the forgeries — 8,965,085 notes with a total value of £132,610,945 — were recorded meticulously by Oskar Stein in his secret diary. That would be $545 million at the official rate of exchange; in today's money at least $6 billion. Less than 10 percent — only £10,368,445 — were top-grade notes actually forwarded to Berlin, but even this was more than $40 million at the wartime rate of exchange, enough to build a small flotilla of submarines.

This is Stein's summary of the total Sachsenhausen production:

£5	3,945,867 notes	=	£17,729,335
£10	2,398,981 notes	=	£23,989,810
£20	1,337,335 notes	=	£26,746,700
£50	1,282,902 notes	=	£64,145,100
Total	8,965,085 notes	=	£132,610,945

Of that total, the following amounts were sent to RSHA (Reich Central Security Office), Berlin:

£5	264,863 notes	=	£1,324,315
£10	176,561 notes	=	£1,765,610
£20	141,046 notes	=	£2,820,920
£50	89,152 notes	=	£4,457,600
Total	671,622 notes	=	£10,368,445

Stein kept no record of how many millions more of almost indistinguishably lower quality notes were plucked from the Sachsenhausen safe and passed into the market.

On September 15, 1943, almost a year to the day after the BB forgeries were first detected, a Yugoslav officer named Dusko Popov arrived in London, opened his bags in front of his British handlers, and dumped out a large cache of silk stockings, a sealed radio set, various written reports, and two packets of money, twenty $100 bills and £2,500 in five-pound notes. Popov was a double agent, and one way he diverted suspicion was to demand hefty payments from his German masters so they would believe his motive for spying was purely monetary. For the British, Popov operated under the code name Tricycle in Lisbon to establish a secret escape route through neutral Portugal for Yugoslavs supporting the Allies, but things had gotten too hot for him. He had flown to London and put himself under the protection of his spymasters. The British found Popov a perch at the Yugoslav legation in London, from which they sent him on missions back to Lisbon. They also sent 500 of his five-pound notes to the Bank of England for inspection and were promptly told that 152 of the notes were counterfeits, which were immediately mutilated. Popov's espionage handlers were nonplussed by his declaration that he had obtained them from a bank in Lisbon. They suspected he had won the pounds and dollars gambling in Portugal's seafront casinos and obtained them on its black-market exchanges, and as one handler scrawled beneath Tricycle's financial statement, "I do not think it worthwhile to pursue further up the trails of the payments." After all, spies also know how to fiddle their expense accounts.

But how did such sums get into circulation? Enter Friedrich Paul Schwend, man of many aliases and one of history's great confidence men. Schwend, or Schwendt, or Dr. Wendig, or Major Kemp, or, on rare occasions, Fritz Klemp, had an international financier's ability to juggle millions casually, which is precisely what he did before World War II. He was born in 1906 in a village near the edge of the Black Forest in Swabia, whose people speak a flat German dialect and know how the world works. Of medium height, blond, slender, hook-nosed, and in his mid-thirties, Schwend was strongly motivated by adventure and risk. In 1929, employed as a mere gas station mechanic, he defied his family to marry into the local aristocracy. His bride was the Baroness von Gemmingen-Guttenberg, a niece of Baron Konstantin von Neurath, a conservative politician who served as foreign minister of the Weimar Republic and continued seamlessly in office under Hitler to help give Germany's new dictator a cloak of respectability.

Schwend's new connections catapulted him into wealth and let him circulate on the margins of celebrity. As was the fashion in his right-wing milieu, he joined the Nazi Party in 1932. He moved to Los Angeles to administer the personal finances of his wife's aunt, one of the Bunge sisters, who had an Argentine grain fortune that eventually grew into an international agribusiness conglomerate. Managing her money earned him $50,000 a year, a huge sum during the Depression. There he also befriended the German consul general, Georg Gyssling, who invited him to parties with Hollywood stars. At the same time, Schwend also sent memoranda to Nazi leaders with unwelcome arguments against the Party line of economic self-sufficiency. Schwend is said to have caught Goering's attention briefly with his nonconformist views, and no doubt the Gestapo's as well.

Schwend lived for a short time in New York City (in the comfortable but unfashionable Queens district of Woodside, where there was a small German colony). On the side he also traded arms in China and the Balkans, then moved to Italy in 1938 to represent the interests of his wife's aunt. He contracted to buy rice, flour, and industrial materials for the Germans; at least half his trades took place on the black market, where he could increase his profits by using Bunge dollars. Schwend based himself at his estate on the picturesque Istrian peninsula in Abbazia, an Adriatic sea-and-ski resort now known as Opatija and part of Croatia. It was then part of Italy, and much earlier was the Riviera of the Austro-Hungarian Empire. There this lover of highborn women and well-bred horses lived a comfortable life at the Villa de Nevoso, "a beach ideal for sun-bathing, my yacht at anchor outside." Unfortunately for him, the war dried up the flow of Bunge dollars from America, and his titled wife divorced him. He soon found another, Hedda Neuhold, the daughter of a wealthy Austrian engineer whom he joined as a partner in various businesses.

In the summer of 1940, as Hitler conquered France, Benito

Mussolini, Italy's Fascist dictator, joined the war in hopes of a seat at the victors' table. The Wehrmacht took up Alpine positions peering down on Germany's new ally, invaded Greece, and thus put Yugoslavia in a pincer by using their Italian allies as the principal occupying force. Croatia became the stronghold of the murderous Ustashe nationalists who allied themselves with Hitler. Resistance began among monarchist Serb partisans known as Chetniks (the word derives from fighters against the Ottoman Turks until an independent Yugoslavia was created after World War I). But the Nazis soon co-opted some of the Chetnik officers, while their Yugoslav peasant conscripts resented being there at all.

Schwend meanwhile plied his trade on behalf of the Abwehr in the section known as the Devisenüberwachtungstelle, literally, the Authority for the Oversight of Foreign Currency. In that job he was supposed to ferret out hard currency from Croatia and deposit it in Switzerland to buy war materiel. Schwend operated among other countries through customs, presumably by giving inspectors a percentage for tipping him off to smugglers. He performed with such zeal that Siegfried Kasche, Germany's minister in the Croatian capital of Zagreb, bitterly complained to his diplomatic superiors in Berlin. This intruder, Kasche griped, was throwing his weight around to line his own pockets. Kasche reported that Schwend was invoking high but unidentified connections in Rome "very compellingly" to muscle into Jewish businesses and threatening anyone who stood in his way with a transfer to the Russian front. (Each must have recognized the other as a nasty piece of work; after the war Kasche was executed for his zeal in deporting Croatian Jews to the gas chambers.) When the Abwehr told the German Foreign Office that Schwend had already been dumped as "unreliable," Kasche demanded "energetic measures" to get rid of him and stop him from besmirching the Reich's good name.

Schwend then went looking for new adventures with an Austrian named Rudolf Blaschke. They had worked together in Croatia, and now they concocted a scheme to trick British agents into buying spurious plans for a new U-boat. Schwend argued that if his plot had succeeded, the British would have been duped into diverting resources for unnecessary defenses. The Gestapo, suspecting him for his business and social contacts with the enemy and unaware that this time he was trying to scam British agents, slapped him into an Austrian jail in the spring of 1942. Schwend might have been executed if not for his old comrade Willi Gröbl, an SS money-launderer in Italy who was buying up weapons. Gröbl urgently needed Schwend's talents to help him manage the expected flow of Bernhard pounds. Schwend said he had never traded counterfeit before, but he nevertheless transferred his always fungible allegiance to Walter Schellenberg's SS intelligence unit. By autumn, just as Bernhard Krueger's presses in Sachsenhausen were starting to roll, Schwend was back in Italy and in business in a big way.

Schwend's real boss was Reinhard Heydrich's successor, an Austrian SS bully named Ernst Kaltenbrunner, of intimidating stature (6 feet 7 inches) and utter loyalty to Himmler. He carried the dueling scars appropriate to the face of an RSHA chief and a taste for the bureaucratic wars, which he conducted continuously against his foreign intelligence chief Schellenberg over how to spend the new Bernhard pounds, needed at that moment to set up a German intelligence network in Italy. Hitler had forbidden German espionage to operate there as long as Mussolini was in power, but now the Fascist regime was trembling. Introduced to the two feuding commanders by Wilhelm Hoettl, Schwend immediately impressed them as someone who, like themselves, could operate on a grand scale. "And yet his conversational style was not brilliant; he affected, deliberately it seemed, the dry manner of a businessman who thought only in figures, and he employed no gestures," recalled Hoettl, who was soon to be Schwend's nominal superior, based in Vienna as chief of SS intelligence for Italy and the Balkans.

Late in November 1942, a man who gave his address as Vaduz, Liechtenstein — then as now the capital of an anachronistic state known for dealings as shady as its steep Alpine valleys — changed some pound notes at the Banque Fédérale in Geneva without incident. A few days later the same individual tried to change £10,000 in notes of small denominations at the American Express office in Zurich. This naturally attracted the attention of the management and, in short order, the Swiss counterfeit police and Switzerland's central bank. The notes were examined and declared "clever forgeries," in the words of Sam Woods, an American diplomat with ties to intelligence who was based at the consulate in Zurich. Washington was less interested in counterfeit pounds than the possibility of fake dollars, but the Swiss Bankers Association immediately sent a circular to all its members warning them to exercise the "greatest caution" in accepting English five- and ten-pound notes. Specimens were sent to the Bank of England, which confirmed with little detail or explanation that they were forgeries. They expressed their sympathy for the Swiss, but the bulk of the circulation was on the Continent and not in England — so why help the counterfeiters improve their product by disclosing their mistakes? Rather unhelpfully, the Old Lady told the Swiss National Bank to test the paper under ultraviolet light and rely on the "feeling and the texture of [the] paper."

The fakes were more of the dangerous Type BB counterfeits, and it did not take the Swiss police long to collar the man from Vaduz. He turned out to be Rudi Blaschke, who had no compunction about fingering Schwend. But they had their story ready: Blaschke said Schwend gave him the notes in Croatia, where Schwend had received them from an agent who claimed to have got them from a Turk in Istanbul, who in turn said *he* had received them from an agent in Iran, where — as everybody surely must know — British and Russian occupation armies were circulating counterfeit money. The Swiss, perhaps speaking the language of diplomacy, said they believed him. But Woods didn't. He telegraphed the State Department that Schwend and Blaschke were probably German agents.

Woods was absolutely right. In fact, Schwend could have been the model for the clichéd agent straight out of a spy novel, that suavely dressed man at the table in the rear under the slowly rotating ceiling fan, with a huge roll of bills in his pocket and a stream of supplicants, some swaggering, others unctuous, all eager to sell him something for hard cash. Schwend, Rudi Blaschke, and Rudi's brother Oskar continued to haul suitcases full of fake pounds into the Vienna SS office, count them out, rough them up, and keep them in stock there until needed. But Schwend was nowhere as much at ease as in disputed territory, trading with rival warlords and trying to come away the winner in any deal. The territory of Istria, his second home, was a no-man's-land of partisans, bandits, and the feckless Italian occupiers who had no stomach for Mussolini's war. Kaltenbrunner asked Schwend to buy as many guns as he could for the always cash-starved SS, and Schwend swooped down the Adriatic coast into Croatia, buying arms from the Yugoslav partisans. The Bernhard pounds, of course, were Schwend's currency of choice, and no one seemed to question their authenticity. They were quickly passed by the peasant deserters from hand to hand, mainly in exchange for food.

When the Italian army started collapsing on home territory in the summer and autumn of 1943, the Wehrmacht scooped up arms there. In Yugoslavia, Schwend bought arms from the fleeing Italian commanders. Communist partisans had begun their campaign of mass Italian executions, dumping thousands of bodies into ravines around Trieste. From the Yugoslav Chetniks, Schwend was an avid buyer of submachine guns that had been air-dropped by the British or delivered by submarine. Such valuable assault weapons quickly found their way into the hands of SS commandos.

In the middle of one of these operations, Schwend and Willi Gröbl were caught behind the unstable Italian lines and ambushed by partisans — Communists, as Hoettl tells it, adding a dubious story of betrayal and confession. Gröbl was killed immediately; Schwend was shot through the thigh and bullets grazed his abdomen. Abandoning his car, he tried to drag Gröbl's body into a vineyard to bury it but, weak from loss of blood, crawled into a culvert under the road and hid there for twenty-four hours, pelted by a downpour but also saved by it, because the rain obliterated his tracks. The next day, he dragged himself to the nearest village and was taken to a hospital on an oxcart. Hoettl obtained a posthumous Iron Cross first class for Gröbl, but Schwend's decoration was only second class because he had survived.

Such borderland activities only increased the flood of counterfeits exasperating and confounding Threadneedle Street. Between November 1942 and June 1943, more than 3,000 five- and ten-pound fakes passed through Swiss banks, especially Geneva's Banque Fédérale and Credit Suisse in Zurich. Swiss bankers could not conceive of an operation on the scale of Bernhard and believed that the notes had probably been drawn from a stock of counterfeits printed for the abandoned Nazi invasion of Britain. Other reports of counterfeits spread as far afield as Denmark, and they substantially undermined confidence in the pound despite the Allies' rising fortunes. During the first half of 1943, the Red Army had surrounded and smashed the Germans at Stalingrad in the decisive battle on the Eastern Front; the British Eighth Army was decimating the Afrika Korps; and Italy's halfhearted military was teetering toward surrender. Yet the pound, which could be exchanged for 14 Swiss francs at the start of the year and should have been buoyed by these Allied military successes, bought less than 10 francs by June 1943 and showed no signs of strengthening on the Swiss foreign exchanges.

More counterfeits turned up in the Chilean embassy in London via its diplomatic pouch from Lisbon, and at the Portuguese consulate in Liverpool. That was home territory, and the Bank of England finally relented, albeit grudgingly. It wrote the Swiss, giving more details about how to examine the deckle edges and the watermark. The letter also gave the precise weight of the paper in a ten-pound note: a square meter of real bills weighed 45.8 grams, while the forged paper was slightly heavier at 54.1 grams.

None of this was of much use to a bank teller, so the Swiss pressed for more. On July 19, 1943, chief cashier Peppiatt wrote Zurich that the Bank of England's officers had carefully considered whether to say more, but "They feel, and I think you will agree, that it would not be feasible to define closely all the technical features." And so on, down to the familiar assurance that the feel of the paper and its appearance under a quartz lamp would be a telling although "not an infallible criterion."

But Swiss banks continued to get stung with bogus bills, and they continued beseeching the Bank of England. On November 8, Peppiatt wrote the Swiss National Bank a meandering letter vaguely warning them to examine "the blackness of the ink, the size of a full-stop [period], the thickness of a line or curve, as well as differences in fluorescence," and finally told them about "definite differences both in the 'sum block' in the lower left-hand corner . . . and in the angle, position or direction of a line or curve and to the point of crossing of, say, a line or curve in certain portions of the wording." These features were shared with the Swiss like state secrets — as if the counterfeiters in Block 19 did not know about them already.

In 1944 the Swiss National Bank sent a personal emissary, a Monsieur Gautier, who plunked himself down in London for two months and refused to go away, even after Peppiatt, in a conversation at the Bank on February 22, "admitted that there were, of course, certain secret devices but . . . these were jealously guarded by our technical experts." Peppiatt's unbudging attitude was summarized by his deputy, H. G. Askwith, who sat in on the meeting and wrote a summary of it. But just one week later, the chief cashier's office had to start backing down.

In a letter to S. B. Chamberlain, the Bank's deputy governor, Askwith reminded him that "we made a New Year's resolution to keep future replies to the Swiss . . . as brief as possible and even try to reduce them to a formula." The Swiss would merely be told whether the notes they had submitted were real or forged, nothing more. He then reported that new forgeries had arrived — thirty-eight of them, to be precise, packed into a seven-page letter from Zurich. It apparently expressed rising annoyance at the stubborn Old Lady; she must have cost the Swiss plenty in money paid out to Schwend, his agents, or his victims when the British bounced back the counterfeits. Peppiatt left it to his deputy to seek permission from Chamberlain for "a further chat with [Gautier] if . . . anything emerges which can usefully be passed on." There is no record of any subsequent meetings. Peppiatt wrote the Swiss again in April 1944 but did not give away anything more about the secret markings. The Swiss obviously were not mollified. Although there was no public announcement, they were stuck with about 1 million Bernhard notes. In response, Swiss banks simply stopped accepting any British pounds at all.

That made little difference to the money-launderers, who by now had the phony pounds circulating throughout the Mediterranean and were ordering even more counterfeits from Berlin. The International Criminal Police Commission, under Nazi management, also helped divert attention by circulating regular notices depicting various specimens of forged pounds — except for their own Bernhard notes, which were never mentioned. Those who paid the highest personal price were the forgers in Block 19, now churning out more than half a million notes every month. Their round-the-clock shifts were monitored with a fanaticism that differed from the random sadism of earlier days, and even the slightest infractions of discipline, such as whispering to a fellow-prisoner at work, were punished with exhausting physical exercise. It was, at long last, time for the Nazis to push their advantage.

Chapter 9

BETTER THAN WALL STREET

By late October 1943, Friedrich Schwend had been placed in command of distributing the Bernhard notes, which he was able to accomplish almost as fast as Krueger's men could print them. Whenever Schwend needed more, he would cable Berlin for *Stahl* (steel), later changed to *Schrott* (scrap metal). If he requested 1 kilogram of steel or scrap, that meant £1,000; and 1,000 kilograms equaled £1,000,000, the maximum permitted for each shipment. Whatever sum was shipped to Schwend was debited against his account, less commission, although the bookkeeping was really notional, as his account was kept in Bernhard pounds and not real money. Schwend's nominal debt was then reduced as he delivered gold, diamonds, jewelry, raw materials, food, weapons, and many other items as disparate as they were useful to the Reich's war effort. The distribution network carried its own code name, Aktion I.

Schwend's gross commission was one-third the face value of all notes converted by his network. In exchange, he agreed to absorb all losses from confiscated notes or theft by his own agents. Their commission was 25 percent. That left Schwend a net 8⅓ percent of the total, which does not seem like much, but no Wall Street underwriter ever did better. By offloading the risks to his agents, he was able to skim a steady flow in commissions for himself. This, of course, was quite separate from the gold and gems he could steal for himself, or the money he could pocket by sharp practice, either in arbitraging foreign exchange or simply kiting the price of goods shipped to Germany for credit to his account.

The cover story that concealed the origins of the money from Schwend's own agents as well as from their victims was simple: The pounds had been taken from the vaults of occupied countries or captured from British troops. This convenient fiction worked because the real extent and nature of the operation lay beyond imagination. Records in the SS administration showed that Berlin sent Schwend at least 6 million Bernhard pounds, or about $24 million. This was a huge sum at a time when even an inhabited monastery could be bought for Schwend for a mere 1 million lire, or £2,000, using his leverage as the agent of an occupying power. Private citizens fared worse. To store his loot, Schwend seized an eleventh-century castle near Merano, Italy, from its owners, who never received a pfennig. This was Schloss Labers, below the Brenner Pass and just across the Alps from Austria, in the friendly German-speaking Tyrol that was only nominally Italian.

Schwend's money-laundering network of about fifty agents and subagents operated mainly in areas radiating out from Trieste, once the Mediterranean entrepôt of the now-defunct Austro-Hungarian Empire. Their activities stretched hesitantly up toward the Low Countries into the great German port of Hamburg, though Schwend tried to avoid the German heartland, lest the Reichsbank get stuck with the fake pounds (although that occasionally happened, too). He was brevetted a commando staff major in the Wehrmacht's famous Panzers, although he wore civilian clothes. Schwend also assumed the *nom de crime* of a predecessor, Dr. Fritz Wendig, an SS officer who had just been killed.

Schwend stationed his five principal agents in Switzerland, Italy, Belgium, Holland, and Yugoslavia. At least two of the more prominent money-launderers were Jews. Wilhelm Hoettl boasted later that recruiting "did not rely on ancestry so much as competence" but admitted much later what was obvious: Schwend preferred Jews as front men because they would be less likely to be suspected as Nazi agents and therefore more successful passing the false pounds.

One Jewish agent was Georg Spitz, raised in the United States before moving back to his native Vienna, where he dealt in carpets and the decorative arts as a cover for swindling. His prewar specialty was passing fake American Express traveler's checks, for which he was sent to prison at the age of twenty-nine. The other was Yaakov Levy, a successful jeweler and art expert in prewar Breslau and then Berlin. Forced to flee with his wife and stepson, he first landed in Switzerland but was turned out of the country as a suspected German agent. He turned up in Budapest with a Dutch passport in 1940, posing as a representative of the International Red Cross under the name of Jaac van Harten. How he got his passport he never said, but most likely he bribed some official.

Van Harten and his family passed four years living in high style on the fashionable Pest side of the Danube and entertaining members of the Hungarian elite in a grand apartment graced by fine paintings, some possibly taken from Jews at forced sales or in exchange for Red Cross papers. His dinners maintained the standards of Budapest's formidably rich cuisine throughout the war. When Jews came to dine, his wife, Viola, who had been a sculptress in Berlin, never failed to remind them that she was a relative of the Schocken family, publishers who were an ornament of Germany's Weimar culture. Van Harten's business front was Transkontinent Import Export, situated in a luxurious office on Budapest's best street. He claimed the company dealt in medicines, resins, and vegetable oils, and perhaps it did. But he certainly distributed Schwend's counterfeit pounds, of which there was no shortage on the Budapest black market.

After the Germans brought down their uncooperative Hungarian puppets in 1944 and occupied Hungary on March 19, van

Harten prospered even more as financier and art appraiser for Obersturmbannfuehrer Kurt Becher. A businessman's son smartly turned out as a cavalryman, Becher ran the commission that purchased arms and horses for the SS's own armed troops, the Waffen-SS. In the process he befriended rich Hungarian Jewish businessmen and incidentally provided cover for van Harten, who now styled himself a baron and was even called in to authenticate a Frans Hals painting destined for Himmler.

For Hungary's prosperous Jewish community, this final year of the war was a historic moment of betrayal, escape, and downright dirty dealing. They had been spared Hitler's wrath until the collapse of the Hungarian Fascist regime; thereupon Adolf Eichmann arrived to complete the murderous task the Hungarians (like the neighboring Bulgarians) had refused to perform. Rudolf Kastner, the head of the Jewish community, was permitted to ransom a thousand Jews and send them to Switzerland in a sealed train, an act of bold heroism or rank favoritism, depending on who was among those saved or left behind. Eichmann also tried to negotiate an exchange of a thousand trucks for Jewish lives, a trade that fell through and may or may not have been supported by the Jewish Agency, the semiofficial organization of Palestine's Jews. Becher offered up Jews, promising more later, in exchange for money but especially for testimony that would help exonerate him after the war. All these and many similar events, the details of which will forever remain in dispute, arouse angry passions to this day.

Van Harten was wheeling and dealing with the rest, and some later regarded him as a hero. But his deals caused surprising leaks in Schwend's money-laundering pipelines. Late in 1944, seeing the handwriting on the wall as clearly as Becher, van Harten got in touch with Peretz Reves, a young Jewish underground leader. He confided that he was a Jew and offered his help. Reves led van Harten to a shelter holding two hundred children and their mothers, and van Harten organized supplies for them. The next time they met, van Harten offered money in British pounds. The contribution was worth about $50,000 at the time, but there was a catch. Reves had to sign a statement, with two witnesses, pledging that the Jewish Agency would reimburse van Harten after the war. Since the underground leader had little hope of escaping the Gestapo dragnet, he signed without hesitation.

The Jewish underground then passed the pound notes to Becher as protection money for Budapest's Jewish ghetto. It was only later that they learned Becher's payoff had been counterfeit, an irony that gave them great amusement in dark times. Reves last saw van Harten in December 1944, fleeing Budapest a day ahead of the Russians. One of van Harten's suitcases dropped and broke open as it was being loaded into his huge car. Out spilled a large amount of jewels and British pounds that were quickly scooped up, and the car sped off for Schwend's castle in Merano.

Georg Spitz, Schwend's other Jewish agent, had first become entangled with the SS by trying to buy his way out of Germany on the claim that he was only half-Jewish. This eventually led him to Schwend, who helped him obtain a clean passport — one not stamped with a J for *Jude* — so that he could make half a dozen trips to Belgium and Holland. Sometimes he was accompanied by Schwend's sidekicks and at least once by Schwend and his wife on a trip to Amsterdam. By Spitz's own account, he spent 600,000 reichsmarks on foreign currency, gold, jewelry, carpets, and paintings. That would work out to roughly 30,000 Bernhard pounds at the nominal wartime rate of exchange. He questioned the validity of only seven of the pound notes, but SS men examined them under a quartz lamp and declared them genuine. Although Spitz would later claim he was pressured by Schwend, he was extraordinarily industrious for someone supposedly operating under duress.

Spitz worked through Alois Miedl, a German businessman long resident in Holland who was known for such schemes as trying to supply wood to Germany by offering to buy up the coast of Labrador in Canada. After the German blitzkrieg of 1940, Miedl inveigled his way into control of Amsterdam's Buitenlandsche Bank and the business of Jacques Goudstikker, Amsterdam's most flamboyant prewar art dealer. Goudstikker threw parties at his country castle and counted the American millionaire publisher William Randolph Hearst as one of his clients. As a Jew, Goudstikker fled to England but fell into an open hatch during a shipboard blackout and died. Taking over his art dealership, Miedl became the confidant of Goering and purchasing agent in the wholesale Nazi looting of Dutch masters and genre painters that had adorned the walls of prosperous Dutch merchants for three centuries. Because of the Reichsbank's currency controls, this huge stock of art had been out of the Nazis' reach until 1940. Now they printed overvalued occupation florins and scooped up thousands of pictures at bargain prices from the conquered and impoverished Dutch. With the economy of the Reich sealed off from the world, fine art was almost as internationally valuable, if not as transportable, as gold, which partly explains the greedy Goering's maniacal art dealings.

By the time Spitz arrived on the scene, most of the best art was already gone, but he used Schwend's counterfeit notes to buy lesser works, which nevertheless had their uses. The continuing Nazi demand drew forth skillfully forged Dutch masters, most famously by a failed Dutch artist named Hans van Meegeren, whose Vermeer fakes were snapped up by the unwitting Nazi hierarchy. One of them, painted in his studio and aged like the others in his kitchen stove, was *Christ with the Woman Taken in Adultery*. Miedl offered it to Goering in September 1943 with a dubious provenance and at a steep price. Goering dickered and finally forced Miedl to accept 150 second-rate pictures in exchange. Few, if any, records remain, but it seems likely that Goering's castoffs were part of some of Spitz's deals involving Bernhard pounds.

Miedl finally fled to Spain with his Jewish wife and held on to a comfortable portion of his gains. Van Meegeren was exposed after the war but escaped with the slap on the wrist of a year in prison (never served because of illness) and wide international acclaim for stinging the Nazi plunderers.

Heavily concealed by the fog of war and therefore operating in his own element of international financial anarchy, Friedrich Schwend succeeded in a confidence game of magisterial proportions, passing more counterfeit money than anyone in history. In his principal area of operations, Yugoslavia and northern Italy, government and indeed all public order had collapsed. In 1943 and 1944, partisans fought the occupying German troops and each other. Those who accepted Schwend's false pounds desperately wanted the currency of what increasingly looked like the winning side. They could not simply go down to their local bank, assuming a bank was operating at all, and ask whether the five-pound note they pushed under the bars of the teller's cage was the real stuff. In German territory, they could have been shot simply for possessing the bills, and for those who reached neutral Turkey or Switzerland, the banks sometimes got it wrong.

So the notes churned across southern Europe in exchange for scarce food and consumer goods. The pounds were preferred to reichsmarks, although they were actually worthless. In Italy, as the pint-size military hero Marshal Pietro Badoglio took over the government late in the summer of 1943 and made peace with the invading Allied forces, new currency was issued at 400 lire to the pound. This was twice the rate of the lire issued by the Nazi puppet state in the north. The Badoglio currency was smuggled to occupied territory, whereupon Schwend bought up the Allied-backed lire from the south with bales of forged pound notes. He then exchanged it for valuables in the north. There, the starving Italians calculated prices in more expensive lire, which Schwend had, of course, obtained for half the price in the south. (If this seems complicated, imagine how opaque it was to the Italians, who ended up on the wrong side of the deal, and also consider how easy it was for Schwend to bilk them.) The goods Schwend swept up even included, according to Wilhelm Hoettl, a rotting Portuguese yacht offering a neutral flag of convenience under which to conduct business. Schwend was moving faster and to more effect than even the legendary American spy chief William J. Donovan, who had already proposed to Roosevelt that the OSS print millions of lire and air-drop them on Italy, accompanied by propaganda loudly warning that Mussolini's money was worthless by comparison. (All espionage masters come up with imaginatively wild ideas from time to time or they would be unworthy of their positions, but this was one that literally never got off the ground.)

The counterfeit pounds were also hidden by their unsuspecting new owners in closets, caves, and castles. Apart from the vaults at Schloss Labers, which stood at the head of a beautiful valley of orchards and vineyards sloping down toward his base in the town of Merano, Schwend maintained storage depots for arms, clothing, food, and other strategic goods not immediately put to use by SS forces. Other supplies, especially modern arms, went to Nazi commandos, including Otto Skorzeny, Hitler's favorite for his daring exploits. Schwend estimated that 30 percent of the guns he handled were of English, American, and Russian manufacture. He even organized the shipments himself, boasting after the war, in a letter to the East German writer Julius Mader, that he had put together three or four trains of ten to twelve boxcars, and "most of the weapons came from the retreating Italian Seventh Army." But apart from bribes probably given to Italian commanders, how much Schwend actually paid for this detritus of war is lost to history. Leaderless Italian troops often allowed themselves to be disarmed, and the Italian generals turned over their equipment to the new and far more fierce occupiers.

In his letter, Schwend further described his operations:

[In Trieste] I had a nice cache of arms and merchandise,
even railroad shipping facilities. In addition, I also had eight
trucks. Soldiers coming from Russia, the East, Poland, and
Romania could use them as needed. My trucks could change
numbers at will. The soldiers served in civilian clothes.
Uniforms were worn very seldom.

The organization became much bigger in Merano,
where I had three big rooms near the city, I believe near the
racetrack. Here, we put together and sent off a train every
fourteen days. We had more modest successes in France,
Holland (with the help of Miedl and Spitz) and Denmark.
You know already how we managed to get the bills out of
there: transporting race horses and oat bins with secret
compartments . . . We were able to get everything that was
in short supply during the war . . . from U.S. jeeps to bottles
of iodine. My people did not work [together] in chains. So
nobody was able to squeal on another.

The elements of Schwend's organization would do credit to
today's multinationals, to say nothing of his own array of identities: Italian passports in the names of Wendig and others; Spanish, Portuguese, Egyptian, and several South American passports.
All his papers were genuine and obtained by bribes, probably paid
in forged pounds. He also carried a partisan laissez-passer, and
Hoettl counted it a great pity that this "unique collection" of documents was later destroyed. Schwend's management team and
senior agents were also uncharacteristically diverse for a Nazi
agency. His closest associates included Rudolf Blaschke, his early
partner who often drank himself into a stupor lasting several
days, and Rudi's milder brother Oskar. Georg Gyssling, the former consul general in Los Angeles, was Schwend's chief adviser,

especially on art. (Gyssling had been brought back to Berlin in an exchange of diplomats but was suspected by the Nazis of Allied sympathies, whereupon Schwend had him transferred to his own service in Italy.) Trusting virtually no one, he put his wife's brother, Dr. Hans Neuhold, in charge of the group's books. Another adventurer was Louis (or Aloys) Glavan, in Schwend's words a man "of strong character, decisive, cunning, and a trader by profession." Of indeterminate nationality but Slavic background, Glavan owned ships and moved goods from one country to another, thus obtaining common items such as cloth, uniforms, and arms for the SS and selling them for high profits in places where they were most needed.

The two ships in Schwend's service were the *Genoa* and the *Trieste,* plying the Mediterranean with pound notes hidden inside their engines in asbestos-lined compartments. Reginald G. Auckland, a propaganda-leaflet specialist serving with the British army in Tunisia, was offered a wad of five-pound notes in Bizerte in exchange for a single pack of cigarettes. Instinctively realizing that something had to be wrong with such an uneven trade, he refused. When Auckland learned later about the Bernhard notes, he was annoyed that he had passed up these high-value collectibles. He also realized that the canny merchants of the Tunisian souk must have figured out very quickly how to distinguish a counterfeit pound from a real one. He never divined their secret.

The most meticulously organized network seemed to exist in Germany itself, with local companies as fronts, but it also did the least business because its members feared the German police. Some were arrested, and Schwend could not help them get out of jail. Occasionally, unsuspecting businessmen were dragooned into handling the Bernhard pounds. Some succeeded in shaking themselves loose; others did not. Johnny Jebsen, a Danish double agent working for the British in Lisbon under the code name Artist, was asked by his SS contacts in 1943 to exchange dollars for pounds that were said to have been taken from bank vaults in occupied Paris. He swallowed the story at first and introduced the SS to a Greek who lived by trading foreign currency on European black markets. The Greek money-trader changed some in Switzerland without incident. Both Jebsen and the Greek trader continued changing pounds (and earning commissions).

Some months later, another Swiss bank spotted the notes as counterfeit, and both Jebsen and the otherwise unidentified Greek stopped dealing in them; the Greek even took a loss on the few left in his portfolio. The Gestapo later arrested the Greek on a charge of espionage, probably trumped up in reprisal for his refusal to continue dealing in false pounds. Jebsen himself was protected by his high Nazi contacts and managed to back out of the business. He even claimed he had warned German diplomats in Lisbon not to touch the notes that arrived in Himmler's envelopes from Germany. Eventually, however, he paid with his life for challenging the Gestapo. The fate of these two showed how poisonous any association with the Bernhard notes could be, except, of course, for those back in Block 19.

Chapter 10

WHAT THE POUNDS REALLY BOUGHT

What did the output of Krueger's money factory and Schwend's money-laundering network actually buy for the German war machine? There is no doubt that it purchased raw materials and gold, although no one knows how much, at a time when Germany was on the defensive. The Bernhard bills also played an important role in reinforcing SS troops in the Balkan theater. Lightly armed as police battalions, the SS was distrusted by the Wehrmacht, which refused to issue heavy weapons to a force loyal only to the fuehrer. Schwend provided heavy weapons from the Yugoslav partisans, who were soldiers of soft loyalty or Communists badly harried and often tempted to head for home.

The pounds generally did not finance SS spies when they were sent out from Germany by Walter Schellenberg's parallel espionage service; the bills were used instead to pay off the Nazis' foreign agents, although to little effect. The British captured, executed, or turned every Nazi spy landing on their home islands. Those allowed to live did so on the condition that they feed Berlin a ration of deliberately misleading information supplied by a committee of twenty British counterespionage officials whose operation was known from its designation in Roman numerals as the Double Cross. The reason Schellenberg hardly ever permitted his own agents to carry counterfeits was that the false money, if detected, might endanger missions that were already dangerous enough.

The Bernhard pounds did underwrite some of the war's most oft-told tales, which upon closer examination turn out to be considerably less effective than advertised. Few were more stirring than Otto Skorzeny's rescue of Mussolini, which happened with fanfare orchestrated by Hitler himself. After Badoglio surrendered on September 8, 1943, the Italian marshal high-tailed it out of Rome the next day and simply ignored his armistice pledge to turn over Mussolini to the Allies. Defeated and deflated, the Duce was confined to a ski lodge in Gran Sasso, a winter sports center in the mountains only 75 miles from Rome. It was accessible by a road and ski lift under complete control of German forces. Rescuing him would have been no more complicated than organizing an armed column of mountain troops to make its way up through the Abruzzi and overpower Mussolini's guards, whose loyalties were uncertain.

What was certain was that Mussolini did not want to be rescued. He had already tried to save his regime by a ridiculous attempt to broker a separate peace with the Soviet Union so the Axis powers could concentrate their forces on defending Italy. Suffering from ulcers and feeling betrayed, Mussolini was through with politics. But Hitler had other, symbolic uses for his former model, later his sidekick, soon to be his prisoner. The fuehrer ordered Skorzeny, his favorite commando, to land gliders on the mountain terrain with enough men to seize Mussolini. Far from having to pay partisans forged pounds to locate and help abduct him (as Hoettl claimed), Skorzeny shared a flask of wine with the colonel in charge of the Italian guard while troops packed their corpulent prisoner into a light plane. Skorzeny joined him and the pilot, the three barely clearing the ground in what was touted worldwide as a sensational getaway.

Landing at Rome, Mussolini demanded to join his family in the countryside but was whisked north to Vienna, Munich, and eventually Hitler's Wolf's Lair in East Prussia. There he was ordered to become the figurehead leader of an "Italian Social Republic," a political false front for the German military occupation of the northern half of the Italian boot. The Wehrmacht's generals resented this maneuver lest it prove a rallying point for royalist Italian officers. The mere existence of this puppet government did in fact serve to intensify a civil war in the north of Italy, though Hitler got what he wanted: an excuse to stop supplying Ruhr coal to a defeated ally, and a captive labor force including hundreds of thousands of Italian troops who now were regarded as prisoners and could be drafted to work for the Reich. As for Mussolini, his enforced return to politics cost him his life. In the final days of the war, partisans publicly strung up his body ignominiously by the heels in Milan's Piazzale Loreto, leaving him hanging naked alongside his mistress.

Several hundred thousand Bernhard pounds did play a role in financing Cicero, the central figure in the best spy story of the war. In the middle of 1943, Elyesa Bazna, an Albanian Turk who had been briefly jailed as a juvenile delinquent, then later worked as a driver, was serving as the valet to the British ambassador in Ankara. Even as a *kavass* (servant) to such a distinguished foreigner, Bazna labored under a social stigma. He later admitted that his intense frustrations in trying to escape his dead-end position at the age of thirty-nine stoked "an obsessional greed for money." His employer, Sir Hughe Knatchbull-Hugessen, occupied a strategic position in wartime diplomacy. It was only natural for someone with such a preposterous name to be known to friends since his school days as "Snatch." The German ambassador to Turkey, Franz von Papen, a smooth politician who had helped grease Hitler's path to power, was as unflappable as his British rival but better acquainted with espionage, having been expelled from Washington as a German military attaché during World War I.

Snatch's instructions from Churchill were impossible to fulfill:

bring the implacably anti-Russian and determinedly neutral Turkish government into the war on the Allied side. Failing that, he was to lever Turkey away from its traditional German commercial partners or at the very least to obtain refueling rights at Turkish airbases for the fighter escorts on the Allied bombing runs over Hitler's Balkan oilfields. Von Papen's task was simpler: block the British however he could.

Bazna, the prospective spy, momentarily filched the keys to the ambassador's safe and dispatch box from his bedside table as Sir Hughe bathed, then quickly made wax impressions to create a duplicate set of keys. He also obtained rods to construct a stand for a camera and a photographic light. They were concealed in his servant's room as rods to hang clothes and curtains, an arrangement he had perfected while working for a German businessman-turned-diplomat who later fired him for prying. Sir Hughe, a diplomat of the old school, of course never bothered to inquire into the checkered past of his valet, who was nondescript except for a receding hairline and a neatly trimmed mustache, spanning the width of his mouth in the local fashion. The ambassador assumed this person who barely understood English (their brief, purely utilitarian exchanges were conducted in French) was only slightly less important and no more dangerous than the wallpaper. A member of the embassy staff had slightly more sensitive personal antennae but nevertheless disdained Bazna as "a clever idiot, suave and always trying to put a fast one across somebody."

Having filled three rolls of film with photographed documents while the ambassador was away from his private quarters, Bazna approached his German contacts by telephone on October 26, 1943. Von Papen, acting on the quite reasonable supposition that a walk-in who peddled his wares by phone was either a fool or a plant, refused to let him bother the local Abwehr agents. That was the prospective spy's first stroke of luck, for Wilhelm Canaris's Abwehr was almost crippled by anti-Nazis who soon would have betrayed him. His next lucky break was von Papen's decision to dump him into the lap of Ludwig Moyzisch, a former Austrian journalist who was Schellenberg's agent at the embassy and the one Nazi in Ankara with virtually unlimited foreign funds. Bazna, who had no idea how long he would have access to the ambassador's locked safe, decided to go for broke on the first try. He demanded £20,000 for two rolls of film.

Copies of secret British documents stolen from the ambassador's bedroom safe by his valet were so illuminating that von Papen code-named the spy Cicero after the eloquent Roman orator.* He never knew Bazna's real name. The photographed documents were flown to Berlin, where tortuous bureaucratic rivalries soon were played out over their credibility. An astounding argument came from Foreign Minister Joachim von Ribbentrop, one of the great political cynics of the twentieth century; he of all people found it difficult to believe Cicero's motive was purely financial and totally lacking in ideology. In due course Moyzisch received authorization to meet Bazna's steep price. The first payment came in real pounds supplied by the German Foreign Office, thus keeping von Papen in the bureaucratic loop and making the secret documents available to him. Bazna insisted on small bills, and the initial reward was so bulky it had to be wrapped in a package covered by newspaper. The next payment, in counterfeits, was fixed at £15,000. The payment thereafter was cut to £10,000 for each delivery, probably to limit the circulation of Bernhard pounds lest a glut yield their secret. Bazna became Schellenberg's proudest prize inside the snake pit of Nazi espionage. Once, he asked to be paid in Turkish lire and some diamonds, which Moyzisch arranged with some difficulty. Bazna had no reason to suspect

---

*Could von Papen have been thinking of the quotation from the Roman orator that forms the epigraph of this book? Perhaps. He had a military and not a classical education, but the historical Cicero's description of money as "the sinews of war" was a phrase known to cultured people like the German ambassador and was in fact used (in quotation marks) in one of the many letters received by the British government urging it to dump forged reichsmarks on Germany.

that his usual compensation might be bogus, since none of the Nazis in Turkey, with the possible exception of Moyzisch, were aware of the German counterfeiting operation.

Cicero continued delivering films without interruption for almost three months until an alarm was sounded from a totally unexpected source. Allen Dulles, America's wartime master spy in Europe and later the head of the Central Intelligence Agency, had a source in the German Foreign Ministry named Fritz Kolbe, who was the polar opposite of Bazna. A committed anti-Nazi, Kolbe made courier runs from Berlin, bringing secret papers to Dulles at his base in Switzerland. In mid-December 1943, he delivered irrefutable evidence in the form of a Cicero dispatch. Dulles quickly contacted his British counterpart and warned him of an undetermined leak in Britain's Ankara embassy. (The British, smug as ever, had rebuffed Kolbe well before Dulles took him on.)

Because of classic intelligence compartmentalization, Kolbe did not know Cicero's identity; probably only Moyzisch did, or at least had a good idea of the identity of his precious source. Dulles told Roosevelt that the Germans had penetrated the president's recent discussion with Churchill about using Turkish airfields. For his part, Churchill wondered whether Sir Hughe had inadvertently let something leak. The British Foreign Office's chief of security and a Scotland Yard detective descended on the Ankara embassy in January and questioned all personnel. Security was declared grossly deficient, but Bazna hardly figured in the investigation. He seemed too obsequious and unlettered to fall under the suspicion of the visiting grandees, who were looking for a professional spy. On their orders, the ambassador's safe was fitted with an alarm. Bazna quickly figured out how to disable it by pulling the fuse to the electricity supply. The British secret service planted a fake document in Snatch's safe, "Peace Feelers from Bulgaria," complete with the forged signature of Foreign Secretary Anthony Eden, but Cicero never took the bait, moving more

cautiously when he resumed his clandestine photography, and finally giving up in March 1944. He tried to squeeze one more payment out of Moyzisch for the details of the embassy's new alarm
system, but no sale.

During his brief but spectacular career as Cicero, Elyesa
Bazna had produced negatives of between 130 and 150 British
telegrams classified as Secret and Most Secret, for which he was
paid about £300,000. That was a fortune at a time when an upper-
middle-class family man in England could maintain a comfortable establishment with servants on an income of £1,000 a year.
Bazna spent with some abandon on mistresses but prudently kept
most of the money flattened under the carpet in his servant quarters, then transferred it to a bank vault. After a decent interval he
resigned from the embassy and dropped from sight. He was never
identified as Cicero during the course of the war.

For their money, the Nazis received about what they paid for
in fake currency, which is to say not much. Von Papen could use
knowledge gleaned from Knatchbull-Hugessen's dispatches to inform his own diplomacy with the Turks, but not too obviously,
lest he arouse suspicion. The pilfered dispatches did provide reas-
surance that Britain was making no progress in persuading Turkey
to enter the war, and this could have been of military value if
properly used. General Alfred Jodl, chief of German military operations, recorded in his diary early in 1944 that "results from
Cicero" convinced him his eastern Mediterranean flank was safe
from British attack. Germany therefore could move divisions from
the Balkans to Western Europe against the invasion everyone
knew was coming soon. (The invasion code name, Overlord, did
slip out of one dispatch but without the essential clue of where
and when it would be launched.) Hitler was not as convinced as
Jodl because the dictator had himself been left in doubt whether
Cicero's information was genuine by the turf battles raging among
his own intelligence agencies. By the time Hitler agreed that it

was safe to move the Balkan divisions to the west, it was too late. Cicero's dispatches might also have provided Germany's code-breakers with a mother lode of cryptanalytical data, but they proved useless because the British used one-time pads to change the key in every transmission. So, wrote the espionage historian David Kahn, one of history's greatest spies "did not — could not — fundamentally alter the course of events."

While Cicero was Operation Bernhard's last hurrah, the activities of Friedrich Schwend's distribution network grew more frantic. One of the money-launderers in Bratislava buried his stock of counterfeit bills in the garden of a friend's house and made a dash for Prague on April 11, 1945, leaving Bratislava one day ahead of the Russians. SS headquarters in Munich, which was much closer to the dirty deals, came to believe that Schwend's men were skimming large amounts to salt away money and gold for themselves. Wilhelm Hoettl regularly crossed into Switzerland, and his colleagues said he deposited money there for his chief, Ernst Kaltenbrunner.

Because of the Nazis' unbridled greed in flooding south-central Europe and the Balkans with fakes, pounds had become deeply suspect currency. By 1944, the total production of Bernhard counterfeits amounted to 13 percent of the £1 billion worth of real notes then in circulation. Even if only half those forgeries were actually distributed by the SS, at least one pound out of twenty in circulation would have been false. If they had circulated widely in the British Isles, such a high proportion of fakes certainly would have been enough to grind, if not completely strip, the financial gears of the British economy. (In those days virtually no worker had a checking account, and most shops dealt in cash; credit cards were unknown.) But the British public had been warned by their newspapers about large-scale German counterfeiting, and the forg-

Authentic five-pound note. COURTESY COLIN NARBETH & SON, LONDON

Counterfeit five-pound note. It is almost impossible even for an expert to distinguish a top-quality Bernhard counterfeit from a real note. In this one, the watermark is slightly misplaced, which is barely visible through the watermark line emerging at the center of the capital N. A more reliable indicator is the quality of the paper and the contrast between its whiteness and the blackness of the ink. After the notes had been aged in Block 19 and crumpled when passed from hand to hand, even expert Swiss bank tellers were fooled. COURTESY COLIN NARBETH & SON, LONDON

An authentic pound-note seal (enlarged), the most difficult challenge to the counterfeiters. They dubbed her "Bloody Britannia." U.S. NATIONAL ARCHIVES

Sir Kenneth Oswald Peppiatt was only the Bank's twentieth Chief Cashier since 1694. His signature appeared on Bank of England notes from 1934 to 1949. COURTESY BANK OF ENGLAND

After being named president of the International Criminal Police Commission, SS-Gruppenfuehrer Reinhard Heydrich, chief of the Reich Main Security Office (RSHA), ordered Interpol's voluminous files on counterfeiters moved to Berlin but refused to authorize the use of professional counterfeiters in Operation Bernhard. U.S. NATIONAL ARCHIVES

This is a previously unknown and unpublished photo taken inside the secret counterfeit plant at Delbrückstrasse 6A. It is one of the more than eighty captured German photos of Operation Bernhard found in recently declassified FBI files at the U.S. National Archives.

On July 20, 1942, four days after Heinrich Himmler authorized a second attempt to counterfeit pound notes, Lieutenant Colonel Hermann Dörner of the business section of Nazi concentration camp administration at Oranienburg signed an order seeking German-speaking Jewish graphic artists and skilled workers already imprisoned in the camps. See chapter 5.

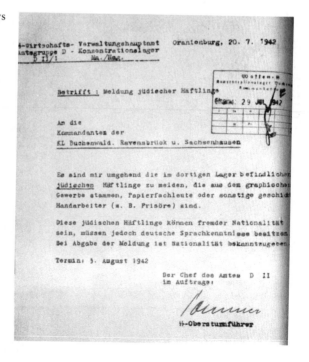

An aerial reconnaissance photograph of Sachsenhausen concentration camp. Barracks 19 is the last one in the group at the bottom point of the triangle formed by the camp's high walls. U.S. NATIONAL ARCHIVES

This undated and uncredited photo showing Barracks 18 and 19 enmeshed in barbed wire is believed to be in the archives of the former Soviet Union. It has been reprinted in several Eastern bloc publications.

Bernhard Krueger was a textile engineer until he lost his job in the Depression, joined the SS, and rose quickly in its technical services. This official photograph shows him in uniform in happier days. U.S. NATIONAL ARCHIVES

Krueger, seen here in disguise in Paris, was sent to Occupied France to gather official stamps, passports, and other documents to be forged by the RSHA. U.S. NATIONAL ARCHIVES

After the German surrender, Krueger laid low for more than a year and turned himself in to the British in November 1946. They told no one and waited three months to take this mug shot, then held him throughout 1947 and handed him over to the French. BRITISH NATIONAL ARCHIVES

These four SS officers knew intimate details of Operation Bernhard, but they were never questioned on the subject at the Nuremberg Trials. Waiting in the Nuremberg Jail to testify are, left to right, Alfred Naujocks, whose failed Operation Andreas paved the way for Operation Bernhard; Captain Viktor Zeischka of RSHA's Vienna office; Dr. William Hoettl of SS intelligence and a link in the distribution of the counterfeit pounds; and Walter Schellenberg, chief of SS foreign intelligence. U.S. National Archives

Salomon Smolianoff, the only professional forger in Operation Bernhard, trying to counterfeit U.S. dollar bills. This sketch by fellow artist and prisoner Leo Haas was discovered in recently declassified FBI espionage files. U.S. National Archives

Shortly after their liberation from Ebensee on May 5, 1945, seven of the forgers posed together. Front row, left to right: Salomon Smolianoff, Ernst Gottlieb from Vienna, unknown, Max Groen. Second row, left to right: Adolf Burger, unknown, Andries Bosboom. COURTESY FAMILY OF MAX GROEN

The sole Norwegian counterfeiter, Moritz Nachtstern, returned to his profession as a stereotyper after the war and published the first eyewitness account of Operation Bernhard in 1949. COURTESY SIDSEL NACHTSTERN

A large crowd of survivors congregates in Ebensee's former roll call area on May 7, 1945. A group at left waves an American flag. UNITED STATES HOLOCAUST MEMORIAL MUSEUM

Arrest photo of Friedrich Schwend, who was Operation Bernhard's chief money launderer and probably the most criminally culpable participant because he helped shield high-ranking Nazis after he escaped to South America after the war.

Schloss Labers near Merano, Italy, with supports for postwar replanting in the foreground. Located in the German-speaking Tyrol just across the Austrian border, the castle served as Schwend's money-laundering headquarters and a storage depot for his loot. COURTESY HOTEL SCHLOSS LABERS

A view of Toplitzsee, where millions of forged pounds were sunk below the oxygen level. Several fortune hunters have perished in the lake or on its steep sides. Peeking over the lakeside cliff are snowcapped mountains of the Totes Gebirge — Death Mountains. PHOTOGRAPH BY GEORG BIEMANN

eries circulated most widely on the embattled Continent, especially in the Mediterranean basin and Hungary, where the proportion of fakes was far higher and the pound even more deeply suspect.

In Budapest, where the Hungarians picked up the BBC's broadcasts, a five-dollar bill could be exchanged for a five-pound note on the black market by the late autumn of 1944. That meant sterling had collapsed by about 75 percent from the official rate, which was about $4 to the pound. Even a fledgling Budapest trader later known as George Soros had been alerted to German-made counterfeit pounds by rumors racing through the markets. Soros, famous a half-century later as the Man Who Broke the Bank of England for trading against sterling at a profit of almost $1 billion, was only fourteen years old when his father used him as a runner during that chaotic final autumn of the war. With George's youth less likely to arouse suspicion, he was sent out one day carrying a heavy gold bracelet to trade on commission for cash. He brought the bracelet to a ring of escaped French prisoners of war operating out of a local café. They left the young man with supposed security of £5,000 while they went off to examine and perhaps fence the bracelet. There he sat, tormented by fear that he had been fleeced with fake banknotes. The money turned out to be real, or at least his father's clients accepted it as genuine. Soros never forgot the sheer thrill of the deal. But someone, somewhere, most likely ended up with a fistful of counterfeits and a very rude shock.

By now it was becoming obvious that the sharp end of the multimillion-pound sting had been blunted by overuse and pure greed, a reflection of the disintegration of the Reich. Hitler himself, secreted in his command post in East Prussia and then his bunker in Berlin, counted on some miraculous reversal of fortune to divide the armies closing in on him. His final throw on the battlefield was his offensive in the Ardennes in December 1944, a sudden thrust that we know as the Battle of the Bulge, to recapture the Belgian port of Antwerp and choke off the Allied supply line. Individual freebooters like Schwend were quietly detaching themselves from the collapsing central will of the Reich and focusing on surviving with their loot. Even Himmler tried to make a separate peace with the Western Allies, using Schellenberg as a go-between with the mad offer of the lives of thousands of concentration camp prisoners to save the SS and his own skin. Anyone who could roll the dice one last time did so, and those in charge of Operation Bernhard were no exception.

Chapter 11

THE DOLLAR DECEPTION

June 6, 1944. D-Day. Cut off from the rest of the world, the prisoners in Block 19 listened to the news over the loudspeaker in absolute and ambivalent silence. With the characteristic distortion of a totalitarian regime, Radio Berlin announced: "The Bolsheviks' allies have launched a dastardly attack against Europe from the West. The German defenders, with fanatic determination and passionate devotion, will defeat that attack." And so on, reporting the enemy losses on the Normandy beachhead, the collapse of the Allied offensive east of Rome (which had in fact just fallen to the Allies), and the crushing of "the Tito-bandit armies" (which had finally begun coordinated and merciless attacks on Yugoslavia's German occupiers). What did the Normandy landings mean for these 120-plus hostages then working in Operation Bernhard? Would their implacable masters redouble their efforts in order to maximize their gains, or destroy the evidence that much sooner and send them up the chimney? Would the invasion advance the date of their liberation or the date of their death? There was no clue.

At one point Berlin ordered production stopped for two days. The alarmed men were quickly soothed by Krueger, who appeared and told them the British had spotted the serial numbers on the counterfeit pounds (as indeed they had) and had warned their own banks (as they actually had not, at least not in much detail). To keep the wheels turning in Block 19, Krueger invented temporary tasks for the counterfeiters. They separated sheets of Nazi propaganda stamps that had already become collectors' items in Sweden; the cross atop the King of England's crown had been replaced by a Jewish Star of David. They sorted boxes of documents confiscated by the Gestapo in occupied countries. Abraham Krakowski came across (and hid proudly in his shirt) a 1921 letter from Vladimir Jabotinsky, the founder of an aggressively nationalist group of Zionists. Felix Tragholz, an offset printer from Vienna, exulted when he found a photograph of his brother and sister in Paris, then collapsed in sobs when he realized it meant they had been deported and most likely were dead. He was denied permission to hold on to this last keepsake. And chief bookkeeper Oskar Stein spotted one important sign: After the Allied invasion, Berlin began ordering notes delivered in the millions rather than thousands. He recorded these shipments in his secret register but did not know whether the SS was vacuuming up the Sachsenhausen stacks prior to liquidating the operation or simply augmenting the flood of counterfeits.

Because of the tight compartmentalization of Operation Bernhard, the name Schwend meant nothing to Stein or any of the other prisoners. What they already knew, however, was that Krueger wanted to expand his counterfeit arsenal to dollars. The new scheme had begun quietly in May 1944, when part of the Block 18 dormitory was cleared for the new dollar workshop, but the work was not going well. This hardly disturbed the Dollar Group (as they quickly became known), who knew the task they faced was challenging. Many false starts would be made, some deliberately. Some prisoners even suspected that Krueger was fully aware of the prospective delays. The longer he could keep his eponymous operation going while every able-bodied man was being called to defend the Reich, the longer he could avoid frontline duty.

One prisoner remembered hearing him worry about what would happen if he had to shut down Operation Bernhard: "I will have to go to the front and you will be killed."

U.S. hundred-dollar bills presented a much more complex task for the counterfeiters than copying the plates for the large, black-on-white five-pound notes and then printing them on a flatbed press. The face of Benjamin Franklin, with his high forehead and knowing smile, is far more challenging to an artist than Bloody Britannia. Furthermore, the bill is engraved with minute details that are excruciatingly difficult to copy. Not only was detailed work demanded on the black-and-white obverse, but also on the green reverse side that gives American bills their nickname. The stiff crinkly paper used by the Bureau of Engraving and Printing in Washington is shot through with microscopic bits of silk thread to add strength, differing from the British bills. Perhaps most challenging of all, the Bureau employs a printing technique known as intaglio. In this process, great pressure forces special ink from the tiny, meticulously engraved strokes on the copper plates into the paper itself, whereupon the thick liquid actually forms a microscopic bas-relief with a distinctive sheen. The bill's almost imperceptible ridges can actually be felt by running a fingernail lightly across the surface or peering at it slantwise against a strong light.

However tiny they were in physical fact, these ridges loomed large to Krueger's Dollar Group. They tried to hurdle them with a process known as phototype or collotype, then widely used in Europe and known in Germany as *Lichtdruck,* "light-printing," which was especially suitable for long runs of a thousand or more prints from a single plate. The small group tried to adapt the phototype techniques that their chief, Abraham Jacobson, had mastered before the war when he managed his own print shop in Holland. The system is similar to lithography; both work on the principle that oil and water do not mix. Krueger brought in a civilian technician for ten half-day lectures and practice sessions. He had no other choice. It took months to engrave a metal plate for intaglio printing, to say nothing of the time needed to learn the technique. This process was then the only possible shortcut.

Unfortunately for the counterfeiters — or perhaps fortunately, for none really knew the odds on their lives — *Lichtdruck* was still not sharp enough to cut corners quickly or precisely enough. At first the glass plate is covered with gelatin impregnated by a light-sensitive solution of potassium bichromate and ammonia, then dried in heat of about 120 degrees. Under a bright lamp, a photographic negative is laid on top of the dried gelatin. The darker areas harden, while the others soften according to the strength of the light passing through the negative. When glycerin is applied, it is absorbed by the soft areas to prevent them from soaking up ink. To repel ink in these lighter, softer areas, the plate absorbs moisture from the atmosphere in the pressroom, which therefore must be kept at a high humidity. Ideally the press should be set in a closed location protected by concrete walls, not the slats of a wooden barracks — a difficulty that provided one of many excuses exploited by Jacobson, the only one who fully understood the process.

Jacobson, a balding, methodical Dutchman, explored many variations in more than two hundred trial press runs. He was careful not to disclose an intrinsic flaw in the scheme: that the microscopic crystals of the chemical would by themselves blur the sharply etched lines characteristic of a genuine bill. As a reserve army captain who had served in the Dutch underground, Jacobson had learned elusive patience during several years outwitting the Nazis before his capture in 1943. His printing experience had won him a reprieve from a death sentence, and he had every intention of using it to survive until liberation.

With Jacobson's skill, the experiments were subtly sabotaged by improperly mixed gelatin and bad photography. Another trick he favored was ordering unnecessary equipment that he knew might take weeks to deliver. Once he ordered a hygrometer "and after some time I got six of them." His chief photographer was the former fashion photographer Norbert Levi, who, despite his name, was not Jewish. The tall, blond, blue-eyed, easygoing Berliner had been condemned to death as one of a ring of food-stamp counterfeiters, then reprieved and sent to Block 19. The third essential member of the Dollar Group was Adolf Burger, a Jewish printer from Bratislava who already knew that his wife had been murdered at Auschwitz. All realized their very existence depended on delivering the next generation of counterfeits, but not whether their chances of survival would improve by producing them sooner or later.

Krueger himself discovered their savior. On August 25, 1944, a short, stateless fifty-seven-year-old Russian with a heavy-lidded poker face and ears like envelope flaps was registered as an inmate at Sachsenhausen. After a fortnight or so in quarantine, his skeletal body was as filthy as that of any other newcomer from the many less privileged camps, but he nevertheless seemed somehow different. Krueger had probably found him by combing the International Criminal Police Commission's files of counterfeiters whom Heydrich had refused to employ for Operation Andreas, then pulled the Russian into his group as quickly as he could. After all, a day, even an hour, could have meant the difference between life and extermination for Smolianoff.

"Good afternoon, you tonsorial beauties," said the new arrival with a smirk, alluding to the contrast between the forgers' barbered hair and his own shaven head. He was led to a table, mounted it, dropped his prison rags, and was formally greeted by

Max Bober, the former Berlin printer whose geniality and quick tongue earned him the role of presiding at camp entertainments.

"Welcome to our clan, *Tovarisch*," said Bober.

"I'm thankful for the great and undeserved honor." The Russian smiled, addressing his new comrades in their lingua franca, which was German. The impromptu master of ceremonies then announced that the new prisoner would be anointed, and proceeded to paint the naked, standing body with random designs in printers' ink, asking the newcomer who and what he was.

"Dear brothers, I am overwhelmed by the royal reception accorded my humble person here today. I come from that famous health resort Mauthausen, summoned by special messenger to work here. I have no knowledge of what you work at here, but I have an idea. By profession I am a counterfeiter and am recognized, even by my enemies, as a master in the field."

And in this fashion, in September 1944, Salomon Smolianoff entered the world of Block 19 and was immediately assigned to Jacobson's Dollar Group. He was not the last of the counterfeiters — a final dozen prisoners would arrive in October — but he was by far the most intriguing. Smolianoff, known to the police across Europe by half a dozen aliases, was the only career criminal behind the wire mesh that enclosed these otherwise respectable artisans and tradesmen. In less extraordinary circumstances, they also would have been adjudged criminal conspirators in the greatest counterfeiting operation in history. But as they all knew, this genuine criminal was probably their last chance to stretch out their unique enterprise.

Smolianoff was born on March 26, 1887, in Poltava, now part of Ukraine. His father, Isaak, was a Jewish ritual slaughterer. From his earliest years he showed extraordinary artistic talent, and at the age of sixteen became a pupil of Ivan Miassojedoff, who had followed in his own father's artistic footsteps. Young Miassojedoff had been awarded Russia's Prix de Rome, his work was exhibited in St. Petersburg, and he was making a career in Kiev and Odessa as a teacher and painter of mystical nudes and mythical scenes in imitation of antiquity. When his world was upended by the Russian Revolution, Miassojedoff fled west and lost everything, while his prize pupil remained for several years in the new Soviet Union, finally escaping in 1925 via Istanbul to Berlin.

The tolerant capital of the Weimar Republic was then host to a thriving colony of some 50,000 argumentative Russian emigrés. They ranged from the world-famous basso Fyodor Chaliapin and his manager Sol Hurok; to the fledgling writer Vladimir Nabokov, whose father edited a local Russian newspaper; and the pioneering abstract painter Wassily Kandinsky.

One Russian artist in Berlin had drifted far from the avant-garde. A judge at his 1924 counterfeiting trial fondly recalled Ivan Miassojedoff years later as a man of great distinction, "like a god from high Olympus with a naturally curled brown beard and beautiful eyes, tall and powerfully built, and with the elegance of a grand seigneur." The accused told the court that, having lost 200,000 rubles to the Bolsheviks in Russia, he felt perfectly entitled to compensate himself by producing his own money — in this case, five-pound notes. Letters from the Bank of England attested that no previous forgeries had been as perfect as his, whereupon Miassojedoff said with a disarming smile, "Well, I have always been a perfectionist." He was sentenced to three years, including the eighteen months already served awaiting trial, which meant he was freed in March 1925. When Smolianoff arrived in Berlin a few months later as his mentor Miassojedoff was released from prison, the young artist's career as a counterfeiter was already made.

Two years later, with police already alerted by a trail of counterfeit fifty-pound notes through Vienna, Prague, Dresden,

Frankfurt, Munich, and the spa resort of Baden-Baden, Smolianoff turned up in Amsterdam under the name of Vladimir Dogranoff. Stockholm police had already cabled the Dutch to look out for one Walter Schmidt of Berlin who had passed a wad of fifty-pound counterfeits to his landlady and skipped town. Questioned under yet another alias (Karl Maier this time), he identified himself as a penniless artist of no fixed address. Smolianoff added that he had found the notes a couple of years before, hidden in the lining of a suitcase at Miassojedoff's home while his old professor was in jail for counterfeiting. To shield his master from the increasingly skeptical Dutch, Smolianoff enhanced his increasingly preposterous story. He now claimed that when he had discovered the notes, they were incompletely printed. Smolianoff himself had added one missing figure and the signature of the Bank of England's chief cashier, finishing the job.

This story was entirely too much for the Dutch authorities to swallow. The examining magistrate challenged the incarcerated Dogranoff-Smolianoff-Maier-Schmidt to prove he could complete an unfinished fifty-pound note behind bars. The prisoner was given drawing materials and engraving tools, and in due course inserted a perfect facsimile of the missing number 5, to the amazed admiration of the Dutch anticounterfeiting squad. But what about the chief cashier's signature? Smolianoff smiled, returned to his cell, and fetched a pair of shoes, extracting from a recess in the heel under the inner sole three tiny zinc plates, two with the number 5 and one with the chief cashier's signature.

Smolianoff was sentenced to two and a half years in prison. Miassojedoff, picked up in a Berlin dragnet, drew a three-year term, which he serenely passed painting frescoes on the prison chapel. Both emerged impenitent. In March 1936, Smolianoff was arrested again, this time in Berlin for passing ten-pound notes, and sentenced to four years. When he had finished serving his time, the war was on, the concentration camp system was writing the rules of German conduct, and Smolianoff was thrown into Mauthausen as an "incorrigible criminal." This death trap — in prison slang *Mord-hausen,* "death-house" — had been designed as a penal camp for "antisocial elements." A Jew, a Russian, and a criminal, Smolianoff needed no three-strikes law to seal his doom. Yet he was saved by Germany's traditional bureaucratic turf battles, which had impeded even the organization of the final solution. Once a prisoner entered the German criminal court system, the judges refused to yield any of their prerogatives to the Gestapo upstarts. Yes, Smolianoff was a marked man, but he had been branded the property of the judicial bureaucracy and not the murderous Gestapo.

Even Mauthausen's commandant had to bow to the court's authority. Instead of assigning Smolianoff to the lethal quarries that surely would have made short work of him, the forger was designated the camp's portraitist. And when Krueger finally located the man he so badly needed, Smolianoff came bearing the Mauthausen commandant's recommendation as a fine artist. Loyal to a fault, Smolianoff also never broke with his mentor. As his home address he listed the Vaduz residence of one Malvina Vernici, Miassojedoff's lifelong companion who sat out the war with him in Liechtenstein.

So there in Block 19 appeared a man with a truly charmed life. Smolianoff's new comrades and even his chief jailer must have hoped that some of his luck would rub off on them.

Hauptscharfuehrer Kurt Werner, the stiff-necked chief of the SS guard who had succeeded the feckless Marock and Weber, explained to Smolianoff it had been decided that the prisoners had already manufactured enough pounds. Now, Werner told the Russian prisoner, they would produce dollars. Smolianoff was then introduced to Jacobson and Levi, who confided that the phototype process was not working. They took the newcomer through the tropical heat of the rooms where the gelatin plates were prepared, a process about which he knew nothing. "We have to produce better work, because if we do not succeed, we are all finished and will be killed," Levi moaned.

The next day, Smolianoff was ushered in to a kindly reception from Krueger. "Well, here you are," the Nazi said. "We have been waiting for you to arrive from Mauthausen. I wonder that you are still alive after long years there." Krueger pulled a hundred-dollar bill from his pocket, a real one, and confirmed that the project to counterfeit dollars was in trouble. What they needed, Krueger said, was a deft and artistic hand to retouch the imperfect negatives. "Do you think you could do that?" Smolianoff assured Krueger that he could, whereupon Krueger spilled out an unprecedented monologue for any SS officer with power of life and death over his prisoners:

"I know that you are all in fear of death, but if you do your work right, I can promise you that nothing will happen to you — as long as I am chief. Inside this barbed wire you are no longer Jews to me. You are my fellow-workers in the fight for the new Europe. Victory is ours. Now we go to work. Do everything to prevent me from falling on my nose in front of Himmler. For if you disappoint me or fail, you will die together with me. All my hope is based on you."

When Smolianoff was returned to the company of Jacobson and Levi, they agreed it was hard to judge exactly what the man they called "the chief" was trying to accomplish. Surely, they reasoned, he could have dredged up a good set of etching tools and a press somewhere in Germany. And surely Smolianoff was not the only competent artist-etcher in all of the Third Reich. As a specialist in the process, Jacobson assured them that no matter how carefully they worked, it would result in a smeared version of the sharply etched strokes that characterized American currency. Although Levi was more hesitant to believe it than the other two, they began to suspect that Krueger was not in quite such a hurry as they had thought.

Nor were they the only ones who thought so. Krakowski had carefully observed Krueger conducting Ernst Kaltenbrunner on a lightning tour of Block 19, declaring all the prisoners "top experts in the field" but chattering incessantly to prevent the SS chieftain from questioning them, and especially from showing off a huge press for printing serial numbers on each bill. (It had been brought from Berlin with great difficulty and mounted on a heavy concrete slab, but no one had ever been able to get it to work properly.) What did impress Kaltenbrunner unreservedly was the huge pile of pound notes stuffed into the camp vault. "Incredible!" he declared. "This must be more notes than in the Bank of England." What they could not determine, Krakowski said, was whether "Krueger intended to save us out of the goodness of his heart, or if he was trying to save his own neck."

As the weather turned cold, the Allies in the west approached the Rhine, the Russians plundered and raped their way through East Prussia and reached the Oder River, only 50 miles from the camp, and almost every night Berlin itself was being pounded into rubble by Allied bombers. Occasionally the planes dumped their explosive cargo near the camp, and after one raid the lights went out. Sitting in the darkened phototyping room, Smolianoff, Jacobson, and Levi agreed to play for time by continually criticizing each other's work. The next day, Levi enlarged a photo of a dollar bill, and Smolianoff retouched it. They were both dissatisfied and said so. They did it again, and again. For weeks they quarreled about the color balance, the chiaroscuro, the precision of the engraving, and much else. Each time, they went back to the camera and the drawing board, "always making photographs of every little detail and fighting continually about the work of the others," Smolianoff said. "Several times the SS had to interfere and separate us because we fought really hard, but they couldn't [dis]miss us, because all the work depended on what we were doing."

Levi tried other tricks. He once insisted that the operation could not proceed without "heavy water" — it is most unlikely that he even knew such a thing existed and was used in making atomic bombs — sending away the puzzled SS men and buying more time. The trio could not carry the entire load of deception, so one of the assistant retouchers, a normally insouciant young artist named Peter Edel, diverted Krueger elsewhere. Shocked by his own courage, the twenty-three-year-old told Krueger that in order to draw some very fine lines, they needed a brush made from the fur of the pine marten.

"And what might these be — magic brushes? Where do you get them?" Krueger asked suspiciously.

"Maybe at Spitta and Leutz at Wittenbergplatz. It's an art shop where I used to . . ."

"Used to!" he interrupted sarcastically, noting that many more beautiful things in Berlin than art shops had been bombed out. "What is the name of this watercolor brush?"

"They're called Chinese brushes, Herr Sturmbannfuehrer. Slim ones with bamboo handles."

"You must be joking. Where do they have to come from — Peking? Am I supposed to send a special commando out to look for Chinese brushes?" A pause for reflection. "But if you do need these things as you say . . ." Then he turned to his senior staff and the other artist-retoucher, Leo Haas, an anti-Nazi cartoonist from Prague who had done a spell at Auschwitz making diagrams for the notorious Dr. Josef Mengele. "Is that really true, Smolianoff? Would this improve things? Haas, what do you think? Well, Burger? Jacobson, Weil, Leonat? Is he right?"

They all nodded yes, astonished but nevertheless indicating that someone ought to try in Berlin.

"So now you tell me! Am I supposed to know where little paintbrushes should be? These excuses are only delaying things. Why didn't you tell me at the start? And if I really believe you, where do I get them without actually stealing them?"

Edel thought they might try his home. "I meant, at my mother's house. My painting equipment should be there. But I'm not sure if it's still there or if my mother . . ." Every prisoner wondered whether his home and family were surviving, even by a thread, as they were. "It was just an idea. I thought I couldn't ask you."

Krueger then led Edel across the courtyard and confronted him in private.

"Have you written your mother?"

"Yes, sir!"

"Did you receive a reply?"

"No, not yet."

"Oh, that's it. All this rubbish about the paintbrush. It was only a pretext for . . . You know exactly what I mean. Now, no more fibbing."

Aware from Krueger's questions that the officer had figured out what was going on, Edel let him ponder without comment. He realized it was a stupid idea after all: Why should this shrewd officer, leading an operation worth millions with a huge arsenal of supplies at his disposal — why should he indulge some prisoner's silly whim?

Still, Krueger sat Edel down at a desk and typewriter, removed the cover, inserted a sheet of paper, and ordered him to start typing.

"About the brushes?" Edel asked.

"What else?"

Edel had never dreamed his plan would get this far and found the scene utterly unreal. He tapped out the letter with two fingers. Krueger peered over his shoulder as the young artist asked for all his China brushes, especially the smallest, size Number 1 to 0.

Edel then extracted the letter and started to write a personal note to his mother. There Krueger drew the line, insisting on a sort of semiofficial request.

"How do you normally address her? *Mutti, Mutter, Mama,* or what? And how do you normally send your regards?"

It then became obvious that Krueger suddenly realized something damning: If Edel coldly asked only about the paintbrushes, his mother's suspicions might be aroused to the point of asking uncomfortable questions. Why did her son need his paintbrushes in a concentration camp? And what was really going on there, anyway? Krueger then instructed Edel to ask for his entire painting kit. "Your mother will surely be pleased to learn that you are being so well treated."

Edel stuttered: "Oil paint. Palette. Easels. Compasses, mixing pots, quills, spray guns?"

"Spray guns, that's good. We will need them. Write down everything properly, one after another."

He wrote it down as ordered, a list that his mother actually received and saved, an extraordinary document with its own life and history, yellowing as the years passed.

"KL Sachsenhausen. Dear *Mutti:* Under the instructions of Herr SS Sturmbannfuehrer Krueger" — who at that point showed the young man the double-lightning SS sign on the special typewriter key and expressed no objection to mentioning his name and rank — "I beg you to give the bearer of this letter the following material." After the list, at the end, he wrote: "Thank you very much for your assistance. Fondest regards from your Peter."

When Edel removed the long list and folded it, he addressed the letter on the reverse to Frau Margarete Edel, which caused Krueger to question why she did not call herself Sarah, as required of all Jewish women under the Nazis. He explained that his mother was not a Jew.

"Aryan? Even better. I don't know all these family trees by heart. I thought always that your father was Aryan and she . . . No, that plays no role for us here!"

Edel bit his tongue. His family name at birth was actually Hischweh; he and his mother both went by her maiden name — but he said nothing. The whole world had been turned upside down — young art students like him had become criminals and criminals had become essential to the functioning of the state. Here was one of Himmler's own officials playing postman for him, and not just postman, a messenger of life.

In due course, suitcases full of the material did arrive to play its part in the dollar counterfeits, but not without another sarcastic Kruegerism about "magic Chinese brushes." Meanwhile, Frau Margarete Edel had been frightened out of her wits when the Gestapo knocked at the door of Kurfürstenstrasse 50, Berlin W35. They scolded her for having mentioned Auschwitz in a letter to him they had intercepted when he was still at that most fearsome of death camps. But now she knew he had been transferred and, best of all, that he had so far escaped the gas chamber.

As the pressure of producing more pounds slacked off, and apprehension rose about progress toward acceptable replicas of dollars, the prisoners amused themselves and even satirized their jailers in a way that was unique in the entire network of Nazi camps. From late in 1943, Die "Moneymakers" von Sachsenhausen had been staging musical evenings. Their easiest task was, of course, printing the programs featuring their own names. But now the Saturday-night cabarets grew increasingly elaborate and purposeful. At the end of Block 19, packing cases from the paper shipments formed the stage and blankets curtained it off. In the front row sat Krueger and his subordinates, starved for entertainment. Krueger occasionally contributed a barrel of beer. As master of

ceremonies, Max Bober welcomed his audience with a flatter-
ing and in fact wholly accurate description of "a distinguished
group of connoisseurs from all parts of Europe. I daresay that
not many artists have ever performed before a more cosmopolitan
public."

The prisoners stirred uncomfortably in their seats lest the SS
take offense. Bober, paying no heed, dripped barracks sarcasm as
he introduced Hans Blass, a Viennese factory worker with the accordion that the disgraced guard Weber had received — "at least
that is what he insisted, as a gift from one of his Jewish admirers."
Blass serenaded them with sentimental German songs and Viennese schmaltz, diverting attention from two Czechs, Oskar Stein
and Alfred Pick, who were sneaking toward the temporarily deserted guardroom. The show must go on — indeed *had* to go on.
"Three troubadours, Max, Moritz, and Harry" — Groen from
Amsterdam, Nachtstern from Oslo, and Stolowicz from Brussels —
were brought forward by Bober to belt out that Maurice Cheva-
lier favorite of the Paris cafés, "Valentine." Groen, the Dutch
newsreel cameraman, who had been based in Paris before the war
and was a boulevardier par excellence, regarded it as his lucky
song and had sung it on the ramp approaching the selection at
Auschwitz. He taught it phonetically to Nachtstern, since the
Norwegian anarchist knew not a word of French.

Suddenly they noticed one guard whisper to another. He rose
and headed toward the guardroom, where Stein and Pick were
stooped down trying to find the BBC wavelength on the radio.
Bober spotted the guard and was prepared: at his signal, Blass
switched harmonies to a shrill, discordant note, as if a key on his
accordion had stuck. The intruders managed to conceal themselves in the guardroom shadows, and the show went on. As the
guard slithered back to his seat, the curtains parted to disclose a
blowup of a dollar bill, roughly three by six feet. Two tiny win-

dows in the bill swung open and out popped the heads of Levi and Groen, singing:

Es geht alles vorüber, es geht alles vorbei;
Nach jedem Dezember, folgt wieder ein Mai.
Es geht alles vorüber, es geht alles vorbei;
Es kommt ja ein schöner Mai, und dann sind wir frei.

Everything passes, gone this will be;
After December, May we shall see.
Everything passes, gone this will be;
One lovely Maytime, we shall be free.

This was a popular song of the time, but the last line was the prisoners' own daring adaptation of the more benign original:

Und zwei die sich lieben, die bleiben sich treu.

And we two who are lovers will ever stay true.

Even Krueger smiled, and his chief disciplinarian Werner had no choice but to join him. What came next was all boffo. A prisoner carrying a Chamberlain umbrella confided he had unfurled it to escape by plane to beautiful Berlin from the horror of bombed-out London, only to land in the famous Block 19. "The Bank of England was only a piggy bank compared to this," he boasted to deafening applause — as Pick and Stein sneaked back in. (They waited until after the show to spread the news of the headlong Nazi retreat before the Red Army.) The onstage gibes continued: at Uncle Sam and his dollars, John Bull laying an egg, and in one skit — passing right over the heads of the Nazis — Levi sitting behind a table full of fake passports as he declared:

"We make everything for the *chaserim*." This Yiddish word, a gross and racist insult, means "swine" — unclean, repulsive, forbidden.

Afterward, in the light of day, the prisoners realized they might be pushing their luck. Krueger lost his cool when Jacobson insisted the dollar counterfeits were not yet ready. "Not yet!" Krueger imitated his Dutch-accented, guttural German: "Well, then, *when*, Cherr Chacobson?" Jacobson shrugged and repeated the problems of matching subtle greens and complex ornamentation. Smolianoff meanwhile was heard boasting that he was working on a fifty-dollar bill "better than the genuine one . . . my life's masterpiece." On another occasion, sliding into what might nowadays be diagnosed as Stockholm syndrome, he said: "It's nice to know one has made something real before it all goes up in smoke."

Finally the senior prisoners brought the stragglers to their senses, warning that their deliberate search for the perfect counterfeit bill was endangering the lives of all. "Leave your work with the magnifying glass and finish the job," one declared. "Prepare a superficial example if you can't do any better." Under such peer pressure, they could no longer maintain the pretense of quarreling. Within two days they had printed what Smolianoff judged a "pretty fair copy of the back of a hundred-dollar bill."

Werner immediately telephoned Krueger, who arrived from Berlin within two hours. Across a table the Dollar Group spread fifteen genuine greenbacks with their fake demonstration bill mixed in. Without a magnifying glass, it was hard even for the forgers themselves to distinguish the counterfeit. Krueger stood before the table studying the array of bills, fearful of making a mistake but probably thinking he would. He finally pointed to one bill — a real one. "We were delighted, he was ecstatic," Smolianoff recalled. Krueger immediately returned to Berlin and presented Himmler with the half-completed hundred-dollar bill as evidence of his team's great progress. That night the barracks heard Himmler was pleased and had ordered them to get on with their work.

The very next day, the Dollar Group turned to the front of the bill. This time they skipped the intermediate step of enlarging the negative for Smolianoff to refine the copy of the engraved face of Franklin. He worked directly on the negative that would be placed directly on the gelatined glass plate. Placing it under a strong light, he picked up a fine needle and, head bent close, began the ceaseless scratching of fine lines to duplicate the original century-note. The guards checked every hour to ensure that he kept at it. He also had to make tiny pinholes in an attempt to match the complex structure of the paper.*

Other departments prepared samples of letters, devised serial numbers, and copied the official government seals on the obverse of the bill. Everyone pitched in to save their own lives, paradoxically aware that success could also lead to their extermination. After a week with little sleep, Smolianoff found his eyes were red and almost swollen shut, but the bill was nearly ready. Werner soon transmitted an order from Berlin for the men to counterfeit $1 million worth of bills a day. By now, late in February 1945, Auschwitz had already been captured by the Russians, Dresden obliterated by the Royal Air Force, and the armored columns of General George S. Patton Jr. were ready to roll across Germany. The final battle for Berlin was about to begin, and the prisoners knew that these dollars could only be Nazi getaway money.

---

*In the 1940s, U.S. banknote paper was half-linen, half-cotton, and milled to withstand pressure of 65 pounds per square inch. It had to remain whole after being folded 2,000 times. It also had a transparency standard of 35 percent when the bill was held up to the light. Under the microscope, tiny pinholes were actually visible. Operation Bernhard's paper suppliers could hardly match those specifications, and certainly not under extreme wartime conditions, so Smolianoff made fine pinholes in the demonstration bill in order to approach its level of transparency.

Suddenly, Stein rushed into the barracks with frightening news. Werner had just informed him that Berlin had ordered the plant to be liquidated. "He laughed maliciously as he told me," said Stein.

Only Krueger could save them now, and he was nowhere to be seen.

Chapter 12

TOWARD THE CAVES OF DEATH

L ike dogs anxiously listening for the telltale step of their master, the prisoners stiffened as they heard Krueger's Mercedes staff car pull past the gate in the fence surrounding Blocks 18 and 19. They peeked out, saw him conducting what looked like a relaxed conversation with Smolianoff, and felt at least a temporary sense of relief. Krueger then strode in and spoke to his men: "Upon my suggestion, our superiors in Berlin have decided to move the plant to a safer location. Our work is too important to have a stray bomb land here and stop it." He continued to address them respectfully as *Meine Herren* and pledged his protection to those who remained devoted and loyal. His attitude and speech allayed their anxieties somewhat, and Smolianoff's explanation was decisive: "We are now going to start printing dollars in such quantities that Wall Street will have to look around for some other business."

That night the prisoners divided up their Red Cross packages for a minor feast, with some extra tidbits for the master forger whose work on the hundred-dollar bill was extending their lives. The next morning they began the brutal job of packing up. The useless numbering machine was dismantled and crated along with the rest of the heavy equipment. The more delicate dollar plates, although still incomplete, were packed more carefully for use in the next camp. Pound notes were put into waterproof crates shaped like coffins and sealed with metal straps. Each packing case weighed about 200 pounds. Loading everything into freight cars during a day and a half was truly backbreaking work. Additional cars carried sealed boxes from the RSHA espionage workshops at Friedenthal. The prisoners themselves, now numbering about 140, were herded into cars equipped with benches and openings allowing them to peer out through iron bars. If asked even by a German general what they were doing, the prisoners were ordered to reply that it was none of his business.

The trip to Berlin alone took four hours, more than three times longer than the regular suburban express. Their rations consisted of sixteen slices of bread for a journey of four days to an unknown destination. With halts for air raids and delays for track repairs, their food was soon exhausted. What they spied through the bars as their train of about fifty cars crawled south from Oranienburg, and February turned to March of 1945, was a wasteland of destruction. When they passed through Dresden, the city was still smoldering a fortnight after the murderous Allied firebombing of the night of February 13–14. In silent horror, the SS guards regarded the historic destruction of this jewel of German Baroque. The blackened wreckage finally demonstrated that Hitler's great Reich was inevitably heading toward collapse. Viewing the grotesquely twisted steel remains of the great railway station, Avraham Krakowski thought of the biblical destruction of Sodom and Gomorrah. He and his comrades rejoiced.

Late the next afternoon the train rolled through Prague. Oskar Stein eagerly took in the sights of his hometown as the train passed the main station and a full view of Wenceslas Square. As they sat on a siding for two hours in an industrial suburb, Morris Gottlieb, a carpenter, spied his own apartment building and silently pondered the fate of his wife and three young children. Other prisoners from Czechoslovakia crowded around the windows, watching their fellow-citizens going quietly about their business and the red-and-white streetcars taking them home. One woman threw them a piece of bread, and even though it fell short, the Czechs especially cried at this display of human feeling, the like of which none had seen for years nor expected, even in their own Golden City.

As the train dragged south, down the Danube valley, old hands recognized that they were heading toward the killing quarries of Mauthausen in northern Austria, where blocks of stone were strapped to human backs and hauled up steps of irregular heights, to be floated downriver on barges to Vienna. In the dark of night, the train ended its 600-mile journey at the station several miles from the camp. *"Raus!"* shouted the guards. Krueger's crew were stripped, deloused, and searched for any scrap of counterfeit currency — possession of which would have brought instant death. Everyone was given a new prisoner's card with a Mauthausen number that wiped away his Sachsenhausen identity with its unique privileges. They could see the camp chimney spewing evil smoke and could smell the repellent odor of burning flesh hanging in the damp air.

Then they were marched up a steep hill, the younger ones helping their faltering older comrades, to Block 20. Some who had previously been at Mauthausen cried out when they saw the number. Block 20 was a way station for criminal prisoners en route to the gas chamber.

The building's walls were spattered with fresh bloodstains. There were bullet holes in the side slats. Hauptscharfuehrer Werner appeared in the doorway to explain. The previous occupants were Russian prisoners who felt they had nothing to lose by trying to escape. Those who were not fast enough for a merciful death on the electrified barbed wire were finished off by machine guns. "So now you know what happens if you are foolish enough to try to escape," snapped Werner, slamming the door.

The forgers were issued damp and moldy mattresses, but

hardly anyone slept. The next day, the younger prisoners unloaded the heavy machinery into warehouses near the railroad station. They were stored next to mounds of potatoes and dried peas that the hungry prisoners dared not touch on pain of death. Up the hill to the barracks they lugged the coffins stuffed with first-grade counterfeit notes and crates holding the more delicate material for the dollar bills. The SS guards shouted for speed: *"Schneller! Schneller!"* Even worse was the sight of about a hundred *Musselmänner,* prisoners whose spirit had already been worked to death, their emaciated bodies soon to follow.* Their clothes were torn from them as they were piled one atop the other, more dead than alive, and loaded into trucks for the gas chamber. Smolianoff, hardened against such atrocities during his earlier years at the camp, was more sanguine than his fellows. "It's impossible to set up a printing plant in this place," he observed. "I could have told you that before. But let them worry about it. Meanwhile, we are gaining time."

For about three weeks the prisoners did little except wait for Krueger and hope that he was in Berlin arguing for his project to continue to the bitter end. Food packages had been stopped, and the watery camp soup offered little nourishment. Krakowski managed to conceal a tiny stock of grain he had swiped from another freight car while their train was stuck on a siding on the slow trip down from Sachsenhausen. On the evening of March 29, observing the rituals with great deliberation, he ground the wheat into about half a pound of flour, kneaded it into a paste with water, and baked it into matzoh in the small barracks stove for the first night of Passover. More than a dozen prisoners shared this meager bread of affliction as they crowded into the washroom for a seder. They chanted the Haggadah in a whisper, lest the guards

---

Musselmann was camp slang, variously spelled. Authorities on camp behavior agree that its origin lies in the German word for "Muslim" because, in the words of the German writer Herman Langbein, "when one saw a group of them at a distance, one had the impression of praying Arabs."

hear this ancient celebration of freedom and its climactic cry, "Next year in Jerusalem."

Two days later the order arrived to pack up once again. It took another week to load everything into about sixteen freight cars, most of them uncovered. The prisoners were packed upright like a tight stand of poplars into two open cars without space to fall if anyone fainted, which some did. Thus on April 23, they made the long day's journey to their next and, they feared, final destination.

The camp was at Redl-Zipf, an Austrian village with an old brewery, lying about 60 miles south of Mauthausen by rail on the freight line through Frankenburg. Redl-Zipf was one of Mauthausen's sixty subcamps, but was kept so secret it was referred to only by its code name, Schlier. The town was nestled in the foothills of the Austrian Alps, midway between Mozart's home base of Salzburg and Hitler's birthplace near Linz, the city projected as the site of his grandiose museum of world art, all stolen. The forested, lake-filled mountain ranges had been chosen as a last redoubt by hard-core Nazis determined never to surrender, partly because they knew what retribution awaited them. Hitler himself disdained the idea because this archdemagogue knew he could never govern from a mountain hideout. He clung to the vain hope that a holdout *Alpenfestung* would split the West from the Russians and allow him to survive by making a separate peace.

In official communications, Redl-Zipf and its 1,500 prisoners did not exist, because the camp was part of the secret production line for the V-2 rockets that had been raining down on London and Antwerp in another of Hitler's final gambles. In the basement of the camp brewery, oxygen was produced for the rockets. The propulsion chambers were machined in huge underground tunnels that had been blasted out of rock with entrances large enough to accommodate a truck. Two dozen workers and their chief engineer had been killed in an explosion during tests the year before. Because of the danger, the underground factory was manned by slave laborers, all dispensable if another rocket should accidentally explode.

As at Sachsenhausen, the counterfeiters took over two isolated sheds, one for their living quarters, the other for their machinery, although nothing was ever printed at Redl-Zipf. The sorting tables took up too much space in the barracks and were moved into Tunnel No. 16. En route, the prisoners crossed paths with other slave laborers for the first time, although they were not permitted to exchange a word. These were Spanish Republican exiles who had been arrested by Vichy France and handed over to the Nazis to help fill the occupiers' quota of slave laborers. The Spaniards had contacts in the local underground and were able to forage for food. They dropped cigarettes on the ground as a way of sharing a smoke with the counterfeiters. Once they left a bucket of food at the barracks gate, which Werner promptly confiscated. The prisoners began to worry that their SS disciplinarian was trying to break their spirit and turn them into *Musselmänner*.

But not enough time was left. Late in April, with the Americans over the horizon, Werner once again issued the dreaded order with his familiar, malicious sneer: "We are going to liquidate." The prisoners were told to burn all banknotes except those of top quality. They worked around the clock for four or five days, incinerating millions of the fake pound notes that were to have been dumped over Britain. Bundles of money do not burn easily, any more than books, and the prisoners had good reason to be painstaking in their work at the smoking, open-air pits: Werner had warned them that anyone found leaving a single scrap of paper unburned would be shot on the spot. So this time the slow pace was not necessarily purposeful, mainly prudent, but it bought more time anyway. (The prisoners were not the only ones covering their tracks. Behind the barracks two Nazi civilians from Berlin buried crates that probably contained counterfeit notes, along with the bodies of two prisoners who had been shot for illness.)

At last, to their amazement, Krueger arrived in his staff car. To some he looked tired, and for the first time even dejected. To others he seemed to be smiling and relieved. As for the future of Operation Bernhard, accounts are not so much contradictory as ambiguous, with some quoting Krueger as saying it would continue "in hiding," others that it was all over for him. But to the end, his mode of address was polite and considerate. He told the printer Fritz Schnapper and a few of the other veterans that at that moment their prospects surely were better than his: "Today I am still wearing my uniform. Who knows what will happen in the next few days?" Putting his arm on the shoulder of the man they all called Tovarisch, Krueger concluded, "I regret we didn't manage to get the paper for the dollar. It would have been such beautiful money. Well, what can't be, can't be. Soon you'll be free again and I wish you all the luck in the future. I have issued orders to have you moved to a place of safety until you are liberated. I shall see you there. Trust me, gentlemen. *Auf wiedersehen.*"

Krueger returned to his car. Later, these men of such precision could hardly agree on the details. Some of the forgers recall that as he drove it away toward Salzburg to the southwest, the vehicle was carrying both a Swiss driving license and Krueger's beautiful young secretary and suspected mistress, Hilda Moeller. But one thing was certain. They never saw Krueger again.

So ended Operation Bernhard.

The prisoners had been left with no trustworthy evidence of Krueger's promises. Krueger had warned his lieutenants (or so he said) that anyone now killing Jews, counterfeiters or not, was in effect committing suicide, as Allied troops were fast closing in on them. The SS men had good reason to fear being stood up against a wall and summarily shot, which was what the Russians had been doing to SS prisoners, partly out of revenge for what the SS had done to Russian political commissars. No doubt the SS would have murdered the Allied elite if the situation had been reversed, and both sides knew it.

For about 30 miles, the general direction of the SS flight from Redl-Zipf followed the winding roads and high passes toward Ebensee, the closest Mauthausen subcamp. Ebensee sat in a hollow, shrouded from aerial reconnaissance by trees and surrounded by hills, just below a lake known as the Traunsee. The camp was the center of a network of tunnels even more elaborate than Redl-Zipf's. Oil was refined and tank and truck parts produced in huge underground chambers blasted out of rock and lined with concrete. Construction had begun in 1943 under the code name Zement — cement — to hide the production of V-2 rockets originally tested and manufactured at the exposed Baltic launch site at Peenemünde. By 1945 Ebensee had become a dumping ground for about 15,000 prisoners death-marched from other camps, including Auschwitz. That gave Ebensee ten times Redl-Zipf's complement of inmates. Only a third were Jews, and the other inmates, slave laborers from all over Europe, were encouraged to mistreat them.

The main road past Ebensee penetrated the mountains, passing through Bad Ischl, over the Pötschenhöhe Pass at more than 3,000 feet, and on to Bad Aussee, another 30 miles beyond Ebensee. At Bad Aussee, a winding spur leads off to the left, first to the Grundlsee and finally the Toplitzsee, both lakes fed by melting snows and underground springs from the Totes Gebirge — the Death Mountains. Toplitzsee, the smaller and more isolated of the two lakes, is in effect a water-filled ravine roughly a mile long and as deep as the height of London's Big Ben. Its isolation and depth made it an ideal naval testing station for U-boat equipment, torpedoes, and the most advanced German rocket. (Fired from the deep, this rocket was eventually developed by its American captors into the nuclear missiles fired from Polaris submarines.)

Back at Redl-Zipf, four heavy Lancia and Mercedes trucks

with carrying capacities between five and ten tons were loaded up. More followed later. They carried Operation Bernhard's crated machinery, possibly some of the SS files, and the coffin-size boxes of counterfeit notes, each containing bills with a total face value of up to £200,000. About May 2 or 3, the trucks started heading south at a grinding pace. Some got only as far as Ebensee, where part of the load was dumped in the Traunsee. Some made it over the snowy pass to the Toplitzsee, where crates covered with metal were unloaded and sunk. Ropes attached to the crates snaked up through the water and were attached to empty rockets that floated just below the surface, marking the location of the counterfeit treasure beneath.

Not all the trucks made it. Probably not by accident, one 700-pound case of notes fell into the hands of an SS officer named Grabau. He was later forced to surrender the money, which eventually ended up with Counterintelligence Corps (CIC) investigators of the U.S. Army. A pair of civilian drivers, Hans Kraft and Josef Zadrappa, veered far off course, dodging American patrols. Their truck broke down, and they found themselves at Pruggern, where one crate popped open. Out spilled gold and silver coins, real American dollar bills, jewelry, and watches, all of which were eventually retrieved from the mud and handed over to the CIC, the vanguard of a vast Allied operation to uncover Nazi war crimes. Crates of machinery and counterfeit notes were dumped in the River Enns. Some wooden crates swelled in the water and burst, releasing pound notes to float downstream with the current. Austrian villagers found some and used them as toilet paper.

Their equipment gone and their production carted away, the Redl-Zipf prisoners meanwhile were searched once again for loot prior to their next transport. (Abraham Jacobson, the master phototype printer, courageously managed to smuggle out a fifty-pound note in the lining of his shoe.) At first Hauptscharfuehrer Werner was able to commandeer only one truck, possibly two. All the prisoners were to be conveyed from Redl-Zipf to Ebensee in successive loads. They jostled among themselves to be last aboard, hoping there would be no room and the stragglers could buy more time. With his pistol, Werner beat as many as he could into the first load. Before leaving, the prisoners warned their comrades that if the truck did not return with a red cross marked on the side as a sign of their survival, they should resist the next transport with all their might. Fifty-six prisoners were jammed into the back. Moishe Nachtstern, as his comrades called the Norwegian printer; Max Groen, the Dutch café habitué; and Adolf Burger, the dour printer, found themselves hustled into the first load. Two guards armed with submachine guns sat on the roof of the cab, and four more were posted at each corner in the rear.

The truck set off from Redl-Zipf with Werner sitting next to the driver, shouting at him to go faster. The driver leaned on his horn to scatter the refugees trudging away from the battlefront. Along the shoulders lay exhausted soldiers of the Wehrmacht. Most had thrown away their weapons.

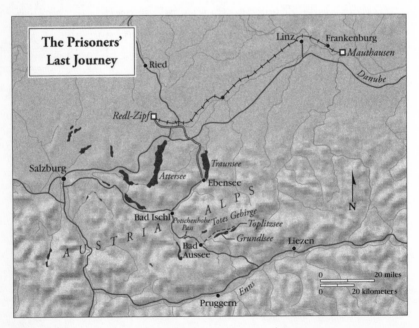

In the rear of the truck, the suspense quickened as it approached a sign reading *Mauthausen* and took a different route. Groen shouted "Bravo!" A guard told him to shut up. They passed another sign, this one reading *Gmunden* and pointing the way toward Ebensee. Groen urged the others to make a run for it if the truck turned the wrong way. He argued that it was better to risk being shot at and possibly missed than face the certainty of being shoveled into the gas chamber.

Then the truck came to a fork in the road. Werner stuck his head out of the cab to speak to a soldier directing traffic. The prisoners could hear the words *Mauthausen* and *die Amerikaner*. The truck turned south, racing around the curves along sharp ravines offering majestic views of the forested valleys and snow-capped peaks of the Austrian Alps, its human cargo more fearful, at least for the moment, of accidental death on the winding road than the diabolical plot to dispose of them. The truck negotiated almost impossible roads to reach Ebensee in less than three hours. The first load of prisoners was dumped out and immediately locked up in a wooden SS bathhouse just outside the camp. SS guards manned the doors, machine guns were trained on the barren building, and it was further surrounded by an outer ring of Hungarian soldiers.

Back at Redl-Zipf, Abraham Krakowski had been awakened at 5:00 a.m. and stood waiting in place outside the barracks for more than four hours. However bone-weary his body, his spirit was aloft: The Nazi swastika was flying at half-staff, marking Hitler's suicide, which had been announced the night before. Krakowski missed the first truck but made the second, which pulled out at about 2:00 p.m. on Wednesday, May 1. Because of engine trouble, it carried only thirty-five men, as well as the meager belongings of the men in the first truckload. When they asked about the machinery, they were told they would find out when they got to Ebensee. These prisoners in the second truck at least knew where they were going, but they had no idea what awaited them there.

They arrived at Ebensee toward dusk and were reunited immediately with their comrades in the crowded bathhouse. Along the way, Krakowski, strengthened by the advice of a young Hassidic comrade, had recited the original Hebrew of the 91st Psalm 91 times: "A thousand may fall on your left side, ten thousand on your right, but it shall not reach you. You will see with your eyes, you will witness the punishment of the wicked." It seemed possible.

But what had happened to the last few dozen of their coworkers? The men in the bathhouse knew that Werner had made one final trip to retrieve them from Redl-Zipf. His orders were to kill every last one of the prisoners, not just most of them, to ensure that all would carry the secrets of Operation Bernhard to the grave.

In fact, when the truck returned to Redl-Zipf, its engine had finally broken down, perhaps sabotaged by motor oil poured into the gasoline tank. Another rumor claimed that the driver, fearful of yet another breakneck trip over the dangerous roads, had joined his comrades and fled. Werner could not drive the truck alone because the prisoners would have pounced on him at the wheel. But he remained fanatically determined to gather all his prisoners under one roof for definitive slaughter, so if he could not get them to Ebensee by truck, they would go on foot.

Looking around, Jacobson counted thirty-eight in this last batch of Redl-Zipf prisoners — twenty counterfeiters and the rest Spaniards. One of those in the last batch was his fellow-Dutchman Dries Bosboom, Max Groen's buddy when the two young café crawlers were arrested in Amsterdam for breaking curfew. The two had remained together through every one of the camps.

The thirty-eight started out late that same day, Werner urging them on with fewer threats of violence than usual. Instead, he turned to Jacobson as the senior prisoner: *Sag das die Leute wei-*

tergehen. Es wird nichts passieren. Die Kameraden sind doch oben. "Tell the guys to go on. Nothing will happen. Their comrades are farther ahead." No one believed him but they slogged on, helpfully slowed by the older prisoners who were winded by the steep hills. Werner urged them on again: *Leute, es ist ja gar nichts los. Die Kameraden nach oben.* "There's absolutely nothing wrong, guys. Your comrades [are] farther ahead." These exhortations carried more menace than they might have in another context, and their effect was precisely the opposite from what Werner had intended. No one had any reason to hurry toward his death. The Spaniards also helped set a measured, deliberate pace.

Reverting to type, Werner occasionally waved his pistol, but his threats began losing force. The accompanying guards themselves began melting away. First one SS man, then another ducked into the woods, as all they saw en route urged their desertion — not Allied propaganda but the stark evidence of Nazi uniforms and weapons already abandoned along the road, ahead of the advancing Americans. Darkness fell, and two prisoners made a break. Norbert Levi, the handsome Berlin photographer, and Eduard Bier, a chemical engineer from Croatia, vanished into the forest while a one-armed SS guard was packing his things to flee. Hans Kurzweil, the chief of the bindery that produced forged passports, tried to follow but did not move quickly enough. Werner waved his pistol under Kurzweil's nose but dared not shoot, lest the remaining prisoners jump him.

Continuing on, the column met a truck loaded with cases of counterfeit notes, and the driver leaned out to warn Werner that American troops were nearby. Then the last two guards deserted. The diminished column resumed its slow if reluctant march under an increasingly powerless Werner, by now their lone captor. Toward the end of the second day, they sat down in the road, accused him of shooting other prisoners, and dared him to shoot them. He backed down, and they dragged themselves toward Ebensee.

By Friday, May 4, three days after starting out, they still had not reached their destination.

Meanwhile, the men in the Ebensee bathhouse waited without food or water, some with anxiety verging on hysteria, others with patience and even insouciance. The longer they waited for their missing comrades, the louder became the approaching sound of the liberating cannon fire. In this impossible situation, Max Groen thought to himself, there was nothing he could do except kick off his shoes and go to sleep on the floor. "I have done that at the strangest moments, as if to say that if they plug me, at least they cannot take away those few hours of sleep." Those awake peeked out through broken glass to see the SS in panic, dragging out desks, filing cabinets, and the files inside them, placing them in a huge pile, and dousing them with gasoline to start a bonfire. Some stripped the SS insignia from their uniforms and headed for the woods. Senior officers changed into civilian clothes and were driven away in staff cars, some with women at the wheel. The prisoners knew that these amazing sights heralded the arrival of the Americans, and that their missing comrades held an invisible ripcord that was somehow keeping them alive. Here was one more perverse result among many: Werner's determination to kill them all in one fell swoop now protected them. When a young guard let a few prisoners out of the bathhouse for a breath of air, the chief of Werner's guard force at the bathhouse, an SS sergeant named Jansen, suddenly appeared and screamed at them to get back in, waving his pistol and threatening the gas chamber. They realized he now was as desperate as they were, maybe more so.

Saturday was the prisoners' fourth day in the stifling bathhouse, Werner's recalcitrant little band still not having arrived. In midmorning, the door was thrown open. *"Raus!"* shouted Jansen. This was it, they thought — until they stepped out into the sunshine to view an even more amazing sight. Down the hill from the bathhouse waved a handful of roughly made flags, like the ragtag standards of a medieval army. They could see the Russian hammer and sickle, the French tricolor, a white flag with the merciful insignia of the Red Cross. There was not a Nazi swastika in sight. One of the Hungarian guards shouted in Yiddish: *Haynt iz Shabbos; hostu mazel!* "Today is the Sabbath; you're in luck!" Krakowski didn't think so because they were still surrounded by armed guards. Almost a mile away stood the main camp, now under control of its former prisoners, flying the rebellious flags of their own liberation.

Half an hour later, Jansen was still conferring with the camp's new masters, and the counterfeiters were still marked men in their makeshift prison. But a guard threw them an incongruous peace offering, a few cartons of soap. It was clear that things were changing fast.

When Jansen returned, he too had ripped off his SS emblem. They all knew the end was near. Jansen announced that they would be moved into the camp proper and issued a stern if ineffective warning: "Soon you'll be liberated. But do not breathe a word to anyone about what you have been doing or you will pay with your lives." As they were marched toward the camp, this handful of prisoners with full heads of hair and motley combinations of used civilian clothing presented a strange sight to the emaciated prisoners with their own striped uniforms and shaven heads. Thousands were milling unhindered about the huge *Appellplatz,* jagged and snowcapped mountains visible in the distance. Inundated by emotion, some were laughing or crying. Others were wandering about in a daze, uncertain of their fate. Just in case, a few of the more vigorous and determined slave laborers had broken into the armory, and random shots rang out.

Could this uprising be one last trick? After a conference between the Red Cross and the remnant of the SS guards to undo bureaucratic entanglements, the camp gate finally swung open. Some of Ebensee's slave laborers had already heard talk of these well-fed civilians engaged in some kind of secret work. The band of forgers was ushered inside the barbed wire and assigned a barracks by a Red Cross officer, a paradoxical kind of liberation in reverse from their SS guards. Suddenly the last of their comrades burst into the barracks. Werner had vanished and they, too, were obliged to talk their way *into* the main Ebensee camp. Soon the full story emerged, Jacobson declaring: "Had we arrived about ten hours earlier, we then would all without any doubt have been executed."

A few days before, the Mauthausen commander, Sturmbann-fuehrer Franz Ziereis, had ordered his subordinate at Redl-Zipf to kill the prisoners, probably by blowing them up in his tunnels. *Nicht bei mir.* "Not while I'm here," replied the Redl-Zipf commander, who had already been warned by the Austrian resistance that he would pay with his own life for any last-minute mass murder. Stymied, Werner had then ordered the emergency evacuation to Ebensee, where the brutality of the commandant, Anton Ganz, was known to his captives and his SS comrades alike. During those final days, Ganz and his guards had worked feverishly to destroy human as well as documentary evidence. But by the time the forgers were assembled at Ebensee, Ganz did not have enough men left to drive the inmates into the Ebensee tunnels. The few remaining SS men tried to coax the inmates underground, claiming that taking shelter in the tunnels was for their own safety and protection from Allied bombers. But the tone of those pleas was suspiciously mild, so the inmates stayed put. Then they refused roll call, in effect revolting by just saying no. Ganz, standing on a table to be heard above the huge, sullen crowd in the *Appellplatz,* announced that work was suspended for the day. He ordered the inmates into the tunnels once again. No one moved. Within an hour, Ganz and his men had disappeared, and the inmates had taken over the camp. The long walk of the men from Redl-Zipf had closed the Nazis' last window of opportunity to kill off all the witnesses to their massive counterfeit.

The American 80th Division had fought across Europe and knew what awaited them in the camps. The troops had passed through Buchenwald and now were spearheading Patton's armored thrust to split the Reich by linking up with Soviet forces from the east. Shortly after the disappearance of the murderous SS, Sherman tanks of the 80th clanked up the highway and into the camp. Max Groen fell into conversation with a tanker sergeant from New Jersey who, in a classic GI reflex, pulled out pictures of his wife and children. Groen glanced at them and, in a classic prisoner's reflex, said, "Just give me one good cigarette." The sergeant had *dritte sorte* — third-class rations — and he offered Groen the whole pack. Forget it, said Max ungraciously. The sergeant was almost apologetic: "That's all I've got. We're moving so goddamn fast that supply can't keep up with us." And then the tanks rolled out.

The counterfeiters had survived the war, escaping their ordained fate only by hours. They had outlasted their tormentors and were indifferent to the whirlwind of counterfeit bills already blowing outside their sealed world. And why should they care about mere money? Life could not be forged, they were alive, and at last they were free.

EPILOGUE

This tale of deception and survival would not be complete without an account of how the survivors got on with their lives. Many proceeded almost as if they had been untouched by the moral ambiguities of this extraordinary experience. What changed was the world around them — a second half-century of relative stability on the soil of Western Europe after it had been drenched in blood by ideologues imposing their own mad utopia on others.

The inhabitants of Block 19 were left with scars, but these were mainly invisible, and all the more worthy of examination for precisely that reason. For example, Max Groen developed a fear of taking orders and could only work as a freelancer. Bernhard Krueger, after a long internment, returned to an anonymous job in industry. Peppiatt and his colleagues at the Bank of England sealed their lips and went into a half-century of denial. The money-launderers' lives were shadowed but far from immediately ruined. Schwend, like some of the most criminal Nazis, escaped to the New World, the place where he had made his first million.

No one swam more adroitly with the tide than Jaac van Harten, who may be accounted the ultimate survivor. When last seen in Budapest, jewels and counterfeit pounds literally popping out of his suitcases, he was headed for Schwend's castle in Merano just across the border in Italy. Van Harten carried a card issued in Budapest identifying him as an agent of the International Red Cross. Although it was only a temporary document, he made the most of it. A file of papers two inches thick recording complaints by Swiss officials, and supported by the Allied military government in Italy, rests in the Geneva archives of the International Red Cross (IRC) under the heading *Abus de Confiance J. van Harten* — "Betrayal of Trust." These official accounts attest he was using a former Nazi newspaper press to forge thousands of Red Cross identity cards for refugees to claim the protection of the Geneva Convention, some of whom received gratuities of 1,000 Italian lire each from the organization to help them get home across the cauldron of Europe.

To the fury of the International Red Cross officials in Geneva, van Harten appointed himself "Swiss Consular Representative for the Province of South Tyrol of the International Committee of the Red Cross." (The real IRC soon began issuing documents not only to bona fide refugees but to Nazi war criminals.) As the war went into its final months, van Harten tried to arrange exchanges with refugees who had been swept up in the Nazi dragnet. He sought help from Georg Gyssling, Schwend's friend and art adviser, and from the Swiss consul general, Alberto Crastan, also one of Schwend's money-launderers and one of many Swiss in the business of profiting from the misery of others. SS troops would snap to attention at the approach of van Harten's big, open Mercedes. He traveled in civilian clothes with his wife, Viola, herself fashionably dressed even in those hard times. He signed Red Cross passes, presumably including one for Schwend. Then van Harten slapped IRC signs on Schwend's warehouses holding the usual complement of clothing, household items, and canned staples. In Merano itself, American troops discovered a warehouse with "thousands of things stolen from merchants in all of Italy, such as: 60 cases of Vermouth, eight cases of Buton Cognac, bolts of silk and wool cloth, linen sheets, silk stockings, cretonne, zebra skins, shaving brushes, hair oil, women's clothes, and children's bathing suits." These hoards led to van Harten's undoing. On May 17, 1945, American troops arrested him for holding stolen goods and contraband, and on May 30 the IRC formally denounced him before Allied headquarters in Rome.

Van Harten boldly replied to IRC directors in Geneva on June 8 with a lengthy account of how he had liberated almost 3,000 prisoners and clothed 7,000 more at the Bolzano concentration camp, set up soup kitchens for refugees, paid local hospitals in advance for treatment of the sick, enlisted the help of the Catholic church, and curbed the worst excesses of the retreating Germans. Moreover, he claimed, he had "sacrificed millions of my own money for this work" (his cover story was that he spent blocked currency from his Budapest company, which of course he neglected to identify as a Nazi money-laundering enterprise). Van Harten told the Red Cross that he had also promised "one million pounds in cash" to the Jewish Agency in Geneva to help Jews establish themselves in Palestine. It is unclear how much money actually reached the Agency, but that these counterfeit pound notes served a historic purpose provides one of the crowning ironies of this tale.

And not the only one. As the war was winding down, a small group in the British Army's Jewish Brigade had dedicated themselves to vengeance against the Nazis and to a new ingathering of exiles. They called themselves the *Havurah* — "the Gang" — or, in a linguistic stew, *Tilhas Tizi Gesheften* (TTG for short) — "The Kiss My Ass Company." Operating from their base in Italy, the gang stealthily kidnapped and assassinated SS killers, and bought or stole arms. Its members helped ship war materiel and thousands of displaced Jews to Palestine aboard chartered old tubs in defiance of British policy designed to placate the Arabs by limiting Jewish immigration. This smuggling operation cost money. Although the TTG was naturally suspicious of his Nazi connections, van Harten with his huge stash of counterfeit pounds served first as willing helper and later as perfect mark. The Jewish Brigade's transport unit, headed by Captain Alex Moskowitz (later a prominent banker in Israel), used trucks to rescue vagrant Jews. These refugees were followed south through the Brenner Pass by trainloads more. Van Harten and his helpers distributed food at the first train station south of the pass.

Near the end of the war, two members of the Hashomer Hitzair (Young Guardians), idealistic collectivists allied to the kibbutz movement, smuggled themselves from Palestine into Italy dressed as British soldiers. Levi Argov and Moshe Ben David wanted to participate in the movement known by its Hebrew name, Brichah (Escape), by organizing routes for thousands of Jewish survivors to flee Central Europe, van Harten's old stamping ground. Moskowitz asked for help. "Of course!" van Harten replied. "Do they have money? Send them to me immediately."

Van Harten handed the young men packets of brand-new British notes with a face value of £40,000 to £50,000. As the money was stuffed into their rucksacks, van Harten asked them to pay off a debt in Budapest. As usual he did not tell them that the bills were counterfeit. Argov and Ben David changed into nondescript refugee clothing, moved north, and got to work — the first as coordinator for the Brichah in Hungary, Austria, and Czechoslovakia; the second as a representative of its youth movement. They established close contacts with Czech Zionists, a delegation of whom used van Harten's pound notes to finance a trip to England. There one unsuspecting Czech was arrested, interrogated, investigated, and harshly informed that his money was fake.

While van Harten's wife wrote frantic letters to the Red Cross extolling his humanitarianism and pleading for his release, Jewish

Brigade officers brought her to the attention of another under-ground escape group, Mossad l'Aliyah Beth, roughly translated as the Organization for Immigration B (the letter *B* meaning illegal, to distinguish it from its prewar function of bringing Jews to Palestine; after the war the British blockaded the coasts of their Palestine mandate to discourage Jewish settlement). An under-ground Jewish leader, learning that Viola van Harten was holding her husband's stock of gold, jewelry, and counterfeit notes, ap-proached her and was given real Swiss francs and fake British pounds, the latter soon traded for gold on the Austrian black mar-ket. The Jewish underground soon realized that the van Hartens were more valuable with her safely in Palestine and him released from his prisoner-of-war cage in Rimini. They shipped out Viola van Harten first by posing her as a nurse; upon arrival in Palestine she was quietly relieved of the valuables her husband had ob-tained from his wartime financial services for the Nazis.

Van Harten himself was released in 1946, thanks to a combi-nation of political pressure on the Americans and less savory in-ducements that probably will forever remain secret. Members of the Gang realized they could squeeze him for hush money and gave him a choice: in exchange for whatever money he could raise quickly, they would keep quiet about his wartime dealings. One of their leaders, Shalheveth Freier, spent hours threatening and hag-gling with van Harten, and one of the members saw this world-class confidence man literally quaking with fear before Freier's restrained but very real threats. The Jewish underground wanted van Harten's money and did not care whether it was counterfeit or real. They passed the bogus pounds to supply Holocaust sur-vivors and help the Brichah smuggle more refugees to Palestine. On the international arms market, they used the money to buy weapons for Jews arming themselves against the British and then the Arabs. They purchased engines, lashed them to the decks of refugee ships, and had them mounted on armored truck bodies that served as makeshift tanks for the Haganah, the nascent Jewish army. (Freier, later chairman of Israel's Atomic Energy Agency, in 1955 gained the dubious distinction of being one of the first Israeli diplomats expelled from the United States, probably for trying to steal atomic secrets; many of his comrades joined him in Israel's nascent espionage service, now known the world over by part of its name — the Mossad, or the Organization.)

Van Harten arrived in Palestine in 1947 after a short spell selling undergarments in Milan, and returned to the jewelry business. When the British found out he was in Tel Aviv — they were still a year away from giving up their mandate — they tried to expel him as a counterfeiter. But van Harten, a master at pulling political strings, made the underground leaders honor their pledge to whitewash his wartime activities. They apparently had no compunction about doing so because of his help to them. No less than Goldie Myerson, then chief of the Jewish Agency's political department and later prime minister of Israel as Golda Meir, was asked by van Harten's lawyer for a testimonial. Her office toned down the attorney's fulsome draft and sent a letter over her signature praising van Harten for saving many Jewish lives at great personal risk and "considerable financial sacrifice . . . [which] entitles him to priority consideration in his application to remain in Palestine." It worked.

But van Harten's *chutzpah* knew no bounds. He sought $5 million compensation from the U.S. government for the contraband seized at Merano. Biting the hand that had just fed him, he filed more modest claims against the Jewish Agency for the note signed by its agents in Budapest. He also tried to obtain money from the Joint Distribution Committee, whose funds helped Jewish refugees. All these outrageous claims failed, but van Harten's jewelry store and other businesses prospered. Because his payoffs had been channeled through men who became powers in the new Jewish state, the hush money lasted right through the trial of Adolf Eichmann until van Harten's death in 1973. The record of Eichmann's interrogation after his capture by the Mossad in 1960 states that the Nazi was believed to have had a Jewish collaborator in Budapest identified only as "Jaac." This page of the Israeli record has remained sealed.

Friedrich Schwend was arrested by the U.S. Military Government in June 1945, probably fingered by a former collaborator who had been caught with a packet of forged pounds. Like van Harten, Schwend tried to ingratiate himself with the winning side, although he was neither as smooth nor as lucky. At first, Allied intelligence agents took him on "bird-dog" missions to dig up buried treasure, hence his code name, Flush. In July he led Allied investigators into the Austrian Alps, where only days before the end of the war he had buried 7,139 French and Italian gold coins weighing about 100 pounds; he put their value at $200,000. The investigators believed the gold was destined to finance die-hard Nazi resistance (instead of Schwend's own retirement), so that was what he told them. The U.S. officers confiscated the haul, and Schwend then took them back to Merano for more loot. Meanwhile, his Jewish money-launderer Georg Spitz led his interrogators to stolen paintings in a Nazi cache near Munich.

As the Cold War began, U.S. intelligence in Germany used Schwend and Spitz to help organize a local counterintelligence network. Schwend tried to insinuate himself into Germany's new intelligence agency (named for its chief, the turncoat Nazi expert on Russia, General Reinhard Gehlen). Spitz meanwhile began mixing in Munich society and feeding Allied intelligence under the code name Tarbaby. Soon their wartime pasts caught up with them. In 1947, Dutch investigators questioned Spitz about his shady art dealings, and the newly formed CIA quickly dropped him. This onetime merchant of fake American Express traveler's checks moved back to his native Vienna to become a banker. When the former SS intelligence officer Wilhelm Hoettl, writing under the pseudonym Walter Hagen, published the first book about Operation Bernhard, Spitz bought up all copies of the first edition. He forced Hoettl to drop half a dozen pages from the next edition and to gloss over Spitz's connection with the counterfeiters. Then Spitz went back to business.

Caught trying to defraud the Gehlen Organization, Schwend fled to Rome, where he was issued a Red Cross passport under the name of Wenceslas Turi and then turned up in Lima, Peru. Ostensibly working as the local Volkswagen manager, he was living comfortably on proceeds of his wartime counterfeits parked in Europe and forwarded by his brother-in-law Hans Neuhold. He Hispanicized his name to Federico Schwend, acted as an informant for Peruvian intelligence, and kept in contact with far more vicious Nazi escapees in Latin America such as Klaus Barbie, known as the Butcher of Lyon for torturing his prisoners to death.

The CIA shadowed Schwend for years. His bridges to the Americans had been burned early in the 1950s when his former comrade Louis Glavan denounced him for living on the proceeds of the Bernhard counterfeits. As late as 1963 the CIA began wondering whether Schwend was counterfeiting dollars for Fidel Castro, and he attracted the notice of James Jesus Angleton, the agency's legendary and paranoid chief of counterintelligence. Nothing came of it. A decade later the Peruvians turned on Schwend and convicted him of blackmail, currency smuggling, and selling state secrets. He was imprisoned for two years and deported to West Germany. He had sunk so far down and out that he was jailed in 1976 for failing to pay a $21 hotel bill. Years before, Schwend had been tried in absentia in Italy for murder, and a German warrant still hung over his head in connection with the mysterious death of an agent who had attempted to abscond with

Bernhard currency in 1944. Tried in Munich, Schwend received a suspended sentence for manslaughter on June 8, 1979, claiming poverty so he could receive legal aid and welfare payments. He also visited Schloss Labers, now returned to its owners, who ran it as a hotel, and walked out without paying his bill. Suffering from diabetes, Schwend returned to Lima, where he died in 1981 at the age of seventy-four — the only person connected to the greatest counterfeiting operation in history to face judicial action. Even when Schellenberg, Naujocks, and Hoettl testified at the Nuremberg war crimes trials, Hoettl alone made only the slightest reference to Operation Bernhard — although he later made a literary career of it.

Bernhard Krueger had a somewhat less adventurous retirement. He gave various versions of how he eluded capture and made his way home to Dassel, near Hannover, hiding for eight days until one of his children called out, "Mama, there's a strange man in the closet." He finally turned himself in to the British occupation authorities on November 25, 1946. They were waiting for him: Krueger's card in the British file of wanted Nazis listed his offense as "Forging Foreign Currency–Passports."

The British held Krueger for slightly more than a year. Already embarrassed by the enormity of what he had done to them, they never breathed a word of his existence, not even to George J. McNally or other U.S. Secret Service agents who were working closely with them in their own hunt for forged dollars. The British also never charged Krueger; forging enemy currency was no war crime. They turned him over to the French early in 1948, who were also ready for him. While Krueger was still a fugitive, Captain S. C. Michel of French intelligence had accurately described his activities and concluded: "Very clever but will probably give up all information if caught especially if convinced it will save his hide."

Krueger said the French secret service offered him his old job of forging passports — for them. Unlike the British, they threatened him with murder charges for the four prisoners killed for illness, meanwhile attempting to recruit him as he sat in Wittlich prison in the French zone of occupation. But Krueger declared he had had enough of forgery, and the French dropped the charges when they released him in November 1948.

Returning as an engineer to the factories of Chemnitz was out of the question: the city was in the Soviet occupation zone (it was renamed Karl-Marx-Stadt in 1953). In 1955, Krueger was discovered by the official census working as a storekeeper near Hannover. He had to undergo a denazification process, during which he made a fairly clean breast of his wartime counterfeiting exploits, although he stressed that he was only a "technical consultant." Several former prisoners later declared that they either testified or sent affidavits in his support. He was exonerated after a brief hearing. For their own propaganda purposes, the Communist government of East Germany pursued him during the 1960s as a murderer of the four prisoners, but the charges had to be filed in West Germany and were dismissed. Krueger eventually found work as a salesman, uncoincidentally at the Hahnemühle paper plant.

Shortly before Krueger's death in 1989 at the age of eighty-three, the marine explorer and biologist Hans Fricke of the Max Planck Institute took him in a miniature submarine to the depths of the Toplitzsee. The vessel's searchlight picked up piles of pound notes still preserved beneath the oxygen line. Krueger stared in amazement and, according to Fricke, uttered the old slogan, still freighted with the code words of Nazi Germany, *Alles für Fürher, Volk, und Vaterland* — "Everything for the fuehrer, the people, and the fatherland." Sobs obscuring his German inflections, Krueger blubbered: "I did everything I could [and] after the war they treated me like a scoundrel" in German, a *Lump*. Self-pitying and unrepentant to the last, he was like so many Nazis who looked straight past the catastrophe they had helped create and valued only their own efforts and their own suffering.

Not a trace remains of the original Reichsfinanzministerium, where the whole thing started — not even on the present-day guideposts to Wilhelmstrasse erected along this historic avenue. Number 61 would have stood just above Leipziger Strasse; the space is now occupied by featureless office buildings and a stylish building housing the embassy of the Czech Republic. The RSHA headquarters on Prinz-Albrecht-Strasse (which has been renamed Niederkirchnerstrasse after a Communist heroine who parachuted into Russian-occupied Poland and was captured by the Nazis and killed in Ravensbrück) was still a pile of rubble overgrown with trees and shrubs sixty years after its destruction. An attempt to preserve the Gestapo's torture cells as a reminder of its terrors has been stymied by a typically German dispute over the meaning of the nation's past and how to memorialize it.

In one of the many accidents of history that have created to-day's Berlin, with its layers stripped bare like those of a geological fault, the RSHA ended up just inside the Allied zone of occupation. Its torture cells stood hard against what would become the boundary marked by the infamous Berlin Wall, remnants of which are visible from the Gestapo site. In what was East Berlin, street names and numbers along Wilhelmstrasse were scrambled by the Communist authorities. Today, the neighborhood is filled with working-class apartments occupied by families with Slavic and Turkish names. But at the corner of Wilhelmstrasse and Leipziger Strasse stands a huge, utilitarian building of Nazi construction that served as Hermann Goering's Air Ministry (some officials there were part of the Russian spy network known as the Red Orchestra). Until reunification in 1990, it housed ministries of the German Democratic Republic, then the organization responsible for privatizing state-owned Communist industry. When the German government moved to Berlin at the start of this century, the building became the seat of the nation's Finance Ministry. Along one side remains a singular historical artifact: a long, colorful mural in the style of socialist realism depicting smiling workers and farmers, determined bureaucrats and technocrats, all united under a sign carried by one group of marchers proclaiming *"Sozialismus."*

Cicero the Spy squandered everything he received. Money went to mistresses, ex-wives, and children. Elyesa Bazna did try his hand at sensible businesses such as used cars, a construction partnership, and a luxury Turkish ski-and-spa resort near Bursa. But even as the first of five floors was being built, a supplier whose bills had been settled in pound notes sent them to his Swiss bank, which bounced them after consulting the Bank of England. Ruined, Bazna spent years defending himself. Criminal prosecutions were abandoned, but civil suits were pursued and he had to repay his victims. Even a concert of classical songs he gave to acclaim by audience and critics ended in financial disaster; his creditors seized the evening's takings. In desperation he turned to the German consulate in Istanbul for reimbursement or a pension. A junior official demanded written proof of his services to Germany and then threw him out. Bazna persisted and in 1954 wrote Chancellor Konrad Adenauer, the founding statesman of the Federal Republic of Germany. In a servile, pleading letter to this confirmed anti-Nazi who had publicly apologized on behalf of the nation for "unspeakable crimes," Cicero could not have come up with a more inappropriate justification for wartime spying: he said he did it out of sympathy for Germany. The German Foreign Ministry rejected his claim outright.

For five years, the British succeeded in hushing up their worst wartime security breach. The Foreign Office's top career diplomat,

Sir Alexander Cadogan, confided to his diary in 1945 that "Snatch, of course, ought to be court-martialled." But Ambassador Hughe Knatchbull-Hugessen drew only a private reprimand and then — the old boys protect their own — was awarded a plum post as ambassador in Brussels to enjoy its delicious cuisine while postwar Britain lived on iron rations. In 1950, Ludwig Moyzisch, Cicero's SS handler, published his memoirs, and the lid blew off. In a statement to Parliament of only forty-five words, the government had to admit through clenched teeth that the story was true.

Darryl F. Zanuck bought the film rights from Moyzisch, and Joseph Mankiewicz's brilliant film *Five Fingers* quickly followed in 1952, starring James Mason as Cicero, which is mainly how he and his story are remembered, if at all. But as with most Hollywood productions, the real-life story was considerably more mundane than the screen version. Bazna did not even receive a payoff in the traditional form of a consultant's fee. The production cost of the movie was about $1 million in real money — slightly less than the face value of the counterfeit pounds paid to Cicero.

Later, Bazna tried writing his own story and sought a collaborator in Munich, who in turn demanded confirmation from Moyzisch that Bazna had been Cicero. Brought together, they sized up what life had done to them in the sixteen years since the war ended. Bazna recalled: "We felt no particular sympathy for each other. Our great adventure had rewarded neither." In vain, Bazna continued pursuing the West German government, suing for 1.7 million marks. He was working as a night watchman in Munich when he died in 1970 at the age of sixty-six, a humble Turkish *Gastarbeiter* in the country to which he had both given and lost everything.

But perhaps no greater loss was suffered than by the Bank of England. The most precious resource of any central bank is confidence in the money it issues, and the Nazis undermined it even from beyond the grave. They forced Britain to issue new five-pound notes with a metallic thread to help detect counterfeits, and what was worse, the Bank had to admit why. This was done in a press release on October 18, 1945, that blamed the "forgery of high sum Bank of England notes in Germany during the war." Even before the war ended, stories persisted that the British were buying up the counterfeits at a rate of one real fiver for two fakes. This was probably too good to be true, but the story demonstrates the widespread recognition of the dilemma facing the Bank.

Huge stashes of counterfeits were uncovered as Allied troops settled into Austria and Germany. Private Allen Cramer of the U.S. Army was guarding a bridge over the Danube when his buddies discovered a chest full of twenty-pound notes. Immediately they debated whether to carry off a lot if it was real, or only a little as souvenirs if it was phony. They correctly decided a little would do, but even though "we knew it was counterfeit, we somehow felt very rich." In Frankfurt, U.S. Secret Service agent George McNally was led to twenty-three coffin-size boxes on a German truck, with manifests describing their contents. McNally alerted the British and soon received a phone call from the Bank in London. He described his discovery and heard a gasp over the line. The Bank quickly dispatched the chief of its printing plant, Patrick J. Reeves, described by McNally as "a tall, angular and reserved gentleman." Reeves dryly reported that on Friday, June 8, 1945, he counted £26 million in counterfeit notes, accompanied by a box of tools to make the plates. He methodically compared the dates, serial numbers, and the Bank's own code numbers on the bills, calculating that as many as sixteen additional crates might be missing with millions more in false pounds. The vast scale of the operation literally stared him in the face. In McNally's somewhat more vivid description, Reeves went "from box to box, riffling the notes between his fingers. Finally he stopped and stared silently into space. Then for several seconds he cursed, slowly and methodically in a cultured English voice, but with vehemence. 'Sorry,' he said at last. 'But the people who made this stuff have cost us so much.'"

Reeves was joined by two officers from Scotland Yard's forgery branch, a chief inspector and a sergeant (appropriately named Minter). They toured the concentration camp complex to which the counterfeiters had been shuttled during their final, uncertain days as prisoners. They discovered the small Redl-Zipf camp had been burned down but were still able to enter its network of tunnels. They began to piece together the jigsaw puzzle of the prisoners' stories. Then McNally, on behalf of the U.S. Treasury, started asking the British uncomfortable questions: How many counterfeits were produced? What were the losses? Had the counterfeits broken through the barrier of exchange controls into Britain's home territory?

The questions were passed to Peppiatt of the Bank, who consulted the British Treasury, which in turn joined with the Old Lady, at least in public, to hide what was fast becoming a national embarrassment. (Even bookies at the London dog tracks had stopped accepting fivers.) Instructions arrived from Edward Playfair, a senior Treasury official, to stiff the outsiders: "I am sorry, as I do not want them to think us uncooperative: but this is a very domestic kind of matter. We at home keep such information inside a very narrow circle, and neither divulge it nor seek to obtain similar information from others." This explanation landed on the desk of Charles A. Gunston, who was on leave from the Bank to serve as chief British financial officer for the Allied Control Commission in Germany. A top scholar at Winchester and Oxford, and a brilliant linguist (German, French, Spanish, Portuguese, and, as a hobby later in retirement, Bardic Welsh), Brigadier Gunston not only understood the situation but could express it in plain English. Next to his instructions to tell this to the Americans — or, to be precise, not to tell them — he wrote in a neat, scholarly hand, *"Let sleeping dogs lie. CAG 14 Sep 45."*

Occasionally those dogs barked, but the principal sound for almost half a century was the silence of an embarrassed cover-up. Even when the Allied Control Commission in Austria wanted to prosecute a gang of seven men for passing false pound notes in 1946, the commission's Public Safety Branch had to plead with the Bank to release enough counterfeits to present as evidence at the trial. When counterfeit pounds of a new type turned up the same year through the Polish Consulate in France, Peppiatt wrote to Scotland Yard demanding immediate action, adducing "the shocks our notes have taken in recent years and are still taking." Like an outraged spymaster in a patriotic thriller, the normally re-strained functionary proposed: "I am hopeful that you may have available a suitable fellow who could take it up and make a real job of it, i.e., to get at the source of supply which is after all al-ways the real target." But a foreign consulate presents a delicate target, and Ronald Howe, the deputy commissioner in charge of relations with foreign police forces, proceeded via the more dis-creet French *police judiciaire* instead of using the more adventur-ous types demanded by Peppiatt. Howe had also been relieved to learn that the unfortunate Hans Adler, the Austrian counterfeit expert whose services had been disdained by Peppiatt before the war, had survived in the Netherlands. Howe noted, "He will be a most useful contact from our point of view." Better late than never.

By now the Bank was worried about more than just its repu-tation for standing behind that inscription on every note that "promises to pay the bearer" (in gold, in times past). Edward Play-fair, who had all the appropriate Treasury credentials — a bril-liant Cambridge classics scholar with a mordant disdain for lesser intellects — remarked that the Bank was "hypnotised by looking at their own beautiful notes." He was on his way to a two-year tour with the occupation authorities and was incensed that his country, which had bankrupted itself in a fight to the death against the Nazis, might have to compensate former enemies "in order to meet the Bank of England's pride." The Bank was painfully aware of the huge potential damage to its reputation if it refused to redeem pounds from unsuspecting foreign banks that had been bilked by the almost perfect forgeries. The Treasury, for its part, put severe limits on any foreign withdrawals based on the presentation of real pound notes, pinching every penny of foreign exchange to feed and rebuild the nation, which had been left exhausted by its victory.

In due course a typically obscure British compromise emerged: prewar pounds only would be exchanged in the "allied" countries of Belgium, Czechoslovakia, Denmark, Greece, and Norway, where, not coincidentally, very few counterfeits had circulated.* Where the counterfeits had been most concentrated, the restrictions were more severe. Exchange arrangements were nonexistent in Yugoslavia, Italy, and Hungary, the latter two under the guise that they had been enemies. Because of suspected Nazi accounts in Switzerland, tight restrictions were enforced there.

But the fakes and even new fakers kept popping up for many years, especially in neutral or pro-Nazi countries that had sat out the war. A regular trade developed in phony fivers that were believed to have been shipped by Swiss banks and officials in Madrid and Rome, then pitched at a discount to unsuspecting buyers along the Mediterranean littoral with the story that they had been

---

*This proved a boon to some of those who had banked on the pound remaining a pound after the war. In 1942, Leo Strawczynski, a Belgian Jewish businessman of Polish origin, had converted most of his assets into pound notes, stuffed them into a bottle, buried it near a bench in a forest outside Liége, and fled with his family to hide in unoccupied France. When they returned in 1945, he dug up the bottle and presented the rotting remnants of the notes to the bank. He got back enough to start up again and eventually to buy a car.

hidden during the war and now could be redeemed by the British. From Stockholm, Harry Söderman, director of Sweden's National Institute of Technical Police, bombarded Scotland Yard with telegrams and letters giving details of Swedish businessmen who had been stuck with counterfeit pounds. And a Hungarian refugee from Budapest arriving in Switzerland in 1946 tried to have a friend change £2,000 at a bank. Could he have been one of the Soros family's clients? No one can ever know, but the refugee soon learned to his chagrin that his pound notes were fakes.

The largest number of counterfeits were dredged up from the depths of the Toplitzsee, preserved in its deoxygenated waters fed by sulfur springs. In 1967 a bundle of Bernhard pounds with a face value of £5 million was found abandoned inside the organ of the San Valentino church in Merano. Argentina, which sheltered many Nazis after the war, also absorbed their counterfeiting tricks during its own Dirty War against leftist guerrillas in the 1970s and 1980s. Ricardo Coqueto, a carpenter, escaped execution in the notorious Naval Mechanics' School in Buenos Aires because he not only learned to forge official credentials but "I can remember making British sterling notes."

For more than half a century, the Old Lady uttered hardly a word about the whole distasteful matter, rather like a well-bred duchess ignoring a spot of red wine spilled on her linen tablecloth. The Bank's archives appear to have been deliberately purged, or worse. A 1949 memorandum reports that two officials destroyed not only an unrecorded quantity of forged banknotes but "photographic copies and records of the plant engaged in the production of the High Sum Plates and Notes." Peppiatt retired from the Bank in 1957 and became a director of Coutts & Co. (a bank whose most distinguished private client was the Queen of England). In old age he particularly enjoyed playing a mean hand of bridge, which is what he was doing in 1983 on the afternoon of the day he died peacefully at the age of ninety. His obituary in the Bank's house organ, *The Old Lady,* did not breathe so much as a whisper about the most singular event in his career.

This obituary was written by his successor as chief cashier, Sir Leslie O'Brien (later promoted to governor and ennobled). Along with the Bank's other senior executives he continued believing that many of the Bank's own records of the Bernhard counterfeits could not be found. The official explanation was that they had been lost or handed over to the security services. Right into the twenty-first century, Sir Eddie George, O'Brien's successor as governor, insisted that it was "conspiracy theory" to suggest that the Bank might have a file copy of the 1945 report from its own man Reeves. In fact, the Foreign Office did have one and declassified it in the 1970s.

The outsize white fivers with the postwar metal thread were finally superseded in 1957, to great public outcry. British traditions were falling away like pieces of the Empire, and this was no exception. It took another two generations for the Bank to acknowledge that the five-pound note was not much good as money anyway. In 1998 John Keyworth, head of the Bank's museum, admitted: "Not only did you have to fold it into your wallet, but many shopkeepers would insist on your writing your name and address on it because it was so easy to fake." Yet the Bank's own promotional film boasting in the late 1990s about how it had maintained the security of its banknotes over the centuries dared not even mention the name Bernhard. The cover-up continued until the old guard died off. Finally, in March 2003, the Bank publicly conceded in a brief but frank account of Operation Bernhard on its website that the scheme had indeed threatened the wartime stability of sterling and that "significant numbers [of counterfeits] found their way into circulation and were a constant headache for the Bank and other financial institutions for years to come."

*   *   *

No one can say the prisoners came out of it well, but they had learned how to gain strength from hope. In Block 19, Salomon Smolianoff had filled his idle hours working on the mathematical probabilities of roulette with Jacob Laskier, a Polish office worker good at figures. They were certain they could devise a system to break the bank at Monte Carlo, which Smolianoff tried after the war but failed. He seems also to have tried to get back into his old game. He wrote his mentor, Professor Miassojedoff, now living under the name Eugene Zotow, in the postage-stamp country of Liechtenstein. Miassojedoff drew, painted, and had, quite naturally, designed some of its postage stamps. Neither could obtain a visa to visit the other, so they arranged to meet at the Swiss border in March of 1946 but could only gaze across a no-man's-land separating them by some 125 feet. Smolianoff claimed to be organizing an exhibition of exiled Russian artists and wrote his friend asking for paintings, but the police figured he really meant a more instantly exchangeable form of art and kept an eye on him.

Sometime in 1946, Smolianoff settled in Rome and in February 1947 married Carlotta Raphael, daughter of an old Italian Jewish family and widow of a professor of engineering. In May the Italian police questioned him about his black-market sale of a five-hundred-dollar bill. He spun a complex tale of exchanging it on behalf of his wife who had been left more such bills by her late husband; of an intermediary who said a bank had certified the money as genuine; and of yet another woman who took a five-hundred-dollar bill to the United States, where it was declared counterfeit. The Italian police seized the money, and in September 1947 Smolianoff took ship for South America. The next year Miassojedoff/Zotow was convicted in Liechtenstein of counterfeiting hundred-dollar bills, the court wisely ignoring an exculpatory statement from Smolianoff in Montevideo. The International

Criminal Police Commission in Paris issued a wanted circular for Smolianoff as a notorious international counterfeiter in March 1948. But he was already working in Uruguay with his brother-in-law, a bookseller, who helped him peddle Russian icons that he occasionally claimed to have uncovered (how they would have turned up in South America was not immediately explained). The professor sailed to join his prize student in 1953 but died just after his arrival in Buenos Aires. In 1955 Smolianoff and Carlotta moved on, settling in Porto Alegre, Brazil, to manufacture toys. Smolianoff stayed straight because his firm and expert counterfeiter's hand was gradually weakened by Parkinson's disease, of which he died in 1978.

The lives of most of the other prisoners took a more prosaic turn, although there was an occasional dash of celebrity. Oskar Stein, the meticulous bookkeeper, was already running his own bar in Pilsen when interrogators came to question him soon after the war. Hirsche and Moshe Kosak, two brothers who were typesetters, emigrated to America and spent their lives working for the Yiddish newspaper *Vorwerts* in New York. Felix Cytrin, the chief engraver of Block 19, entered the United States in 1950 as a displaced person; the Secret Service kept him under surveillance almost until his death in New Jersey in 1971. Norbert Levi adopted the name Norbert Leonard, gravitated back to the high life, and spent some time as a photographer for Aristotle Onassis. Hans Kurzweil, chief of the bindery that produced fake passports, got revenge of a sort. When SS officer Hoettl published his book reporting falsely that Krueger had used criminals to forge sterling, Kurzweil sued and won on the basis of a sworn deposition from Krueger that he had not. Kurzweil's legal victory in a Viennese court deprived Hoettl of his government license to run a school, which he had to close.

At least five survivors published memoirs or cooperated in them. The first was Moritz Nachtstern's, still fresh with anecdote;

he returned to work as a stereotyper, employed by *Hjemmet* (Home), a Norwegian family magazine, and lived until 1969. Adolf Burger worked closely with the police from the time of his return to Prague, publishing his memoirs in Czech and then in German. Avraham Krakowski settled in Brooklyn and resumed work as an accountant, still so pious that his Flatbush neighbors knew him as "the rabbi" even though he wasn't one. Peter Edel became an author, man of the theater, and novelist celebrated by the Communist government of the German Democratic Republic. Max Groen, whose father had been the prewar manager for 20th Century Fox in the Netherlands, subtitled imported films, which permitted him the leisure to enjoy the café life he loved. To the end of his life Groen insisted he had never doubted for a moment that he would outlast his captors: "I knew the future. I'd be free." Even his last wish was fulfilled, that death come peacefully and without suffering, as it did one morning in 2004 at his home on a placid Amsterdam canal at the age of eighty-six.

But the hands-down winners were the tourist operators around the Toplitzsee, who have in recent years turned it into an Austrian Loch Ness, complete with its own website. The lure of sunken treasure made the lake a cynosure for fishermen, divers, and assorted adventurers, not all of whom survived. Only weeks after the war ended, the first catch was made innocently by a real fisherman who hooked a bundle of fake fivers with a face value of £400,000. He turned them over to the American occupation forces. U.S. Navy divers based in Cherbourg also went down that spring but were stopped by the logs that regularly slip down the steep mountainsides and form an interlocking, almost impenetrable mantle floating about a hundred feet below the surface. Others were more determined and less lucky. In 1946, two former engineers from the abandoned naval research station who had been camping on the lip of hills above the lake were found dead in mysterious circumstances. In 1950 two more alumni of the station tried to slither down its steep sides; one lost his grip on the brittle limestone and fell to his death.

The most ambitious underwater expedition was mounted in 1958 by the German magazine *Der Stern*. It retrieved a printing press and millions in counterfeit sterling before being stopped by the publisher, possibly on the orders of the Austrian government. This gave rise to persistent stories that *Stern*'s crew of divers and reporters had located — or was about to — SS records including the numbers of Swiss bank accounts. Representatives of the Bank of England were present when the counterfeits retrieved from the deep were burned in the boilers of the Bank of Austria. Their official report contains no hint of secret accounts that might lead the Old Lady to recover hidden treasure on deposit in Zurich, to which it might be entitled as profit from the counterfeits. In 1963 the Austrian government put the lake off limits to treasure-hunters and conducted its own survey of the bottom with a sounding device and underwater video camera. It declared there was nothing more to be found. Again neither the Bank nor the Yard made mention of any SS records in its reports, and the next year Scotland Yard formally closed the case.

Predictably, this only intensified the search. Hans Fricke, the underwater biologist, spent three years scouring the bottom in a miniature submarine, filming with the aged Krueger as a passenger on one dive. Fricke discovered more forged pounds, various rockets, missiles, and other detritus of experimental Nazi ordnance, as well as a previously unknown worm that lived without oxygen. Fricke said there was no more to find. Nevertheless, in 2000 the World Jewish Congress, prompted by an Israeli adventurer who declared himself a Mossad operative, advanced most of the $600,000 needed for a month's sonar mapping of the lake and five weeks of diving for hidden SS archives. The operation was filmed by CBS News. Still, nothing was found aside from a case of

EPILOGUE

beer caps and more counterfeit fivers, the latter on display at the Simon Wiesenthal Museum of Tolerance in Los Angeles.

As of this writing, yet another undersea adventurer, Norman Scott, who went after the wreck of the *Republic,* an American Civil War steamship that foundered off the coast of North Carolina with a cargo of gold, has obtained a three-year license from the Toplitzsee's state proprietors to hunt for gold. He claimed to have turned up new leads in the archives in Washington and Berlin and expressed confidence he would find "something damn big." After more than half a century, perhaps he will finally recover an underwater Treasure of the Sierra Madre, assuming that it has not blown away.

NOTES

ABBREVIATIONS USED IN THE NOTES

ACICR	ARCHIVES DU COMITÉ INTERNATIONAL DE LA CROIX-ROUGE (SWITZERLAND)
B/E	BANK OF ENGLAND ARCHIVES
ADM	Administration Department
BNO	Bank Note Office
C	Chief Cashier's Department
G	Governors and Secretary's Department
M	Museum Holdings
PW	Printing Works
FDRL	FRANKLIN D. ROOSEVELT PRESIDENTIAL LIBRARY
NARA	NATIONAL ARCHIVES AND RECORDS ADMINISTRATION (UNITED STATES)
RG 56	Records of the Department of the Treasury
RG 59	Records of the Department of State
RG 65	Records of the Federal Bureau of Investigation
RG 72	Records of the Bureau of Aeronautics, U.S. Naval Technical Mission in Europe
RG 84	Records of the Foreign Diplomatic Posts
RG 87	Records of the United States Secret Service
RG 226	Records of the Office of Strategic Services
RG 242	Records of the Collection of Foreign Records Seized
RG 243	Records of the United States Strategic Bombing Survey
RG 260	Records of the Office of the Military Government, Germany
RG 263	Records of the Central Intelligence Agency
RG 407	Records of the Seventh Army, G-2
PRO	PUBLIC RECORD OFFICE, THE NATIONAL ARCHIVES (U.K.)
FO	Foreign Office Papers
HW	Government Communications Headquarters Papers
MEPO	Metropolitan Police Papers
KV	Security Service Papers — MI5
T	Treasury Papers
WO	War Office Papers

SBA   Swiss Bankers Association
SFA   Swiss Federal Archives

Chapter 1: Attack the Pound the World Around

3 Wilhelmstrasse: Photographs and descriptions of these prewar ministries, which were destroyed during World War II, can be found online at www.topographie. de/wilhelmstr/. Connoisseurs of financial architecture will note similarities between the prewar German Finance Ministry and the Federal Reserve Bank of New York, constructed in 1924.

4 Details were put forward: Interrogation of Heinz Jost, chief of SS foreign intelligence until 1941, by Allied officials. Camp 020 Interim Report on the Case of Heinz Karl Maria Jost, May 12–December 5, 1945, Appendix XI, "Forgery of Bank of England Notes," pp. 16–17, PRO KV 2/104.

4 ambitious, opportunistic: Höhne, *Order of the Death's Head*, 87, 356–58.

4 The International Criminal Police Commission (ICPC) was known by its German initials, IKPK, in Germany; not until 1956 did the term Interpol come into use. The reconstituted Commission, then housed in Paris, is now based in Lyon. Five presidents of the ICPC — Otto Steinhaeusl (1939–40), Reinhard Heydrich (1940–42), Arthur Nebe (1942–43), Ernst Kaltenbrunner (1943–45), and Florent Louwage (1946–56) — were SS officers and Nazi Party members, as was Paul Dickopf, who served from 1968 to 1972, when his Nazi past caught up with him. Kaltenbrunner, nominally a policeman, was hanged at Nuremberg in 1946 for war crimes.

4 gaining access to fifteen years of case files: Deflem, "The Logic of Nazification." Heydrich, then president of the ICPC, was shot by assassins in May 1942 and died the next month. Arthur Nebe, as chief of the Reichskriminalpolizeiamt, became the provisional president for a year, during which he removed all ICPC archives from Vienna to Berlin.

4 adapt the mobile gas van: "The Development of the Gas-Van in the Murdering of the Jews," Jewish Virtual Library, pp. 4–5, http://www.jewishvirtuallibrary. org/jsource/Holocaust/vans.html.

5 Nebe proposed mobilizing: The great Nazi hunter Simon Wiesenthal thought Nebe had actually done so. See Wiesenthal's memoir *Justice, Not Vengeance*, 253–54.

5 Federal Bureau of Investigation: Passport forms requested, April 17, 1939; Heydrich circular, October 11, 1940; also, correspondence between Arthur Nebe and J. Edgar Hoover; invitation (with fare reductions and free hotel) to ICPC conference planned for Berlin; Hoover's internal memo to cut all contact with ICPC, December 4, 1941, NARA, RG 65, FBI–Interpol Files.

5 an avid reader of spy stories: Höhne, 215.

5 the single initial *C:* The designation originated from the name of Captain (later Sir) Mansfield Cumming of the Royal Navy, the first chief of Britain's Secret Intelligence Service in modern times. The SIS, also known as MI6 (for military intelligence), was formally established in 1909, with Germany's naval buildup as its principal target. Cumming initialed his memos with C (or *MC*) in green ink, and the code name stuck right into the twenty-first century and his successor in the intelli-

gence brouhaha leading up to the Iraq War, Sir Ian Scarlett. Until this was publicly confirmed by the British government in 2005 when it established a Secret Service website (www.sis.gov.uk or www.mi6.gov.uk), no one covered by Britain's Official Secrets Act could confirm or deny anything about the identity of C, past or present. The name of Stewart Menzies, the World War II chief of the Secret Intelligence Service, was inadvertently disclosed to the British public in 1966, although Heydrich's SS knew it (but misspelled it "Stuart"), as well as the name of his predecessor. Menzies, whose organization was notoriously penetrated by Communist double agents such as H.A.R. (Kim) Philby, had been a British agent during World War I. Dispatched to Madrid to assassinate Wilhelm Canaris, then a young intelligence officer accurately monitoring Allied shipping in the Mediterranean for U-boat captains, Menzies could not even *find* Canaris, let alone kill him. No wonder James Bond was a fictional character. The Nazis also knew the address of the SIS and even the location of the nearest Underground station (St. James's Park), as evidenced by the Nazi handbook for the supposedly imminent invasion of Britain, a copy of which fell into British hands in 1945 and was lodged in the Imperial War Museum in London. See *Invasion 1940: The Nazi Invasion Plan for Britain* by German general Walter Schellenberg, published in 2000 in cooperation with the museum; and Jörgensen, *Hitler's Espionage Machine*, 45.

5 He had his office: Reitlinger, *The SS*, 31–35.

6 The only serious objection: interrogation of Jost, PRO KV 2/104.

6 Funk, a homosexual former financial journalist: Taylor and Shaw, *Penguin Dictionary of the Third Reich*, 102–3.

6 legal advice from the military: Wilson, memorandum on the Tricycle/Artist group, November 20, 1943, NARA, RG 226, entry 119, box 23, folder 177A. The legal adviser to the Oberkommando der Wehrmacht (OKW) was Count Helmut von Moltke, scion of a famous military family and member of the Christian pacifist Kreisau Circle (named after his family's estate), which believed Nazism could evolve toward postwar social justice. The information in this memorandum from Wilson originated with the British. Tricycle was the code name of Dusko Popov, double agent (see chapter 8). Artist, who provided further information about the forgeries when they started appearing, was Johnny Jebsen, a Danish businessman who worked for the Abwehr out of Lisbon but often traveled to Berlin, according to Breitman et al., *U.S. Intelligence and the Nazis*, 133 n. 4. Jebsen and Moltke were executed by the Nazis in the final weeks of the war, the former by his SS enemies, who had long believed him (correctly) to be an insufficiently zealous supporter of the Nazis, the latter for his Kreisau connections.

6 Joseph Goebbels also found: *Die Tagebücher von Joseph Goebbels. Im Auftrag des Instituts für Zeitgeschichte und mit Untertzutzung des Staalichen Archivdienstes Russlands,* Teil I, Aufzeichnungen 1923–1941, Band 7, Juli 1939–März 1940, bearbeitet von Elke Frölich, Munich, 1998. Translation by Ingeborg Wolfe.

7 Hitler had refused to endanger: Kindleberger, *A Financial History of Western Europe*, 405.

7 a letter from Michael Palairet, chief of the British legation: Palairet to William Strang, Foreign Office, November 21, 1939, B/E PW 17/5. Palairet's dispatch was ignored for years by the Bank of England's own historian and others, probably because a typed copy was filed away at its printing works. The original was not immediately found in

the British National Archives. The dispatch and Paul Chourapine's memo were literally unearthed in the Bank's windowless archives, four levels below busy Threadneedle Street, the principal crossroads of the City of London.

9 Herschel Johnson, the highly respected senior career diplomat: Herschel V. Johnson, Deputy Chief of Mission, to Secretary of State, Confidential Memorandum No. 229, February 29, 1940, NARA, RG 59, Central Decimal File (1940–44), London Embassy, Classified General Records, 811.5158/2632.

9 This kind of obfuscation characterized: In a memo of January 4, 1940, to the Bank's governors titled "Forgeries," the chief cashier, Sir Kenneth Peppiatt, recalls the Athens dispatch and other warnings, B/E G 14/27, Committee of Treasury Files, Notes: Forgeries. But in *Promises to Pay: The First Three Hundred Years of Bank of England Notes,* published for the Bank by Spink (London), in 1994, Derrick Byatt, a career Bank official for forty years, wrote (p. 145) that in December 1939, the Bank had been alerted by the British embassy in Paris that Fernand Romano, "an Italian Jew with British sympathies," reported the Germans were counterfeiting one-pound notes to circulate only in distant countries, or to give to Germans who wanted to exchange their reichsmarks for foreign currency at 65 to the pound. Romano told his British handlers in Paris he was heading to Switzerland the next month, then vanished. No mention of any other, more detailed warnings appeared in this semiofficial volume. Moreover, the Romano story was not based, strictly speaking, on the Bank's own files, which apparently had vanished, but on a postwar police report filed in the Bank's Note Issue Office: C 5/136, Scotland Yard Report 16/1/46. Romano surfaced in 1954, when he wrote on company stationery from Milan to the Metropolitan Police in London demanding a medal and compensation for having told the British embassy in Paris in 1939 about the Germans' forging pound notes. On June 24, 1954, Scotland Yard noted that it had no evidence of this and rejected Romano's request. Either the police did not bother to tell the Bank about what Scotland Yard obviously regarded as yet another crank letter, or the Bank was told and simply ignored it. "Production of Bank of England notes 'BB' series by Nazi Government during World War II, 1945–64," PRO MEPO 3/2400.

10 transferred to the British secret services: Advice in September 2002 to the author from Henry Gillett, Bank of England chief archivist, whose retirement in 2003 has helped make this book possible.

10 destroyed some records: See Epilogue, p. 203.

10 "the most successful counterfeiting enterprise": C. Frederick Schwan [and] Joseph E. Boling, *World War II Remembered: History in Your Hands, a Numismatic Study* (Port Clinton, Ohio: BNR Press, 1995), 164. The study is known to specialists; when I began my researches, it was the first publication cited to me by William Bischoff, former curator of the numismatic collection of the Newark (New Jersey) Museum.

10 Between the wars: For more detailed and technical background on which this passage is partly based, see Kindleberger, *Financial History of Western Europe,* and also Skidelsky, *John Maynard Keynes,* vol. 2, 180–232.

11 sailors coming off ships were mobbed: Kindleberger, 318.

12 they went back on the gold standard: Probably the best way to explain the gold standard, even in this oversimplified manner, is to trace its history. British paper

money began as promissory notes for gold that was held in safekeeping by London goldsmiths late in the seventeenth century. What turned these pieces of paper into real money was the Bank of England's declaration on every note that it "promises to pay the bearer the face value on demand." As long as confidence in that promise held firm, paper money was literally as good as gold — and weighed less in your pocket, too. Right up to World War I, the Bank made good on that promise, but ordinary people, observing the huge cost of the war, started hoarding gold coins. His Majesty's Treasury made up for the shortage of money by issuing notes signed by its chief civil servant, John Bradbury. These notes, known as Bradburys, helped pay for the war but also served to exacerbate suspicion of paper money, and with good reason: During World War I the pound lost half its value to inflation. Even when Britain tried to return to the gold standard, anyone attempting to test the Bank's promise to exchange notes for gold was first asked to explain why. The minimum redeemable amount was an inconveniently heavy gold bar of 400 ounces, which meant that only the savings of the rich were protected by a gold guarantee. The poor paid in another way: In those days, countries settled foreign trade deficits in gold, so when gold was transferred from England to America, for example, the stock of gold-backed pounds had to be reduced. Money became tight, interest rates rose, business and trade stagnated, and so did wages. The Great Depression forced the world off the gold standard. After 1931, a pound note could be exchanged only for another, although the Bank was so confident of its ability to detect counterfeits that it would exchange even badly damaged or deteriorated notes.

13 Hitler called his military chiefs: Reitlinger, 97.

14 "What now?" Kershaw, *Hitler,* 223.

14 Approximately $3 billion more came from German Jews: A fascinating if speculative accounting of prewar Jewish wealth in Europe was compiled by Helen B. Junz for the Independent Committee of Eminent Persons (known as the Volcker Commission). Its conclusions were published in 1999 as *Report on Dormant Accounts of Victims of Nazi Persecution in Swiss Banks*; see its Appendix S, pp. A-127–206. The committee was headed by Paul Volcker, former chairman of the board of governors of the U.S. Federal Reserve System, who appointed Junz, a former U.S. Treasury economist and herself a survivor of the Holocaust. She reckoned prewar Jewish wealth in Austria, the Netherlands, Germany, Hungary, and France at $12.9 billion and estimated that the Germans got all but $3 billion of it.

15 Hitler even prohibited German espionage: Kahn, *Hitler's Spies,* 347.

15 "which everyone knows and can trust": Churchill speeches in the spring of 1925, quoted by Kindleberger, 341.

CHAPTER 2: OPERATION ANDREAS

17 Marshal Mikhail Tukhachevsky, a Bolshevik hero: Höhne, 230–32. In addition to Churchill, some Nazis believed the story, among them Walter Schellenberg and Wilhelm Hoettl of SS intelligence, as evidenced by their memoirs. The tale of the Tukhachevsky forgery also made its way into the mythology of Operation Bernhard through its most important Western popularizer, Murray Teigh Bloom, in a 1956 *Harper's* magazine article, "Bernie and Solly," reprinted a year later in Bloom's history of great counterfeits, *Money of Their Own.*

17 Marked money with a face value in the millions: Schellenberg, *The Labyrinth*, 28.

18 Heydrich was the son of a provincial: Höhne, 161–64; Reitlinger, xvii, 31–35.

18 the considered view of Schellenberg: Schellenberg, 11–14.

19 But Hitler ignored, perverted, and even rejected: Taylor and Shaw, 238.

20 the man who fired the first shots of World War II: Kahn, 280–81; Reitlinger, 122; Höhne, 227, 264; Peis, *The Man Who Started the War*, 94–100; Crankshaw, *Gestapo*, 101.

21 the muscle man in the kidnapping: This was the notorious Venlo affair. Major Richard Stevens and Captain S. (Sigismund) Payne Best of British Secret Intelligence were lured to the German border at Venlo, the Netherlands, in the belief that they had intelligence from anti-Nazi officers whom they had been cultivating in the hope of promoting a coup against Hitler, the prevention of which was a prime mission of the SS. After a gun battle, Naujocks and his SS men captured the two officers and rammed their big Buick across the frontier barrier. Stevens and Payne Best were held in concentration camps for the remainder of the war and interrogated for what they knew about British intelligence.

21 the security service's technical section: Section F of the foreign intelligence service of the RSHA (Reich Central Security Office). The section's Bureau 4 forged documents and therefore was ordered to produce counterfeit currency. In 1939 Himmler and Heydrich divided the RSHA into six departments, or *Amter*: Amt I handled personnel and training; Amt II administration and economic and judicial affairs; Amt III internal security; Amt IV was the notorious Geheime Staatspolizei, the secret state police popularly known as the Gestapo; Amt V the Kriminalpolizei, known as the Kripo; and Amt VI the Auslandsnachrichtendienst, or foreign intelligence service. Amt VI was the RSHA's own espionage service, which ran spy networks and performed sabotage. Officers of these departments were generally members of the Sicherheitsdienst, the SD (Security Service).

The most infamous of these disparate security organizations brought under Heydrich's command was, of course, the Gestapo. This secret police did not originate with the Nazis. In the 1920s it was Department IA of the Prussian political police under the Weimar Republic, and its job was the surveillance of Communists. What made the Gestapo notoriously evil after Hitler snuffed out Germany's ill-fated experiment with democracy was the power quickly assumed by the Nazis to arrest and hold anyone in "protective custody" without trial or even explanation. Himmler later devised a means to make some victims vanish forever in *Nacht und Nebel* — night and fog — so that relatives would never even know where their loved ones were buried. (See Reitlinger, 38, and Crankshaw, 15.) Once established, this technique did not go away. In South America during the counterterrorist regimes in the 1970s, suspects were arrested, tortured, and dumped anonymously into the sea from airplanes or buried in common graves, a fearsome weapon that turned the word *disappear* into an active verb. Students of antiterrorist activities in Britain and America after September 11, 2001, may find a chilling similarity in powers claimed by the executive branch to arrest and detain suspects without charge in the two nations with the deepest traditions of habeas corpus — the Latin term for the state's obligation to produce a prisoner and publicly explain why he is being held, and a foundation stone of Anglo-Saxon law. This dubious claim was overruled by the highest courts in both countries, but only after several years and not definitively.

21 Naujocks's technical command put him in charge: Copy of replies by Alfred Naujocks to Bank's questions, B/E PW 17/5 Forgery: 12 July 1929–11 December 1963.

22 Nebe had ultimately walked out: Jost, PRO KV 2/104.

22 Langer . . . had served in Austria's code-breaking: Isolde Langer (widow of Albert Langer), interview by David Kahn at her home in Austria, September 14, 1973. Kahn has generously provided his notes to the author.

22 to build a code-breaking machine: "Translation of Report Dated 22.6.1945 by Dr. Albert Langer of Valden am Woerthersee on the Technical Section of Amt VI of the RSHA," NARA, RG 226, entry 109, box 66, folder XX 11587–99 (22 June 1945 — Langer), hereafter cited as Langer report. This report is somewhat hysterical under the shock of defeat, although the anonymous U.S. intelligence officer who summarized it found the report "very entertaining reading." Langer, born April 29, 1895, in Graz, Austria, was assigned NSDAP number 614388 on May 1, 1938, only six weeks after the *Anschluss* between Germany and Austria (NARA, RG 242, MFOK, roll M-81, frame 1532).

22 mental processes in curing cancer and another: War Room Comment on Langer report.

23 Langer, a fragile, thin, bespectacled man: Or so Naujocks remembered him almost five years later. M.I.5. Interim Interrogation Report on the Case of Alfred Naujocks, NARA, RG 226, entry 108B, folder 2082 XX 3980, pp. 36–37.

23 Langer wrote in the only official account: "The Counterfeiting of the Pound," NARA, RG 226, entry 155, box 2, folder 13. Internal evidence confirms Langer is the author of this unsigned and undated eleven-page Top Secret memorandum, which is the source of information attributed to him in this chapter unless otherwise noted. The memo was probably composed in 1952 or 1953. He had regained his mental equilibrium (partly through the security of postwar employment by U.S. intelligence in Germany, according to his wife) and gave a more coherent account of events that occurred "12½ years back." In the unsigned report, he described himself as the technical director reporting to Naujocks, and the only civilian in the operation aside from the printers, etchers, and other craftsmen. This description fits Langer precisely. Documents at the National Archives in the same box from the files of the wartime Office of Strategic Services and its successor, the Central Intelligence Agency, make it clear that the CIA's Eastern European section was trying to get to the bottom of the Germans' World War II counterfeiting operations once and for all, probably to ensure that they had not somehow been taken over by Communist espionage after the war. See the memo from E. Parmly III of the CIA's Eastern European section, October 8, 1953, and the reply from McGregor Gray, October 26, 1953, NARA, RG 226, entry 155, box 2.

24 (footnote) A wrinkle in this story has been repeated so often: The story first appeared in Hoettl, *Hitler's Paper Weapon*, 27.

25 an 1855 drawing by Daniel Maclise: Byatt, *Promises to Pay*, 96.

25 a professional named Artur Rau: Translation of a Report Given to the American Authorities (by Capt. [Serge] S. G. Michel, French liaison officer, who interviewed Rau), p. 23 (see paragraph 11), NARA, RG 65, box 62, no. 937.

26 engraver in his late sixties named Walter Ziedrich: Identified by Langer only by last name in his written account but named in full as an RSHA employee in its telephone directory (July 1943) of the technical section headquarters on Berkaer Strasse (ext. 331). Langer's extension was 208, Schellenberg's 251 (and his home number 80-79-84). The directory is in NARA, RG 242, T-175 (Records of the Reich Leader of the SS and Chief of the Kriminalpolizeiamt), roll 232. RSHA 1943 directory begins at frame 2720276 and ends at 2720417, where Ziedrich's name is listed.

26 Paper was delivered to the ground floor: Diagram accompanying Naujocks's replies to questions submitted on December 14, 1944, by Kenneth Peppiatt, chief cashier of the Bank of England, to Sir Norman Kendal of Scotland Yard, for Naujocks's interrogation, B/E PW 17/5.

26 August Petrich, a Nazi Party veteran: Born in Berlin in 1901, joined NSDAP (Nazi Party) (no. 5584607) on May 1, 1937, Captured German Records of the NSDAP, NARA, RG 242, roll A3340-MFOK-QO68 Ortsgruppen.

26 They proudly posed for photographs: The photos ended up in the custody of the FBI in 1945, along with falsified documents that FBI agents in Europe thought could help track fleeing Nazis. Many of the fake passports, visas, entry permits, and so on, were copies of documents from South American nations, some perhaps lifted from diplomats cavorting at Salon Kitty. NARA, RG 65, Class File 65-47826-297, boxes 50, 51, section 12 (4 parts).

26 Naujocks thought the notes: B/E PW 17/5.

26 code name . . . *Andreas-Angelegenheit:* Langer report.

27 Even the Bank of England realized that: John Keyworth, curator of the Bank of England museum, in an essay "The Sinews of War" (regarding the documentary film *The Great Nazi Cash Swindle,* http//:www.channel4.com/history/microsites/H/history/n-s/swindle.html) writes: "If the original plan had been carried out . . . everyday life would have been severely disrupted as people lost confidence in banknotes, and large areas of the country would have reverted to barter."

27 According to the former SS officer Wilhelm Hoettl: See Hoettl, *Hitler's Paper Weapon,* 21. The same quote ("Dollars no.") is repeated on behalf of Naujocks, also without any source, in Peis, 137. The quote also appears in Bloom, *Money of Their Own.* No evidence whatever, either in a document or in the direct report by any German, including Hoettl himself, has been found in research for this book to substantiate that Hitler ever made this comment. This has not stopped it from appearing in many repetitions of this tale.

27 Hitler rarely put any orders on paper: Kershaw, 33.

28 it had a strong "literary make-up": Deposition for trial of Adolf Eichmann taken at Bad Aussee, Austria, June 22, 1961, by Senior Judge Egon Kittl, www.nizkor.org/hweb/people/e/eichmann-adolf/transcripts/Testimony-Abroad/Wilhelm_Hoettl-08.html.

28 One Simon Graham wrote: Miriam Kleiman and Robert Skwirot, Interagency Working Group Researchers, "Analysis of the Name File of Wilhelm Hoettl," p. 6, n. 36, NARA, RG 263.

29 *Evening Standard:* B/E C 12/111, Note Issue Files.

29 The Swiss Bankers Association did not issue: Counterfeit circular No. 961 (in French and German), Basel, December 3, 1942. Copies provided to the author by James Nason of the SBA.

29 the Bank was still nodding: Byatt, *Promises to Pay,* 147. This authorized account was written by the retired records adviser of the Bank and published under its auspices. After its publication, members of the press and public seeking information about the wartime counterfeits were directed to the book, and only to it, by the office of the Archivist until his retirement in 2003.

30 "as usual, lost his temper": interrogation of Jost, PRO KV 2/104.

30 the Delbrückstrasse factory was diverted to rubles: Mader, *Der Banditenschatz* (The Bandit's Treasure), 59. Julius Mader was a propagandist writer with connections to the Stasi, East Germany's security service.

30 left around 1942 with back problems: Kahn interview with Isolde Langer.

30 about £3 million in false pounds: This is also the figure given in an unpublished memoir by Bernhard Krueger, the SS officer who revived the counterfeiting operation in 1942. See notes to chapter 5.

30 "It became more and more unorganized": Langer report.

31 a graphic account appeared in a Frankfurt newspaper: *Frankfurter Rundschau* article, December 24, 1945, NARA, RG 65, box 51, Class File 65-47826-378.

CHAPTER 3: WHITEHALL AND THE OLD LADY

33–34 Churchill letter to Simon: "Suggested distribution by aeroplane of forged German currency notes over German territory. 1939 Sept. 6–1945 Feb. 1," PRO T 160/1332. Unless otherwise noted, this and other letters, internal Treasury memoranda, and exchanges with the Bank of England cited here and in the following paragraphs are lodged in this file at Britain's Public Record Office in Kew. Most of the originals of the Bank's correspondence on the subject are missing from its archives or, if they remain, have not been declassified.

35 Keynes wrote at the conclusion: John Maynard Keynes, *The General Theory of Employment, Interest and Money* (1936; reprint, New York: Harcourt, Brace & World, 1964), 383.

36 not the first time the English had thought: Bloom, *Money of Their Own,* 236.

37 During the American Civil War, confidence men: Currency exhibit, Federal Reserve Bank of San Francisco, 2001.

37 When the Soviet Union was starved: W. G. Krivitsky, "When Stalin Counterfeited Dollars," *Saturday Evening Post,* September 30, 1939, 8ff.

37 the rogue nation North Korea: John K. Cooley, "The Rogue Money Printers of Pyongyang," *International Herald Tribune,* October 24, 2005, 8. Mertin Fackler, "North Korean Counterfeiting Complicates Nuclear Crisis," *New York Times,* January 29, 2006, 3.

40 dropped forged German ration books: [probably H. Merle] Cochran to Henry Morgenthau, Jr., quoting Britain's Treasury representative in Washington, *Morgenthau Diaries* (1938–1945), vol. 306, leaf 4, FDRL. Lord Lothian, unsigned memorandum (prepared by Gerald Pinsent, British Treasury representative and financial counselor of the British embassy in Washington, according to subsequent memorandum to Morgenthau on September 14, 1940) to Morgenthau, September 12, 1940, ibid., leaves 180–82.

40 In 1943 Radio Berlin reported: "Berlin Raiders Accused of Adding Insult

to Injury," *New York Times,* May 29, 1943, 4. See also Auckland, *Air-dropped Propaganda Currency:* "a directive issued by the War Cabinet to the British/American psychological teams stated that on no account were German banknotes of any description to be completely forged." During the war Auckland had actually encountered the counterfeits in North Africa (see p. 137 of this book). Afterward he was the editor of *Falling Leaf,* the journal of the PsyWar Society, and presumably had seen this secret directive or was told about it. The psychological warfare units nevertheless forged the face of German bills, and on the reverse printed propaganda slogans, sometimes bawdy ("Ich bin Hitlers Arschwisch . . .").

41 Waley had the wit to put himself: So did the thriller writer Margery Allingham, who plotted her 1941 novel *Traitor's Purse* (published in the United States as *The Sabotage Murder Mystery*) around Nazi counterfeits spread through Britain to destabilize the economy.

41 "Perhaps it is a fairy story": Waley to Catterns, November 27, 1939, B/E PW 17/5.

41 In May 1939, as war loomed: Sir Frederick Phillips exchange with Catterns of Bank of England, 19 May 1939 et seq., PRO T 160/1344.

41 "could be silent in several languages": Keynes's obituary tribute to his colleague in the *Times* of London, quoted in Skidelsky, 146.

41 torpid superiority: When a wealthy American Anglophile proposed placing a Foucault pendulum in the well of the Bank in 1939 as a symbol of permanence, Edward Holland-Martin, an executive director who went by the nickname of Ruby, commented, "I am not quite sure what a Foucault pendulum is." Correspondence of Edward Holland-Martin, B/E ADM 245.

41 the Bank had actually printed up excellent counterfeits: Herbert G. de Fraine of the Bank's printing plant, quoted by Bloom, "Uncle Sam," 350. Maurice (later Lord) Hankey, secretary to the War Cabinet, wrote in his diary on January 25, 1916, that an official identified only as Montagu — presumably Edwin Montagu, an MP then serving in the subcabinet post of financial secretary to the Treasury — "called on me to explain a scheme of his for placing forged German bank notes in circulation, in which I promised to try and help. It appears that the Governor of the Bank of England, with the knowledge of the Chancellor of the Exchequer and the Prime Minister, has produced some marvelous forgeries. It seems rather a dirty business, but the Germans deserve it and Napoleon used to do it. There is some reason to suspect that the Huns have played this game on us." On January 27, Hankey also sought help from the British Admiralty's intelligence chief in the scheme, a Captain Hall. Quoted in Roskill, *Hankey,* vol. 1, 246.

42 fear of public embarrassment if the device failed: Byatt, *Promises to Pay,* 137.

42 slightly more than half of all notes in circulation: *Bank of England Quarterly Bulletin,* June 1967.

43 K. O. Peppiatt — who, like the Treasury's Waley: *Who Was Who* and Peppiatt's obituary notice in *The Old Lady,* September 1983, 144. This obituary in the Bank's staff magazine was signed L. K. O'B, for Leslie O'Brien, Peppiatt's successor as chief cashier and later the Bank's governor, ennobled as Lord O'Brien. His obituary is also the source of the description of Peppiatt's cool manner.

43 the cleverest man in England: See the author's chapter on Keynes in *The Horizon Book of Makers of Modern Thought.*

43 "always absolutely charming, always absolutely wrong": Skidelsky, 554.

45 The chancellor recounted the conversation: Untitled memo initialed by Simon, April 6, 1940.

45 kill any other newspaper stories: On December 5, 1939, the Bank of England drafted a notice to newspaper editors, saying: "No information should be published without submission to censorship which is likely to undermine public confidence in any notes which are legal tender in the UK. In particular it should not be stated, without official sanction, or suggested that any series of currency or other notes are forgeries." The very existence of such "D-notices" — Defense Notices — is secret even in peacetime, so it could not be ascertained whether one was actually issued, but official behavior such as Simon's indicated that some kind of notice was in force. B/E ADM, Holland-Martin correspondence, p. 416A.

45 Peppiatt refused the offer of the French police: Copy of Peppiatt letter dated 9 Feb. 1940, Forged Bank of England Notes, PRO T 401/5.

46 a plea from Vienna for help in finding refuge: Notes, Printing, Coin and Silver, 1935–47, Chief Cashier's Policy Files, B/E C 40/889.

46 the Bank banned the repatriation of its own banknotes: *Promises to Pay,* p. 142. Bank of England Archives G14/27 Committee of Treasury Files: Draft Notice, dated December 1939.

CHAPTER 4: NOBEL PRIZE–WINNING IDEAS

48 had already been received in the Oval Office: *Steinbeck: A Life in Letters,* 206–7.

49 Letter from Steinbeck to Roosevelt: President's Official File (OF)3858, Steinbeck, John, 1939–1940, FDRL.

49 James Rowe: Ibid.

50 a twenty-minute meeting with Roosevelt: White House Stenographer's Diaries, 12 September 1940; White House Usher's Diaries, 12 September 1940, FDRL.

50 Steinbeck's highly dramatized version: Steinbeck, "The Secret Weapon We Were AFRAID to Use," 9–10. At least Steinbeck did not make the mistake of putting Roosevelt in a wheelchair. The president, whose legs were paralyzed by polio, moved around the White House in a wheelchair, but in the Oval Office he was lifted by his aides into an ordinary desk chair. Curtis Roosevelt (the president's grandson), communication to the author.

50 addressed them as Uncle Henry and Aunt Elinor: Ibid.

51 Also at the meeting was Herbert G. Gaston: Gaston, confidential memorandum to Henry Morgenthau, September 12, 1940, *Morgenthau Diaries,* vol. 305, pp. 116–17 (reel 83), FDRL.

52 blunt when the occasion called for it: During the first two desperate years of the war, Britain spent almost 90 percent of its gold and dollar reserves, and Churchill knew he could obtain financing only from the United States. Lord Lothian, returning in October 1940 from London with instructions to strike a deal with Washington, lost no time in going public. Deplaning at New York's LaGuardia Airport, he greeted the waiting American reporters: "Well, boys, Britain's broke. It's your money we want." Skidelsky, 96; chart of depleted reserves, 134. The precise figures for the declining reserves were £519 million in September 1939 at the start of the

war, and £69 million on its second anniversary, September 1941, which was close to the low point of World War II. In dollars, at the official rate of $4.03 to the pound, that represented a collapse of Britain's reserves from $2.09 billion to $279 million.

52 memorandum prepared by Gerald Pinsent: Morgenthau-Lothian exchange and Pinsent memo, September 12 and 16, 1940, *Morgenthau Diaries,* vol. 306, 179–82 (reel 82) FDRL.

54 Morgenthau quickly wrote to thank: Henry Morgenthau Jr. to Philip Kerr [Marquess of Lothian], British ambassador to the United States, September 16, 1940, *Morgenthau Diaries,* vol. 206, 179–82 (reel 84) FDRL.

54 "a deadly little plan": Steinbeck, undated letter to Archibald MacLeish, quoted in *Steinbeck,* 212. (The original was not found in MacLeish's papers at the Library of Congress or in the MacLeish collection at Greenfield Community College in Greenfield, Mass.)

54 The author would later encounter the president: Cliff Lewis and Carroll Britch, eds., *Rediscovering Steinbeck: Revisionist Views of His Art, Politics, and Intellect* (Lewiston, N.Y.: Edwin Mellen Press, 1989), 194 et seq. Cliff Lewis, *Steinbeck: The Artist as FDR Speechwriter.* For minority rights, see Jonathan Daniels, *White House Witness, 1942–45* (New York: Doubleday, 1975), 234.

54 dismissed him as a "spluttering" moneybags: Steinbeck, "The Secret Weapon."

55 Central Intelligence Agency had the idea: Financial measures "would include attempts to dislocate the enemy economy through . . . dumping of counterfeit currency to promote inflation, etc." NARA CIA Crest Database, CIA-RDP79-01084A00100050002-1 [declassified June 13, 2000], p. E-6. "Foreign Economic Intelligence Requirements Relating to the National Security."

55 "Know Your Money" campaign: "Secret Service To View Fake Money Films," *Washington Post,* January 8, 1940, 1.

55 "sometime soon Germany and Japan may try to panic": *Life,* August 24, 1942, 66.

55 sent the German chargé d'affaires, Hans Thomsen: Pierrepont Moffatt, Chief, Division of European Affairs, memorandum of conversation with Dr. Hans Thomsen, German chargé d'affaires ad interim, January 26, 1940, NARA, RG 59, Central Decimal Files (1940–44) 811.5158/2612, box 3916.

55 a report by the Turkish ambassador: Letter from the Turkish Ambassador to the United States by Ambassador Mehmet Munir Ertegün to the Office of the Adviser on International Economic Affairs, April 3, 1940, ibid., 811.5158/2630. In 1947, Ertegün's twenty-four-year-old son Ahmet founded Atlantic Records in Washington, D.C.

56 reporter called "black bourses": "Europe Is Nervous Over Bogus Money," *New York Times,* January 26, 1940, 6.

56 Herschel Johnson's London memorandum: Herschel Vespasian Johnson II (1894–1966), born in Atlanta and named after an ancestor who was a governor of Georgia, served in the U.S. Army in World War I, and was U.S. minister to Sweden, 1941–46; U.S. ambassador to Brazil, 1948–53. He also served as acting chief of the U.S. mission to the United Nations in its crucial formative years, 1946–48. In 1940 Johnson was chargé d'affaires ad interim, in charge of the U.S. embassy in London

following what Roy Jenkins (and many others) called the "unlamented" departure of Joseph P. Kennedy as ambassador. Jenkins, *Churchill: A Biography* (New York/London: Penguin, 2002), 262.

56 the American embassy in London was told curtly: James Clement Dunn, Assistant Secretary of State, to American Embassy in London, Confidential Memorandum (No. 100), April 1, 1940, NARA, RG 59, Central Decimal File 811.5158/2612, box 3916.

56 arrested in neutral Turkey for passing counterfeits: "Turkey Rounds up Counterfeiters in Plot to Debase British Pound," *New York Times,* January, 2, 1941, 2. London *Evening Standard,* January 2, 1941, copy in B/E C 12/111. Headline and page number obscured.

56 a Chilean diplomat and a number of attractive women: "Chilean Diplomat Vanishes in Turkey," *New York Times,* January 19, 1941, 16.

57 as high as £100 were circulating in Switzerland: "Forged Bank Notes in Switzerland: Yard Warned," London *Evening Standard,* January 7, 1941, B/E C 12/111.

57 a typically tut-tutting editorial: "Paper Money in Germany," *New York Times,* January 11, 1941.

57 another reader, Manfred A. Isserman: *New York Times,* January 30, 1941. Isserman would later serve as an interrogator at the Nuremberg war crimes trials.

57 Private N. E. Cortright of the Weather Squadron: Letter from Cortright [no addressee], December 22, 1941, NARA, RG 226, entry 9, box 28, folder 46. This folder also contains the comments on Cortright's letter.

58 a letter from a "very able Colorado publisher": Edwin C. Johnson, Senate Committee on Military Affairs, to William J. Donovan, Coordinator of Information, January 6, 1942; Emile DesPres, interoffice memo to Dr. James P. Baxter re letter from Johnson to Donovan, January 9, 1942, NARA, RG 226, M-1632, roll 23, frames 644–45.

58 These were elaborated in a letter to the president: G. Edward Buxton, Acting Director, OSS Washington Director's Office, to the president, July 14, 1943, NARA, RG 226, M-1632, roll 3, frames 644–45.

58 permission to drop fake lire: William J. Donovan, Coordinator of Information, Memorandum for the President (No. 269), February 19, 1942, NARA, RG 226, M-1072; Report titled "Historical Instances of Political Counterfeiting," February 11, 1942, is not attached to the Donovan microfilm copy of his memo; original copy in President's Secretary's Files, Subject File: Office of Strategic Services Reports, February 12–20, 1942 (box 148), FDRL.

59 Lovell's first job was to manufacture: Lovell, *Of Spies and Stratagems,* 23–27.

59 a young New York lawyer: Murray L. Gurfein, "Project for a Secret Printing Press," memorandum to Hugh R. Wilson and Allen W. Dulles, July 13, 1942, NARA, RG 226, entry 92, box 102, folder 22, no. 9373 (Paul Wolf of Washington, D.C., first located the document at the National Archives). Wilson noted that the project "deserves real study." Gurfein's memo was passed to David Bruce, soon to be sent to London as chief liaison with British espionage. "Let's implement it," wrote Bruce, and they did, since no self-respecting espionage agency could operate without

forged passports and similar paraphernalia. Gurfein, then an assistant district attorney working in the office of the racket-busting Thomas E. Dewey, tacked on a supplementary suggestion noting recent "discussion of the possibility of creating artificial inflation in enemy countries through the manufacture and distribution upon a large scale of the enemy's currency." He also concluded that introducing counterfeit might be practical in a weak country like Italy, and his contribution to the debate was to suggest funneling it through the black market. (This was around the same time the Nazis returned to their far more serious counterfeiting scheme.) Gurfein would soon enter the armed forces as an intelligence officer. He had a distinguished postwar legal career, first serving as an assistant to Justice Robert Jackson at the Nuremberg War Crimes Trials. In 1971, shortly after being appointed a federal district judge, Gurfein made the historic decision refusing to stop the presses when the Pentagon Papers were first printed by the *New York Times*. His last law clerk was the young Michael Chertoff, himself later a federal judge and secretary of homeland security in the administration of President George W. Bush.

59 "vital to us if we weren't to be closed up": Lovell, 24.

60 only one known to have been put in writing: Bloom, "Uncle Sam," 352, 356.

61 to stay on the lookout for counterfeit dollars: Ulius L. A. Moss, in an OSS interoffice memo to Major David Bruce, October 13, 1942, forwarded the request of the U.S. Secret Service to "get all reports possible on enemy counterfeiting of occupied or other nations' currency. . . . The Secret Service fears an eventual flood of counterfeit American money." NARA, RG 226. Major David K. E. Bruce, then director of the U.S. Secret Intelligence Branch, later director of the OSS in London, was a political patrician who later became a distinguished postwar American ambassador to France, West Germany, and London.

61 Copeland, who believed that this great: Bloom, ibid., 352–53.

61 an Army Air Force major: Major Clifford H. Pangburn, letter to Major General William J. Donovan, July 6, 1944, accompanied by memo "General Plan for Morale Operations Against Germans as Holders of Cash," NARA, RG 226, M-1499B, reel 221, frame 32,043 (first located by Paul Wolf).

61 Reddick, the master printer, could feel the wartime pressure: Bloom, ibid.

CHAPTER 5: THE COUNTERFEIT CHAIN OF COMMAND

63 "the greatest counterfeiter the world has ever known": "I Was the World's Greatest Counterfeiter," by Bernhard Kruger (*sic*) as told to Murray Teigh Bloom. Bloom, an experienced reporter and World War II counterintelligence agent, met with Krueger more than a decade after the war, having already made himself an expert on counterfeiting and published a minor classic on the subject, *Money of Their Own*. He interviewed Krueger and chose to turn his notes into a first-person account under Krueger's name for greater impact (and tabloid sales). Later Bloom posed more detailed questions, to which Krueger replied in German. They were never cast into narrative form, but the two kept up an extensive correspondence in the hope of making a film. Bloom has kindly allowed me to view and quote from the surviving fragments, which cover Operation Bernhard during only the first year of Krueger's involvement. These have been translated by Ingeborg Wolfe and are re-

ferred to in these notes as "Krueger fragments," with the pagination referring to the copies of the original German pages in the author's possession.

63 described him as slightly bowlegged: PRO WO 354/26, Judge Advocate General's Office, Military Deputy's Department: War Crimes, Europe, Card Indexes of Perpetrators, Witnesses and Accused, Second World War, Box: Kruber-Lamschultz, 1942–48.

63 peered into the camera for his mug shot: PRO WO 309/1772, Judge Advocate General's Office, British Army of the Rhine War Crimes Group (North West Europe) and predecessors: Registered Files (BAOR and other series) Detention Report 208 449, Bernhard Friedrich Walter Krueger. He was arrested at 8 p.m., November 26, 1946, and photographed three months later.

63 "It was technical perfection": Krueger interview filmed in 1984 and included in the German television documentary *Der Fluch des Toplitzsees* (The Curse of Lake Toplitz), broadcast on ZDF in 2003.

63–64 Born November 26, 1904: Krueger's birthplace was Riesa, Germany, and his parents were Franz and Wella Marx Krueger. NARA, RG 242, A-3343-SSO, roll 217A. Krueger's SS number was 15,249, his NSDAP number 528,739. His thick SS file is devoted almost entirely to disciplinary action involving a drunken episode at a restaurant in Stettin in 1938 (*Lebenslauf*), which did not impede his rapid promotion in a service known for its brawlers and sadists.

64 constructing locomotives out of concrete: Speer, *Inside the Third Reich: Memoirs*, 268.

64 By profession an engineer of complex textile machinery: The details of Krueger's career — broadly confirmed in Bloom's articles — are contained in a dossier on Krueger compiled immediately after the war by United States, British, and French intelligence as part of a fuller description of Operation Bernhard. Judging by the spelling and military abbreviations, the dossier was written by an American official attached to Supreme Allied Headquarters in Paris, but the most complete version was located in the Swiss Federal Archives in Bern: E4323 (A) 1988 Band 73 F11.1 (Appendix "A 1"). A slightly shortened version on a different typewriter is in the U.S. National Archives (RG 260, box 451, 950.31) and carries an anonymous handwritten notation "From the report of Capt. [S. C.] Michel, French Army." Michel was probably with the U.S. Counterintelligence Corps detachment of the 80th U.S. Infantry Division, which is credited in the postwar report with doing "elaborate work" on the investigation.

65 forwarding packets of French identity cards: Krueger to Naujocks, 23 November 1940, NARA, RG 226, entry 155, box 2, folder 13.

65 obtain and forge passports and other identity papers: "German Police–Germany," NARA, RG 65, Class File 65-47826-294, section 12 (4 of 4), box 50 (declassified in 2003). In Schellenberg's memoir, *The Labyrinth,* 364, he tells the story of an Allied interrogator who refused to believe he had never visited the United States, showing Schellenberg an American passport in his name, complete with visas. Stumped momentarily, Schellenberg remembered that Krueger's technical department had presented him with this fake passport in 1943 as its first perfect product.

65 designated Section VIF4: Kahn, *Hitler's Spies,* 262.

65 visited military intelligence posts in unoccupied France: SFA, E4323 (A), "Part I," p. 3.

65 Krueger was summoned "on an urgent matter": Krueger fragments, 1.

66 The seventh child of a Saarbrücken piano manufacturer: Background and description of Schellenberg from Kahn, 255–61.

66 "the better type of people": Schellenberg, *Labyrinth*, 3.

66 foreign economic intelligence flowed in: Kahn, 92.

66 Its arrest wish-list of 2,820 individuals indicated: Schellenberg, *Invasion 1940*, xxvi, 175.

67 Schellenberg's office, although deeply carpeted: Schellenberg, *Labyrinth*, 214–15.

68 As Krueger entered Schellenberg's lair: Krueger fragments, 1–5, describing the encounter and exchanges with Schellenberg.

69 Far from being elated: Krueger fragments, 6–10, 36–38. Krueger, "I Was the World's Greatest Counterfeiter," part 1, June 8, 1958.

70 "the narrow gate between duty and crime": Krueger, 1984 ZDF interview.

71 he visited Delbrückstrasse 6A: Krueger fragments, 49–52.

72 In Himmler's personal daybook: Himmler, *Der Dienstkalender Heinrich Himmlers 1941/2*.

73 ceaselessly engaged in bureaucratic empire-building: Kershaw, 313.

74 He loved imaginative but untried projects: Speer, 144.

74 Cash was also donated: Baron Kurt von Schröder, letter to Himmler, submitted in evidence at the Nuremberg trials; copy of newspaper account of the "Friendly Circle" forwarded to the chief of the U.S. Secret Service, NARA, RG 87, box 69, folder 109, Germany through 1937.

75 had to beg for a loan of 80,000 marks: Höhne, 421–22.

75 yielded only 178 million reichsmarks: Milton Goldin, "Financing the SS," 9. (Reichsmarks are converted at the official — and notional, as well as artificially high — rate of 40 U.S. cents.) See also Taylor and Shaw, 202, 218.

76 "wasted as a result of unrealistic fantasies": Schellenberg, *Labyrinth*, 367–69.

76 Goering's Luftwaffe was not even able to resupply: Reitlinger, 233.

76 the perfect cover for the scheme: In his extensive postwar interrogation, Schellenberg barely mentioned the plan to dump the counterfeits on Britain and concentrated on how they were otherwise employed. NARA, RG 226, Schellenberg OSS IRR Personal XE001752, Appendix VII, "Financial Affairs of the RSHA and Amt VI."

77 The following directive soon went out: A photo of the original is published opposite p. 82 in Mader, *Banditenschatz*. Mader, who had contacts with the propaganda and security services of the former German Democratic Republic, wrote the book to draw attention to Nazi criminals — former forgers, including Krueger — still living in the West. He cites many Western publications, but to make his book more credible, the Stasi presumably supplied him with some Nazi documents in its files, and this would have been one of them.

77 signed by Lieutenant Colonel Hermann Dörner: Although the name *Dörner* is illegible in the printed copy of the order, it was certainly signed by Obersturmbannfuehrer (Lieutenant Colonel) Hermann Dörner, chief of the technical division of foreign intelligence. SFA, E4323(A) 1988 Band 73, F11. See Part IV, "List of Per-

sonalities." See also Burke, *Nazi Counterfeiting*, 7; Sem and Mayer, *Report on Forgery in Sachsenhausen Concentration Camp*, 9. The latter is based on extensive interviews by Czech police immediately after the war.

78 two more appeals were circulated: Mader, 214.

CHAPTER 6: INGATHERING OF THE EXILES

80 Avraham Krakowski, a pious young Polish accountant: Krakowski and Finkel, *Counterfeit Lives*, 122; Krakowski, author interview, Brooklyn, N.Y., November 10, 2002.

81 Auschwitz, Majdanek, Treblinka: *Auschwitz: Inside the Nazi State*, part 2, Laurence Rees, writer/producer, aired on the Public Broadcasting Service in 2005.

81 "Keep in mind": Suchomel in Claude Lanzmann's film *Shoah* (1985).

81 the Nazis' political opponents: See entries in Taylor and Shaw, under *concentration camps, Pohl, SS, Wannsee*. See also Sofsky, *Order of Terror*, 28–30.

81 A punishment camp for Communists and Social Democrats: Sachsenhausen details here and below are from Sofsky, 50; Taylor and Shaw, under *Sachsenhausen*; Burger, *Des Teufels Werkstatt*, originally published in Prague as *Ďáblova Dílna*, Prague, 1991, reprinted by Verlag Neues Leben GmbH, Berlin, 2001, 115. (Further references to Burger are to this 2001 edition.) Burger was himself a prisoner, who arrived at Block 19 in 1944; his book also drew on details, maps, and archival photographs in Mader, *Banditenschatz*. The level of assistance offered to Burger by Communist authorities is uncertain. The camp's few remaining buildings, now part of the Brandenburg state museum system, have their own curator-historian to do research and to guide tourists, schoolchildren, and, as was evident during a visit by the author in 2004, soldiers of the German *Bundeswehr*, lest they forget. An imposing memorial building and a monument to the murdered Russian soldiers were erected by the German Democratic Republic before German reunification. Both were virtually deserted on that visit in favor of a lively and more comprehensive exhibit of camp life in a barracks reconstructed in the style of those occupied by the prisoners of Operation Bernhard and containing some of its artifacts. The dispute between these rival versions of history will no doubt persist, and the camp itself will continue to be a cynosure for the memories, myths, and horrible fascination of this dark period in history. On December 14, 2005, two drunken women, ages eighteen and nineteen, were arrested at the Oranienburg station for giving the Nazi salute and singing a neo-Nazi song as a foreign tour group alighted from the train. The nineteen-year-old, a repeat offender, was sentenced to ten months in prison, the other to a symbolic few hours under Germany's strict laws banning Nazi symbols. *Deutsche Welle*, December 14, 2005. www.dw-world.de/dw/article/0,2144,1822224,00.html.

82 Then he decreed that the prisoners' output: Georg, *Die wirtschaftlichen Unternehmungen der SS*, 111, quoted in Höhne, 390.

82 The greatest success proved to be: Sofsky, 177.

83 Another slave group produced a fuselage: R. Antelme, *Das Menschengeschlecht* (Munich, 1987), quoted in Sofsky, 173.

83 each prisoner would yield profits: Quoted in Eizenstat, *Imperfect Justice*,

207. A note on p. 374 attributes the statement to "SS Profitability Calculation Regarding Use of Prisoners in Concentration Camps," quoted in Bernd Klewitz, *Die Arbeitssklaven der Dynamit Nobel* (The Slave Workers of Dynamit Nobel) (Schalksmühle, Germany: Engelbrecht, 1986). The document is also in the U.S. National Archives.

83 At Dora-Mittelbau near Nordhausen: Eizenstat, 205 and note, 374, citing "Quotations Showing Nazi-German Mentality," U.S. Army document for the Dachau war crimes trial of Kurt Andrae et al., August 7, 1947, in the Friedmann Collection at the U.S. Holocaust Memorial Museum in Washington, D.C.

83 During the first six months, almost 3,000: Sofsky, 180.

83 more than 3,000 in this *Kommando Speer:* ibid., 176.

83–84 complained that mere extermination wasted: Reitlinger, 259.

85 suitable guards for Block 19: Krueger fragments, 3–5. Krueger recalled his superior as an SS-Gruppenleiter (lieutenant general) named Faustin, but there is no such officer in SS records.

86 Next Krueger summoned August Petrich: Ibid., 25ff.

86 Krueger paused to consider the inherent contradiction: Ibid., 25–35. This description of Krueger's selection process is also in the same passage.

89 The prisoners' recollections of Krueger's selections: Nachtstern and Arntzen, *Falskmynter i blokk 19.* Translated privately, 32–33, 43–50. This prison memoir is based on the notes typed by Nachtstern's wife as he told her his story shortly after he returned home. A copy of this draft — the original is still in possession of his daughter Sidsel — was then turned over to Ragnar Arntzen, a Norwegian journalist who edited and polished it for publication. Written so soon after the event, Nachtstern's memoir is probably the most reliable and comprehensive of the prisoners' memoirs. It is quoted here and elsewhere in this book by permission of Nachtstern's son, Jan Howard Nachtstern.

89 part of the Hollerith classification system: See Edwin Black, *IBM and the Holocaust: The Strategic Alliance between Nazi Germany and America's Most Powerful Corporation* (New York: Crown, 2001). These Hollerith numbers were also the basis of the infamous tattoos on the arms of all Auschwitz inmates. Black presents new evidence of the link between IBM and Auschwitz in the German paperback edition of his book. The evidence has also been posted on the Internet at the History News Network and, Black promised, would be included in future English-language editions of his book.

90 Around the same time: Krakowski, 105.

91 Adolf Burger, a Slovak: Ibid., 112–13.

91 Max Groen and his boyhood friend: Author interview, Amsterdam, October 12, 2002; Kors, *De tocht opnieuw* (The Return Journey), portions translated for the author by Toby Molenaar; additional material was supplied by Anne Makkinje, Groen's former wife, who also accompanied the author to the interview. Groen, always the dandy, recalled that when he received his tattoo at Auschwitz, he tried to suck it out of his skin but succeeded only in blurring the final numeral 1.

92 the classic prison "jungle tom-tom": Kors, 59

92 "We have beaten England in the military field": Nachtstern, 50.

93 Those of you who have long and involuntarily: Krueger fragments, 39–40, which includes Krueger's recollection of the speech and his prisoners' response.

CHAPTER 7: THE COUNTERFEITERS OF BLOCK 19

95 just over 140 prisoners: An approximation; see Appendix for a full accounting.

95 "even if they had been looking for sword-swallowers": Nachtstern, 52.

95 in a nearby forest at Friedenthal Castle: Krakowski, 129. Krakowski was sent there occasionally to pick up inks, dyes, and other materials.

96 Krueger's story was that the prisoners: Krueger, "I Was the World's Greatest Counterfeiter," part 1.

96 retouched the Friedenthal plates: Ibid.

96 "counting strips of paper": Nachtstern, 83 (quoting Cytrin).

96 first and most difficult production problem: Byatt, *Promises to Pay*, 153–54.

97 Krueger tested more than a hundred sample batches: Krueger fragments, 82–85. Also the source of his description below of the problems of paper manufacture.

97 The washbasins and toilets: Ibid., 25–35.

98 New arrivals were issued a towel: Groen notes via Anne Makkinje (Zora cigarettes); Krakowski, 112–13 (hot oatmeal); Nachtstern, 42–49; Burger, 119–21.

99 When a fire broke out: Krakowski, 142.

100 Visas, date markings, and rubber stamps: Abraham Jacobson, statement to Dutch authorities, June 6, 1945. Several versions, all in agreement, are gathered in PRO Home Office file 63938/67. Jacobson, a reserve captain in the Dutch army, was arrested as a regional commander of the resistance around Groningen, condemned to death, reprieved, then assigned to Operation Bernhard as chief of the phototype department because he had managed a printing plant in Haarlem. His professional account of conditions in the camp is one of the most reliable. PRO FO 1046/268: SS Forgeries of British Currency and Banknotes 1945.

100 Artur Springer, a fifty-five-year-old Czech businessman: Nachtstern, 74. From prison records it appears that his business either manufactured or processed paper.

100 paper production could be erratic: Sem and Mayer, 13.

101 "It was a nerve-wracking period": Nachtstern, 52.

101 believed their system to be virtually inscrutable: B/E C 12/103, Note Issue Files, 16 December 1922–29 December 1964. From a memorandum to the chief cashier from the Note Issue Office, 7 February 1938:

> The dating of Bank of England notes of £5 and upwards is controlled, not by the Printing Department, but by the Issue Office, who when ordering notes to be printed indicate the dates they are to bear. These dates are settled in accordance with a Dating Scale prepared in advance by the Issue Office. What the Printing Department do is to give every date a particular cypher, the letter of which is determined according to the denomination of the notes to be printed . . . As not more than 100,000 notes of any denomination are ever printed with the same date, it is obvious that, in the case of notes of £5 in particular, the dates must be constantly changed. The Cypher rota is so constructed that the same cypher is never repeated within a period of 40 years. Thus, as no chief cashier is likely to hold office for that period, the cypher of a note always provides a key to the date

and vice versa . . . The Bank Note Registers all show dates as well as numbers but not cyphers. These latter, however, can always be ascertained by reference to the Cypher Book kept in the Bank Note Office . . . A reason for the retention of both is that the fact of the cypher and date always corresponding is very little known outside the Bank and consequently is frequently a stumbling-block to forgers.

102 then copy the batch and serial numbers: Many authors have spilled much ink speculating on how Langer, a cryptographer by trade, and then the Reich codebreakers who provided numbers to Krueger cracked the British numbering system. Some go so far as to speculate that Krueger had information from inside the Bank. Even Byatt's officially blessed *Promises to Pay* concedes the "Dating Scale" (in Bank jargon) was sufficiently well known on the inside for a mole to have transmitted it to Berlin. But Byatt wanly concludes it was "far more likely" that this supposedly redoubtable stumbling block "was readily deducible by sampling notes still in circulation" (p. 150).

102 It was known as Frankfort black: Burke, 22.

102 the Reichsbank recognized this and asked: Byatt, 119.

103 The Britannia medallion itself always had three secret marks: Ibid., 234–37.

103 almost invisible dots they called "flyspecks": Nachtstern, 141; Krakowski, 136.

103 "Look at this, gentlemen": Nachtstern, 70.

104 about 650,000 notes a month: Report of Capt. Michel, NARA, RG 260, box 451, file 950.31.

104 Six flatbed presses, including four of the latest: Burke, 27–28; Sem and Mayer; Major George J. McNally, Currency Branch, U.S. Seventh Army, Report, 24 January 1946, p. 3 NARA, RG 226, entry 155, boxes 2–3 (hereafter cited as the McNally Report). George J. McNally (1903–1970) joined the U.S. Secret Service in 1935. He was assigned to the counterfeiting division for six years and then to the White House presidential protection detail. After joining the Army in 1942, he was assigned to the White House Signal Corps. In 1945 he was sent to Europe on special assignment to investigate Operation Bernhard with Scotland Yard. Under Presidents Truman and Eisenhower, McNally served as chief of the White House Communications Office and was in Dallas with President Kennedy on November 22, 1963, the day he was assassinated. Forrest V. Sorrels, one of McNally's associates in the Bernhard investigation, was riding in the motorcade's lead car when Kennedy was shot. In 1982, McNally wrote a book about his presidential travels but never mentioned a word about his role in unraveling the largest counterfeiting scheme in history. He had already told that story, although with some lacunae and inaccuracies, in an article coauthored with Frederic Sondern, "The Great Nazi Counterfeit Plot," *Reader's Digest,* July 1952.

104 The room was sectioned into areas: Krakowski, 123.

104 A double line of prisoners: Nachtstern, 83–87, 141; Krakowski, 135–37; Kors, 68.

105 stabbing her in the eye: Byatt, 149.

105 a nearsighted SS sergeant named Apfelbaum: SFA, E4323 (A) 1988 Appendix A1, Part IV "List of Personalities."

105 Glanzer began boasting that the counterfeits: Nachtstern, 140–41.

106 had learned all the peculiarities of the bills: Ibid.

106 counted and indexed the notes in a ledger: McNally Report, 8.

107 "good enough to fool anyone but an expert": Ibid., 6.

107 Felix Tragholz: Krakowski, 123.

107 "You are collectively responsible": Ibid., 124.

107 "We must pay our agents well": This revelation is dubious. It hardly seems plausible that Krueger would give away the essence of the plot, even to prisoners he expected would be executed. The text appears in an English translation of the Czech edition of Burger's book provided to the author, but not in the edition published in Germany after the demise of the Communist secret services. This passage should appear on p. 121 of the German edition, but does not, and Krakowski did not mention espionage in his interview with the author.

107 only the first-class notes: Max Nejman, released prisoner, Brussels, July 9, 1945. McNally Report evidence, NARA, RG 260, box 451, file 950.31.

107–8 shipped directly to German commercial attachés: Max Bober, printer in Block 19, undated statement, McNally Report, and cited by McNally with diagram, 8–8a.

108 "for his personal use": Former prisoners Georg Kohn and Jack Plapler [Isaak Plapla], statement volunteered to U.S. investigators in Leipzig, 1945, PRO FO 1046/269.

108 Auschwitz was a plum: *Auschwitz: Inside the Nazi State* (PBS).

108 The elderly Artur Springer was caught: Nachtstern, 87.

109 Sven Hoffgaard, a *Mischling* Danish bank teller: Ibid., 107.

109 A wrinkled little man named Hermann Gütig: Statement of Schnapper supplementing previous, 5/9/45, NARA, RG 260, box 451, file 950.31; also Nachtstern and others.

109 a young teacher from Poland named Izaak Sukenik: Burger, *Des Teufels Werkstatt* (2001 edition), 181; Krakowski, 163.

110 In the end, Marock and Weber proved more dispensable: Nachtstern, 103–5. This was also reported by Bloom and other sources.

111 performed small acts of sabotage: Max Bober statement, p. 1, included in McNally Report.

111 "We agreed, however, to sabotage the orders": Jacobson, Home Office file no. 653938, in PRO FO 1046/268.

111 During working hours, the prisoners' minds: Burger, 179.

111 "This is England": Nachtstern, 70.

111 The lugubrious Cytrin declared such stunts: Ibid., 68–69.

112 Max Groen, the Dutch newsreel cameraman: Author interview.

112 Krakowski, reproached for not extinguishing: Author interview; Krakowski, 138.

112 "we will need divine mercy": Krakowski, 131.

112 asked Springer one day whether he thought: Nachtstern, 94–95, 152.

CHAPTER 8: "THE MOST DANGEROUS EVER SEEN"

114 To inspect the bound ledgers: B/E BNO 3A56/1, 1871–1955.

115 The new fakes were designated Type BB: M5/533, Museum Book and Document Collection Secretary's Department. War History, Vol. 1: Internal Finance.

Unpublished (Microfilm), "Forged Notes: £5 and upwards," pp. 231ff. Also, Byatt, 146.

115 had sent one of their number rushing out to buy: In the more stately language of the unpublished war history, "A quartz lamp now purchased was of great assistance," 231.

115 According to the Bank's own war history: War History, 1, p. x.

115 the Bank's clerks wrote their litany: B/E Note Office 3A56/1, Memorandum Book, 249–50.

116 The chancellor of the exchequer, Kingsley Wood: *Times* of London, March 17, 1943, 8.

116 the minutes of its senior management committee are completely silent: B/E G 14/27, Committee of Treasury Files. Bank Notes: Production and Issue 10 January 1940–2 July 1969. Notes: Forgeries. Includes papers relating to Nazi Forgeries of BE [Bank of England] Notes. Alas, only *one* such paper, a memo from Peppiatt to the Governor dated June 26, 1945, is entered in the Committee's files as C/T/27/6/45, upon which a handwritten notation remarks: "Previous Minute 10/1/40." The Committee of Treasury is composed of the governor, his deputy, and senior department directors.

116 recorded meticulously by Oskar Stein in his secret diary: "Interview with Oskar Stein alias Skala [his Czech name], head bookkeeper, at his home in Tabor, Czechoslovakia, Sept. 16, 1945," McNally Report, 16a.

116 in today's money at least $6 billion: I am multiplying conservatively by a factor of only 10, basing my calculation on the long-term increase in the price of gold, roughly tenfold in recent years but rising (during the war years it was fixed at $35 an ounce). Of course, many asset values, from beachfront property to Harvard degrees to Old Master paintings, have increased far more than that, and so have many military costs. The economist Fred Hirsch called these items of intrinsically limited supply "positional goods." The rise in their prices is offset by the decline in inflation-adjusted prices of many manufactured goods in everyday use. And some mass consumer goods of great utility, such as tape recorders or personal computers, would have been priceless then or simply unavailable.

116 enough to build a small flotilla of submarines: In the command economy of Nazi Germany, with the exchange rate of the reichsmark fixed artificially high, there is no way to estimate the real price of anything, especially when production inputs included slave labor and raw materials that had been stolen or even paid for in counterfeit pounds. Not even the economists of the postwar U.S. Strategic Bombing Survey (*German Submarine Industry Report,* Washington, D.C., Munitions Division, 1947) published cost estimates of what had been destroyed. So to give a sense of the enormity of only the top-grade Bernhard counterfeits in tradable currencies, I have used the wartime estimates of the U.S. Navy's Bureau of Ships, or about $3 million per submarine. At $40 million on the open market, if there were such a thing for submarines in wartime, that would mean about a dozen U-boats. Michael Thomas Poirier, Commander, United States Navy: Chief of Naval Operations: Submarine Warfare Division, *Results of the German and American Submarine Campaigns of World War II,* October 20, 1999, footnote 124, citing the $3 million estimate of the Navy's Bureau of Ships. *Ships Data: U.S. Naval Vessels* (Washington, D.C.: Government Printing Office, 1945), vol. 1, 88.

117 Stein's summary of the total: Figures in McNally Report, 8, 16a.

117 a Yugoslav officer named Dusko Popov arrived: PRO KV 2/854, Records of the Security Services, Personal Files, World War II, Double Agent Operations, August 26–October 7, 1943.

Popov had already played a role as a double agent in the United States, although the failure of that mission was not his fault. Dispatched by the Germans in August 1941, Popov informed his British masters, who told him he had to obtain J. Edgar Hoover's permission to erect a bogus espionage front on U.S. soil. Popov attempted to demonstrate his bona fides by telling the FBI chief that Hitler's Japanese allies had shown intense interest in the destruction of a sizable part of the Italian fleet in Taranto harbor. British carrier-based torpedo bombers had made the attack the previous November, and Popov told Hoover that his German spymasters had ordered him to travel to Pearl Harbor with "the highest priority" and report in detail on the naval installations in Hawaii. Hoover, whose own agents had scouted out Popov as a womanizer and a spendthrift, dismissed him as an untrustworthy foreign playboy trying to gather American secrets to sell to the Germans. "I can catch spies without your or anyone else's help," said Hoover. He never passed on Popov's tip, which was delivered six months before the Japanese attack on Pearl Harbor brought the U.S. into the war. See Persico, *Roosevelt's Secret War,* 138–41.

118 Enter Friedrich Paul Schwend, man of many aliases: Breitman et al., *U.S. Intelligence and the Nazis,* 123–25; Robert Wolfe, "Analysis of CIA Personality File of Friedrich Schwend," prepared as background for *U.S. Intelligence,* of which he was a coauthor. Wolfe was for thirty-four years the chief of Foreign Records Seized (RG 242) at the U.S. National Archives, who has kindly shared his analysis with me; RG 226, entry 190C, Dulles Files, and a secret record of Memo from "399" [Gerhard P. Van Arkel, general counsel of the National Labor Relations Board, 1946–47] to "100" (Allen W. Dulles), April 17, 1945, re: Conversation with Georg Gyssling [code numbers defined at http://archives.gov/iwg/declassified_records/rg_226_oss/rg_226_contents.html_]; also Michael Horbach and Wolfgang Löhde, "Geld Wie Heu," *Der Stern,* August–October 1959; Schwend CIA Name File released by the Nazi War Crimes and Japanese Imperial Records: NARA, RG 226, Interagency Working Group (IWG), CIA; description of Schwend by Georg Spitz and details from Bertha von Ehrenstein (customs violators, 3). NARA, RG 226, Georg Spitz CIA Name File. Interrogation of Bertha von Ehrenstein. Schwend's Nazi Party number was 874-181; PRO KV 2/412. Records of the Security Service, Personal Files, World War II, German Intelligence Officers, August 1, 1944–August 1, 1945, Hoettl's interrogation by the British, p. 13.

119 lived a comfortable life at the Villa de Nevoso: Schwend to Julius Mader, August 18, 1966, NARA, RG 226, Schwend CIA Name File (Part II). Mader had published *Der Banditenschatz* the year before but may have still been looking for material, presumably on behalf of East German intelligence. Schwend's letter to Mader was intercepted, opened, photographed, and translated by the U.S. Army Operations and Research Department in Frankfurt, according to a December 21, 1966, cover letter from J. Edgar Hoover, director of the FBI, to the CIA's Deputy Director, Plans. The copy in Schwend's declassified IWG file (Part II) is marked WARNING NOTICE: SENSITIVE SOURCES AND METHODS INVOLVED. The FBI forwarded a photocopy of the envelope, which was addressed to Mader on Französiche

Strasse, Berlin W.8 — the heart of the government district in East Berlin. In 2003 the author asked Markus Wolf, whose memoirs he had edited, whether Wolf knew of Mader. With characteristic indirection Wolf replied, "It is a long time since I have heard that name." He then quickly changed the subject.

120 minister in the Croatian capital of Zagreb, bitterly complained: NARA, RG 242, Microfilm Publication T-120, A Catalog of Files and Microfilms of the German Foreign Office, Germany Department, Section DII, Internal DII, Secret, 23/4 Record; top secret excerpts concerning the matter of Schwend, Fritz, Blaschke, and Hedda Neuhold, from DII 136 top secret to DII 285 top secret 1943.

121 buying spurious plans for a new U-boat: NARA, RG 242, German Foreign Ministry Archives, May 27, 1942.

121 "And yet his conversational style was not brilliant": Hoettl, 44.

122 were examined and declared "clever forgeries": Sam[uel Edison] Woods, American Consul, Zurich, telegram no. 268, to Secretary of State Cordell Hull, December 3, 1942, NARA, RG 59, Central Files 1940–44, box 4969, 841.5158/38/.

122 Washington was less interested in counterfeit: NARA, RG 84, American Legation, Bern, Confidential File 1940–49, box 13 (1943), 851.51.

122 Swiss Bankers Association immediately sent: Counterfeit Circular No. 961, December 3, 1942.

122 ultraviolet light and rely: Byatt, 151.

123 Schwend and Blaschke were probably German agents: Sam Woods, American consul, Zurich, telegram to Cordell Hull, January 15, 1943, in reply to State telegram no. 1, January 2, 1943, NARA, RG 59, 1940–44, box 4969, 841.5158/41.

123 dumping thousands of bodies into ravines: "Italy opens sad pages of history," *International Herald Tribune,* February 12, 2005, 3.

124 Schwend and Willi Groebl were caught: Hoettl, 104–7. For corroboration, see unsigned SS telegram, Berlin to Rome, September 19, 1943: "Ref. GROEBL'S death. WILLI was murdered by partisans 16/9 between TRIESTE and ABBAZIA. SCHWEND seriously injured," NARA, RG 226, entry 122, box 2 (Decoded SS Message Traffic, August to October 1943). These tattered flimsies are typed decrypts of GP [German Police] Code No. 3, and are in PRO HW 16/27: German-language decrypts, Government Code and Cypher School: German Police Section. This and other messages cited here originated in the Government Code and Cypher School and Government Communications Headquarters at Bletchley Park, England. Intelligence derived from them was coded Top-Secret Ultra. That the British had broken the German Enigma code was the most decisive espionage coup and the best-kept secret of the European war. It was not revealed until 1976.

124 Between November 1942 and June 1943, more than 3,000: Walter H. Sholes, American consul general, Basel, memorandum to Leland Harrison, American legation, Bern, re "£5 and £10 Pound Notes Counterfeited," June 7, 1943, NARA, RG 84, American legation, Bern.

125 It wrote the Swiss, giving more: Byatt, 152.

125 Peppiatt wrote Zurich that the Bank of England's officers: Text of letters in Byatt, 151–54.

125 a personal emissary, a Monsieur Gautier: B/E C 5/136, Note Issue Files, 18 September 1942–5 December 1950. "Bank Note Forgeries ("BB" Type). H.G.A. [H. G. Askwith], 23 February 1944.

126 "we made a New Year's resolution": Askwith to Chamberlain, 29 February 1944, B/E, Note Issue Files.

126 they were stuck with about 1 million: Swiss Public Prosecutor to Dr. Motta, director of the Swiss National Bank, enclosing report "on the counterfeiting of foreign bank notes and passports by the German Reichssicherheitshauptamt," October 24, 1945, Swiss Federal Archives, E4323 (A) 1988 Band 73 F11.1.

126 simply stopped accepting any British pounds: Sam Woods, American legation, Lisbon, telegram no. 1601 to Secretary of the Treasury re DEPTEL 1448, May 25, 1944, NARA, RG 56, International Statistics Division/Country Files: Germany 1931–1952. (Germany: Currency Counterfeit & Captured.)

126 The International Criminal Police Commission, under Nazi management: Sem and Mayer, 4.

127 even the slightest infractions of discipline: Nachtstern, 138.

CHAPTER 9: BETTER THAN WALL STREET

128 Schwend had been placed in command: Message, Berlin to Rome, October 21, 1943, reads: "The pounds question cannot be dealt with at this end as CDS [Chef der Sicherheitspolizei, i.e., Kaltenbrunner] has confided central control to WENDIG [Schwend]. If possible get in touch with the latter in TRIESTE HOTEL DELLE CITTA. HOET. [Hoettl]," NARA, RG 226, entry 122, box 2 (Decoded SS Message Traffic, August to October 1943).

128 Whenever Schwend needed more, he would cable: Allied interrogators got the figures and code words from Lieutenant Rudolf Guenther, private secretary and bookkeeper to Lieutenant Colonel Josef Spacil, who became chief of the administrative section (Amt II) of the RSHA in the summer of 1944. Six million Bernhard pounds was Guenther's figure. He was in a position to know, and far enough down in the hierarchy not to be seriously implicated and therefore relatively trustworthy. But even he admitted he did not know the total for sure, and his accounts were almost certainly wanting. For example, Hoettl's Munich account already showed 750,000 Bernhard pounds unaccounted for when Guenther arrived. CI [Counterintelligence] Intermediate Interrogation Report No. 47, February 6, 1945, NARA, RG 65, Class 65, entry A1-136P, box 185, case file 65-56600.

129 a mere 1 million lire, or £2,000: Telegram no. 7165, Berlin to Rome. NARA, RG 226, entry 122, box 2 (Decoded SS Message Traffic, August to October 1943). The sale apparently was negotiated by a priest known as Pater Michael, who was investigating "the possibility of inducing the tenants of the house to move as quickly as possible." This forced sale appears to have been confused by some authors with the seizure of Schloss Labers. The castle was owned by the Stapf-Neubert family, descended from a Danish textile magnate who bought it in 1885. The family reclaimed the castle after the war and turned it into a hotel. The present owner and proprietor, Georg Stapf-Neubert, assured the author in a fax message on March 16, 2006, that "the sale never came through." See Ralph Blumenthal, "The Secret of Schloss Labers," *New York Times*, June 22, 1986.

129 Schwend's money-laundering network of about fifty agents: NARA, RG 226, Georg Spitz name file, SCI 6th Army Group, Spitz interrogation, May 16, 1945.

129 Schwend stationed his five principal agents: James Jesus Angleton, CIA Deputy Director, Plans, memorandum to Chief, U.S. Secret Service, citing information received from the CIA representative in Peru on October 11, 1963, NARA, RG 226, Fritz Venceslav Schwend CIA Name File, Part 2.

129 "did not rely on ancestry": Hoettl, 60.

130 One Jewish agent was Georg Spitz: PRO MEPO 3/1182, Office of the Commissioner, Correspondence and Papers — Special Series: International Crime, Sergeant's Special Report, SB 15019/25, 6 February 1926, to the Chief Inspector, Metropolitan Police, English translation of memo from Police Headquarters, Vienna [page 38 B], Feb. 2, 1926. MEPO CID Extradition Report. April 9, 1926. "To the Examining Magistrate at the County Court of Frankfurt am Main" and MEPO CID Extradition Report dated 9 April 1926 [p. 14a].

130 The other was Yaakov Levy, a successful jewelry and art expert: NARA, RG 226, London X-2, PTS-13, SCI Twelfth Army Group, "RSHA Financial Operation," 20 and 28 July 1945. See also Braham, "The Nazi Collaborator with a Jewish Heart"; Elam, *Hitlers Fälscher*. Braham, a professor at City University of New York, is an expert on wartime Hungary; Elam is an Israeli investigative journalist based in Switzerland.

131 Obersturmbannfuehrer Kurt Becher. A businessman's son: Höhne, 564–65.

132 had first become entangled with the SS: Spitz interrogation, May 16, 1945. NARA, RG 226, Spitz CIA Name File.

132 Alois Miedl, a German businessman: Nicholas, *Rape of Europa,* 102–10.

134 new currency was issued at 400 lire to the pound: Hoettl, *Hitler's Paper Weapon,* 98.

135 even the legendary American spy chief: William J. Donovan, Coordinator of Information, Memorandum for the President, February 19, 1942, NARA, FDR Library, President's Secretary's Files, Subject File, OSS Reports, 2-12 to 2-20-1942 (Box 148); RG 226, M1642, roll 22, frames 1075–1078.

135 "came from the retreating Italian Seventh Army": Letter from Schwend to Mader, August 18, 1966 (passages also quoted in paragraph that follows).

135 Italian generals turned over their equipment: Porch, *Path to Victory,* 470; Elena Aga Rossi, *A Nation Collapses: The Italian Surrender of 1943* (Cambridge: Cambridge University Press, 2000), 111–2. Garland and Smyth, *Sicily and the Surrender of Italy,* 535.

136 In his letter: Schwend to Mader, August 18, 1966.

136 Italian passports in the name of Wendig and others: Hoettl, *Hitler's Paper Weapon,* 55.

136 His closest associates included: Interrogation of Bertha von Ehrenstein, 25 May 1945, NARA, RG 226, Schwend CIA Name File.

136 Georg Gyssling, the former consul general in Los Angeles: Lt. Charles Michaelis QMC, memorandum to Commanding Officer, X-2 Germany, re "RHSA Financial Operations," 5 June 1945; Spitz interrogation, dated 16 May 1945, NARA, RG 226, Georg Spitz CIA Name File.

137 Glavan owned ships and moved goods: Secret Dispatch, 14 March 1960, from Chief, WHD, to Chief [redacted], CIA, re "Transmittal of Traces on Friedrich Schwend and Additional Information on Aloys GLAVAN," NARA, RG 226, Friedrich Schwend CIA Name File, Part 1.

137 inside their engines in asbestos-lined: Hoettl, *Hitler's Paper Weapon,* 97.

137 Reginald G. Auckland, a propaganda-leaflet specialist: Cited by Burke, 37. See Auckland, *Air-dropped Propaganda Currency.*

137 The most meticulously organized network: Report of Detective Sgt. J. Chadburn, Criminal Investigation Department, Metropolitan Police, New Scotland Yard, 18 February 1946, PRO FO 944/4, German Section, Finance Records, 1943–1956, Counterfeit and Foreign Currency, Germany and Austria 1945–7.

137 Johnny Jebsen, a Danish double agent: The origin of this information is clearly British intelligence, which handled Jebsen under his code name Artist. D. I. Wilson, memorandum on the Tricycle/Artist group, November 20, 1943, NARA, RG 226, entry 119, box 23, folder 177A.

CHAPTER 10: WHAT THE POUNDS REALLY BOUGHT

139 The pounds generally did not finance SS spies: Kahn, *Hitler's Spies,* 300. Kahn's source was not only German archives but his own interview with Georg Duesterberg, finance officer of the Abwehr, the military intelligence service eventually swallowed by Schellenberg.

140 Skorzeny's rescue of Mussolini: Lamb, *War in Italy,* 23–24. Richard Lamb was an Italian-speaking British officer who served with the royalist Italian army, and his account of the military situation at Gran Sasso can be regarded as a primary source. See also Keegan, *The Second World War,* 351; Porch, 470; Garland and Smyth, 536–39.

140 Far from having to pay partisans forged pounds: Hoettl, *Hitler's Paper Weapon,* 68, claimed, "It was forged bank-notes that found the vanished Duce: a fact unknown to this day." This remains uncorroborated by any other source, although it has been repeated by others eager to pass on the myth.

141 Bernhard pounds did play a role in financing Cicero: The story of Cicero is taken mainly from Wires, *The Cicero Spy Affair,* by far the most reliable and comprehensive account because, like me, Richard Wires was able to examine previously sealed archives and thus weigh conflicting and often self-serving accounts of the principals as well as apologists for embarrassed British officialdom. Wires's book is one of a series on intelligence history edited by David Kahn, whose own *Hitler's Spies,* 340–46, also served as a useful source.

144 a source in the German Foreign Ministry named Fritz Kolbe: See Bradsher, "A Time Act," part 2, p. 7.

144 Dulles told Roosevelt that the Germans had penetrated: Undated Secret memo, "Germans Secure British Reports," from OSS, Washington. "Shortly prior to the 4th of November, 1943, Ambassador von Papen came into possession of certain documents on which he clearly placed great value and which, seemingly, were secured from the British Embassy in Ankara by an important German agent. Among the cables was a list of questions which the British Ambassador took to Cairo for his own guidance in consulting with Eden." NARA, RG 226, entry 210, box 440, folder 1: Boston Series No. 5, copy no. 8 of 8.

145 never identified as Cicero during the course of the war: The official story was told in considerably less dramatic terms, perhaps deliberately to protect the reputations of those still alive. On April 1, 2005, the British National Archives

released additional records (KV 6/8), which document official efforts to piece together facts relating to "a serious wartime espionage case." The file bin includes a summary of the case, written in 1979 by a research assistant to the official history "British Intelligence in the Second World War."

146 buried his stock of counterfeit bills: Preliminary Statement of Agi Zelenay in connection with RSHA Financial Operations, 4 June 1945; Continuation of Statement, 26 June 1945. NARA, RG 226, Friedrich Schwend CIA Name File.

146 SS headquarters in Munich, which was much closer: Memorandum, 30 May 1945, re SCHWEND Alias WENDIG, based on "Interrogation of Josef Dauser," NARA, RG 226, Georg Spitz CIA Name File. Dauser was the SS intelligence chief in Munich.

146 Hoettl regularly crossed into Switzerland: Interrogation of Theodor Paeffgen of the SD (Security Service), December 1945, NARA, RG 269, box 630. Cited by Goñi, The Real Odessa, 64. Hoettl's explanation for the visits to Switzerland — that he was trying to negotiate peace terms with the Americans — is not confirmed by any memoir, although such negotiations were under way at a much higher level.

146 amounted to 13 percent of the £1 billion: In 1944, there were a total of £1,077,464,198 genuine pound notes in circulation. Bank of England Quarterly Bulletin, June 1967.

146 public had been warned by their newspapers: "Germans Mass-Forge British Bank Notes," London Daily Mail, January 18, 1944.

147 fledgling Budapest trader later known as George Soros: Kaufman, Soros, 49; details elaborated by e-mail exchange between Soros and the author via Soros's spokesman, Michael Vachon, March 14, 2005.

CHAPTER 11: THE DOLLAR DECEPTION

149 Radio Berlin announced: Nachtstern, 144.

149 for these 120-plus hostages then working in Operation Bernhard?: Although the prison roster was maintained with bureaucratic precision in this camp as in all camps, it was possible only to approximate how many men were enrolled at any given time — probably a few more than 120 in June 1944. Late in that year the last draft of about one dozen arrived from the Nazi roundup of Jews in Hungary, bringing the probable total on the final list to 143 prisoners (see Appendix).

150 To keep the wheels turning: Krakowski, 148–51.

150 And chief bookkeeper Oskar Stein spotted: Stein interview, McNally Report, 2.

150 The new scheme had begun quietly: Jacobson statement to Dutch police, June 9, 1945, p. 2, PRO FO 1046/268.

150 Some prisoners even suspected that Krueger: Krakowski, 171.

151 "I will have to go to the front": McNally Report, 6.

151 However tiny they were in physical fact: This description of the prisoners' first attempt to surmount the difficulties of counterfeiting dollars is based on McNally Report, 3, 5; Burger, Des Teufels Werkstatt (2001), 163–64; interview with Burger, who was the printer in the Dollar Kommando, by chief inspector Julius Sem

of the Prague police, September 15, 1945, NARA, RG 260, box 451, file 950.31; and Sem and Mayer, *Report on Forgery in Sachsenhausen,* 17–19.

152 more than two hundred trial press runs: Sem and Mayer. The precise number of experiments given there is 220.

152 a reserve army captain who had served: Jacobson statement, p. 1.

153 His chief photographer was . . . Norbert Levi: Krakowski, 160.

153 On August 25, 1944, a short, stateless, fifty-seven-year-old Russian: Smolianoff's personal prison record, NARA, RG 242, A-3355, Mauthausen, roll 7: *Häftlings-Personal-Karte.* Smolianoff gave his profession as *Kunstmaler* (artist) and his Mauthausen number was 138498. In addition to several memoirs by his fellow prisoners, Smolianoff's Mauthausen record definitively contradicts earlier authors who have incorrectly given Smolianoff a major role in counterfeiting pounds sterling.

153 Krueger had probably found him: In April 1938, a month after the annexation of Austria, the Nazis installed Otto Steinhaeusl, president of Vienna's police, as president of the International Criminal Police Commission (ICPC). When he died of tuberculosis in June 1940, Arthur Nebe, head of the RKPA (Reich Criminal Police, the Kripo), became the nominal president until Reinhard Heydrich proclaimed his own "election." The ICPC had been compiling dossiers on international counterfeiters since its creation in 1923. They were sent to the RKPA office in Berlin. In August 1945, the U.S. Army discovered the ICPC dossiers containing records of 18,000 international criminals at the Wannsee house in suburban Berlin that had served as the commission's headquarters. According to Paul Spielhagen, the archivist who had overseen the records for fifteen years, the files had been carted off in 1939 to the four-story mansion that was used as a guesthouse for foreign police visitors and, more recently, to imprison two generals who had been part of the July 20 plot against Hitler's life. After a review of the files, the FBI decided they had no interest in keeping them. FBI Interpol files at www.fbi.gov. Special Agent Frederick Ayer, Jr., Frankfurt, memorandum to J. Edgar Hoover, Director, FBI, re "Records of International Police Commission," August 10, 1945, quoting article by John M. Mecklin, in the New York newspaper *PM,* "World Police Files Found/18,000 Small Criminals in Berlin Lists," dated August 2, 1945. See also Deflem "The Logic of Nazification."

153 "Good afternoon, you tonsorial beauties." Nachtstern, 142–44; Krakowski, 158–59. Krakowski writes that the initiation was administered not by Bober, but by the barracks chief Felix Tragholz, and that he covered Smolianoff with soot from the stove. In this case, as in most, it is preferable to rely on memory recorded closer to the event, which is Nachtstern's by at least forty years.

154 And in this fashion, in September 1944: This date can be deduced from Smolianoff's admission date plus his period in quarantine. It is further confirmed by Krakowski, who writes that Smolianoff appeared "several days" after they had celebrated the Jewish New Year (p. 158), which in 1944 fell on September 18. For these prisoners held in total isolation, fixing such dates became increasingly difficult during the final days of World War II. They often ignore or do not agree precisely on dates, and Burger even disagrees with himself in different editions of his own book. However, Krakowski, a deeply observant Jew as well as an accountant, followed the Jewish calendar assiduously in order to celebrate the holidays on time. These now

can easily be converted to secular days of the month with the help of Spier, *The Comparative Hebrew Calendar.* In the chaotic early days of 1945, Krakowski's citations of the Jewish holiday calendar probably provide the most reliable check.

154 Smolianoff was born on March 26, 1887: *Häftlings-Personal-Karte.*

154–55 Young Miassojedoff had been awarded Russia's Prix de Rome: Hermann, *Ivan Miassojedoff/Eugen Zotow,* 18–19.

155 The tolerant capital of the Weimar Republic: Otto Friedrich, *Before the Deluge: A Portrait of Berlin in the 1920s* (New York: Harper Perennial, 1995), 82–92.

155 "like a god from high Olympus": Francis M. Kayser, Scarsdale, N.Y., to Murray Teigh Bloom, May 10, 1959. Kayser, a young judge serving on the Berlin criminal court in 1924, was driven from Germany by the Nazis, settled in the United States, and wrote Bloom after reading about Zotow's trial in Bloom's *Money of Their Own.*

155 Two years later, with police already alerted: J. W. Kallenborn, "An International Counterfeiting Champion," *International Criminal Police Review* (journal of Interpol), August–September 1957, 209–18. Kallenborn, chief of the Interpol counterfeit office in The Hague, presaged his own story in an illustrated "Visit to the Interpol Counterfeits and Forgeries Museum," published in the same journal in 1950, identifying the counterfeiter only by the letter *S* and his Berlin confederate only by the letter *M.* In addition, the real names of both are not given in Kallenborn's journal article. The reason for this, according to Interpol's spokesman at its present headquarters in Lyon in a conversation with me in 2004, is that Interpol never releases the names of suspects, even after they have been arrested and convicted, without the formal permission of the government that has supplied them to the international police organization. This is logical in cases where a suspect is not aware he is the object of an international police dragnet, but it makes no sense in this one, when all involved are dead. However, Interpol rarely maintains historical files, even on such notorious cases as this one, not only to my amazement but to that of incoming Interpol officials trying to penetrate its labyrinthine bureaucracy, now largely French in nationality, style, and obstructionist culture.

156 Smolianoff was sentenced to two and a half years: "Forged Bank Notes/Berlin Discoveries/Russian Emigres on Trial," *Times* of London, October 25, 1932, datelined Berlin, October 24.

156 for passing ten-pound notes, and sentenced to four years: Burger, 161.

157 Yet he was saved by Germany's: "Without control of the criminal courts the RSHA and the Gestapo were nothing like as omnipotent as is generally supposed. The best refuge from the Gestapo was to be in the custody of the court. It is true that the Gestapo might keep a man out of the court's reach, and it could pounce on him if the court freed him, but such is German protocol that, once a man possessed a judicial record, it was no longer possible for the Gestapo merely to spirit him away. His legal existence continued even in a concentration camp. And if he happened to be a Jew, he was not whisked into the gas chamber . . . His court record traveled with him; he was given a registration number in the camp files and, protected by his criminal record, he had a chance of survival. This Erwhonian justice prevailed until the end of the war, a monument to the incompleteness of the Gestapo system." Reitlinger, *The SS,* 212.

157 the Mauthausen commandant's recommendation as a fine artist: "Report

about 'F.6.4' secret Counterfeiting Camp in Sachsenhausen from Sali Smolianoff," PRO MEPO 3/2766: Trafficking of forged Bank of England notes by the Nazis, 1946–1948 (Document 17E). This is a seven-page, single-spaced typewritten report of Smolianoff's postwar interrogation at a refugee camp in Rome by U.S. Secret Service agent A. E. Whitaker. He regarded Smolianoff's account as reliable and forwarded a copy to Scotland Yard, which only recently declassified it. According to a 1985 statement written by Whitaker and provided to the author by Murray Teigh Bloom, the Secret Service agent had written "a lot of reports. They are probably microfilmed in the archives somewhere." But according to the Secret Service's helpful archivist Michael Sampson, the agency had apparently already purged the main file on Operation Bernhard (CO-12,600) in February 1980.

157 the Vaduz residence of one Malvina Vernici: Smolianoff's personal prison record.

157 the stiff-necked chief of the SS guard: Smolianoff interrogation, 2–3.

158 "Well, here you are" et seq: Ibid.

159 Krueger conducting Ernst Kaltenbrunner on a lightning tour of Block 19: Krakowski, 171; Krakowski interview; Nachtstern, 166.

159 For weeks they quarreled about the color balance: Smolianoff interrogation, 4.

160 the operation could not proceed without "heavy water": Krakowski, 168.

160 a normally insouciant young artist named Peter Edel: Edel, *Wenn es ans Leben geht,* 145–55. Also quoted and attributed by Burger.

160 Leo Haas, an anti-Nazi cartoonist from Prague: Mader, 77.

163 had been staging musical evenings: Nachtstern, 146–51; Kors, 85–89; Groen interview; Burger, 185–90.

166 "Well, then, *when,* Cherr Chacobson?": Edel, 145; Nachtstern, 165.

166 Smolianoff meanwhile was heard boasting: Nachtstern, 156, 169.

166 brought the stragglers to their senses: Exactly who belled these headstrong cats is unclear. Smolianoff told the whole story to Whitaker, the U.S. Secret Service agent, in his interrogation, p. 5. He said the message was brought by "the eldest" of the prisoners but did not name him, and the list of prisoners does not make clear who that was. The oldest on record is one Georg Jilovsky, a Prague painter born in 1884, whose Sachsenhausen number is not recorded and was not prominent enough to figure in any other account. More likely it was Artur Levin, the chief printer from Berlin, who at fifty-six was only a few years younger. Smolianoff was also approached by Kurt Levinsky, a thirty-six-year-old Viennese, who in chatting with him around the chessboard warned that the dollar bill "had better be finished quickly" (Nachtstern, 169). Whoever it was, as Smolianoff confirmed to Whitaker, the Dollar Group changed course immediately.

166 with their fake demonstration bill mixed in: Burger (p. 170) writes that two dozen forgeries were printed from which the best were selected, and then another two hundred by the night shift. Smolianoff speaks of only one bill, but even if Burger is correct about the work in his print shop, they had nevertheless completed just one side of the bill before Krueger arrived, an important detail Burger omits.

166 "We were delighted, he was ecstatic": Bloom, 259.

167 to counterfeit $1 million worth of bills a day: Burger, 170.

168 "He laughed maliciously": Nachtstern, 170.

CHAPTER 12: TOWARD THE CAVES OF DEATH

169 stiffened as they heard Krueger's Mercedes staff car: Nachtstern, 171–73; Krakowski, 172; Smolianoff interrogation by Whitaker, 5; Jacobson statement, 2. Burger (p. 214) gives a more unsettling version in which the order is issued not in February but on March 13, rescinded as the prisoners start packing up, and then reissued a day later. Burger also makes no mention here of Krueger, although the other memoirists do. Perhaps he was standing by the version he gave the Czech Interior Ministry's investigators late in 1945, or perhaps the Communist Party functionaries who ran Czechoslovakia for more than forty years were forcing on him their habit of rewriting history. While this kind of revisionism usually appears convoluted and opaque to outsiders, it appears that in this case their motives — like Julius Mader's in East Berlin — were to mention Krueger's undisturbed existence in West Germany as support for the Communist argument that their enemies in Bonn still harbored unpunished Nazis. This they certainly did, but far bigger fish than Krueger.

169 The next morning they began the brutal job of packing up: Smolianoff interrogation, 5. Operation Bernhard material and men: Burger, 215; Krakowski, 173, who gives the final day of packing as the Jewish holiday of Purim, which in 1945 fell on February 27. Krakowski gives the total number of boxcars as fifty, with twenty prisoners to a car and intelligence material from Friedenthal filling most of the other freight cars. Nachtstern, 175, says there were fifty men to a cattle car.

170 In silent horror, the SS guards: Krakowski, 174.

170 the train rolled through Prague: Burger, 215–16; Nachtstern, 175.

171 the killing quarries of Mauthausen: Krakowski, 175–85; Smolianoff interrogation, 5–6; Nachtstern, 177–78; Max Groen, notes provided to the author by Anne Makkinje.

172 (footnote) *Musselmann* was camp slang: Herman Langbein, *Menschen in Auschwitz* (Vienna: Europaverlag, 1972), 114. Quoted by Robert Jay Lifton in *The Nazi Doctors* (New York: Basic Books, 1986), 132.

173 load everything into about sixteen freight cars: Harry Stolowicz, interviewed September 7, 1945, McNally Report.

173 In the basement of the camp brewery: Fritz Kretz, manager of the oxygen works, and Hermann Weidner, chief engineer, statements to U.S. and British investigators, July 13, 1945, 430th CIC Detachment, Appendixes B and C to McNally Report.

174 As at Sachsenhausen, the counterfeiters: Smolianoff interrogation, 6; Nachtstern, 179–82; Jacobson statement, 2. His estimate of £180 million burned and £10 million dumped in the water is likely exaggerated. Only Burger alone (p. 222) writes that the Spaniards were veterans of the International Brigade and that they kept up their morale by singing Spanish songs with guitar accompaniment. This seems unlikely, but during the Cold War there were political reasons for mythologizing this largely Communist unit, which had few if any Spanish troops.

174 nothing was ever printed at Redl-Zipf: Stolowicz, McNally Report; Jacobson statement. Georg Kohn and Jack Plapler to British interrogators, PRO FO 1046/269. Kohn and Plaper are also the source for the statement that banknotes were burned around the clock — in their words, "day and night."

174 two Nazi civilians from Berlin buried crates: Fritz Schnapper, Operation Bernhard printer, interviewed September 5 and September 25, 1945; Richard Luka, interviewed October 8, 1945, McNally Report.

175 Krueger as saying it would continue "in hiding": Krakowski, 189–90.

175 Putting his arm on the shoulder: Nachtstern, 132. In Smolianoff's version to Whitaker (p. 6), Krueger appears twice, first to give the order to break camp, then to order the prisoners to break open the boxes of third-class notes and burn them, while the first- and second-class notes were carried away on trucks. Smolianoff would be unlikely to stress to an American interrogator how closely they came to counterfeiting dollars. But in a memoir written when he was safely back home in Norway, Nachtstern would feel no such constraint.

175 both a Swiss driving license: Stolowicz, McNally Report. He said he knew Krueger had Swiss and Paraguayan passports. All documents probably had been forged in Krueger's own shops.

175 suspected mistress, Hilda Moeller: Smolianoff, who calls her Krueger's "girl-secretary" (p. 6), was one of the few to talk privately with Krueger on his last day with the prisoners. Bloom, 259, describes her as "an attractive 24-year-old blonde with an arresting, high-cheekboned face" who worked as an artist at RSHA headquarters in Berlin. But her name is not listed in the June 1943 internal telephone directory (*Fernsprecherzeichnis*) of the security police. Krueger is listed at Extension 220. NARA, RG 242, microfilm T-175, roll 232.

175 had warned his lieutenants (or so he said): Krueger, "I Was the World's Greatest Counterfeiter," part 2.

176 the general direction of the SS flight from Redl-Zipf: Nachtstern, 182–83; Burger, 226; Groen interview; Krakowski, 192; Smolianoff interrogation, 6. Once again, it is uncertain whether there was only one truck to make several trips, or two trucks in relay. Smolianoff remembers three. Among these understandably panicky recollections, Nachtstern's seem more reliable because they were recorded close to the event and not under police interrogation.

176 a dumping ground for about 15,000: Goetz, *I Never Saw My Face*.

176 and the most advanced German rocket: NARA, RG 72, entry 116: Reports of NTE/Europe, 1945–1946, box 12: serial 1470, U. S. Naval Technical Mission in Europe Technical Report No. 500-45, German Underwater Rockets (October 16, 1945). The report is based in part on interrogation of Dr. Determann, director of underwater research at the Toplitzsee Naval Research Laboratory, who became a primary source of information for investigators into what happened at the Toplitzsee in the last days of the Third Reich.

176 four heavy Lancia and Mercedes trucks: Statement by Hans Kraft, truck driver, and statement by Engineer [Viktor] Doubrava, July 13, 1945, to detectives Minter and Chadburn, Appendix D, McNally Report. A copy of the latter was given to the U.S. 430th CIC Detachment, also working on the case. Doubrava was a district partisan leader who showed the investigation team to a number of the local sites for abandoned or buried Bernhard material. Other versions, none contradictory but necessarily slightly different given the confusion of those final days, can be found in a number of the memoirs and interrogations already cited. Smolianoff, for example, counted "approximately 10–15 trucks with trailer." Sem and Mayer's account, which was based partly on Burger's testimony, says some crates contained Operation Bern-

hard's account books and "secret archives" of the Sicherheitsdienst (Security Service), the alleged existence of which was to become a postwar bone of contention (p. 21). In his book (p. 225), Burger says the papers were driven away during the night of April 28 aboard two military vehicles carrying about forty crates. Out of all this slightly variant material, I have tried to piece together as coherent and factual a story as possible.

177 used them as toilet paper: Bloom, 263.

177 a fifty-pound note in the lining of his shoe: Jacobson statement, 3.

179 flying at half-staff, marking Hitler's suicide: Krakowski, 192. Hamburg Radio announced Hitler's death after 10 p.m. on May 1, Hitler having committed suicide in his Berlin bunker at 3:30 p.m. on April 30. Shirer, *Berlin Diary,* 1350.

180 its engine had finally broken down: Burger, 230; Nachtstern, 182; Krakowski, 205; Kors, 24–28; Groen interview. Groen's account of the march was based on what he was told by his friend Dries Bosboom.

183 Some of Ebensee's slave laborers had already heard: Krakowski, 195–96; Nachtstern, 185, 188; Kors, 26–27; Groen interview; Sem and Mayer, 22; Jacobson statement, 3; Goetz, 71; Tenenbaum, *Legacy and Redemption,* 157ff.

184 "Had we arrived about ten hours earlier": Jacobson statement, 3. This account of their last-minute reprieve is fully confirmed from inside the camp in a statement written by Burger in German, translated by Sergeant Chadburn of the London Metropolitan Police, and dated 8 June 1945, PRO MEPO 3/2400.

184 Sturmbannfuehrer Franz Ziereis, had ordered his subordinate: Krakowski, 211. Probably drawn from the text of Zieireis's deathbed confession. See *Nuremberg Trial Proceedings,* vol. 11, p. 330, Testimony of Dr. Ernst Kaltenbrunner on Document Number 3870-PS, USA-797, quoting "Confession of Frank [*sic*] Ziereis," p. 2. http://www.yale.edu/lawweb/avalon/imt/proc/04-12-46.htm: "According to an order by Reichsfuehrer Himmler, I [Ziereis] was to liquidate all prisoners on the instructions of SS Obergruppenfuehrer Dr. Kaltenbrunner; the prisoners were to be led into the tunnels of the Bergkristall works of Gusen and only one entrance was to be left open. Then I was to blow up this entrance to the tunnels with some explosive and thus cause the death of the prisoners. I refused to carry out this order." The confession is controversial, and when it was entered in evidence at the Nuremberg trials, all concerned tried to distance themselves from it. Nevertheless, the prisoners uniformly recall that the SS tried to lure them into the tunnels.

184 "Not while I'm here": Kors, 24.

184 standing on a table to be heard: Samuel Goetz, e-mail to the author, April 2, 2003. Goetz was an inmate of Ebensee.

185 clanked up the highway and into the camp: Notes from Anne Makkinje and Groen interview. Krakowski, 206, says the troops were from the 11th Armored Division, whose historians do not confirm his designation. The U.S. Holocaust Museum and U.S. Office of Military History give units of the 80th Infantry Division credit for liberating Ebensee, although clearly it was the inmates who liberated themselves before the troops arrived to guarantee their survival. Krakowski recalled years later that the troops were "visibly shaken," but this seems unlikely since elements of the division had already seen far worse at Buchenwald and elsewhere. Ebensee appears to have been the last camp reached by Allied troops.

EPILOGUE

187 A file of paper two inches thick recording complaints: *Abus de confiance, J. van Harten,* Band G 61, Archives de la Comité internationale de la Croix-Rouge, Geneva (hereafter cited as *Abus*).

187 Van Harten appointed himself: "Red Cross [Does] Not Recognize Italian representative," published in *Il Tempo,* June 6, 1945, copy attached to letter dated June 16, 1945, signed by Dr. H. W. de Solis, Delegation Chief, International Red Cross in Rome, in *Abus*.

187 not only to bona fide refugees: Vincent La Vista, "Illegal Immigration Movements in and through Italy," report to Herbert J. Cummings, assistant chief of the Department of State's Bureau of Foreign Activity Correlation, May 15, 1947, NARA, RG 59, Central Decimal File (1945–49), 800.0128/5-1547. This thirty-five-page document, originally classified Top Secret, was compiled by a lawyer serving as military attaché at the U.S. embassy in Rome, perhaps as cover for intelligence work. The report, which details Vatican and International Red Cross complicity in securing travel documents for fleeing Nazis, was made public in January 1984 after an expert on Nazi war criminals, Charles R. Allen, Jr., discovered it.

187 sought help from . . . the Swiss consul general, Alberto Crastan: La Vista Report, Appendix C, 4.

187 a warehouse with "thousands of things stolen": Ferris and Bickel.

188 the IRC formally denounced him before Allied headquarters: Telegram, (in French) signed F[rédéric] Siordet, 30 May 1945, and letter, dated May 30, 1945, signed Albert Lombard, vice president of the CICR (International Red Cross), May 30, 1945, *Abus*.

188 Van Harten boldly replied to Red Cross directors: "Action for a declaratory judgment," 8 June 1945, by "J. Lewis van Harten, Merano, Hotel Stefanie" (trans. Fiona Fleck), *Abus*.

188 counterfeit pound notes served a historic purpose: Ronen Bergman, two articles in the weekend magazine of the leading Israeli newspaper *Ha'aretz,* "Jacques Van Harten: Collaborator or Hero?" April 28, 2000, and "The Van Harten Affair: New Evidence," May 19, 2000. It is to the credit of the Schocken family that it has not objected to the publication of these balanced articles (with which the van Harten family at first refused to cooperate) by the distinguished newspaper in which it still holds a substantial interest.

188 a small group in the British Army's Jewish: Blum, *The Brigade,* 231ff.

189 transport unit, headed by Captain Alex Moskowitz: Elam, *Hitlers Fälscher,* 140–41. This part of Elam's account is heavily based on Bauer, *Ha'bricha,* 108; *Ha'aretz* weekend magazine, June 7, 1994; Professor Yehuda Bauer is a leading Holocaust historian, and his book was simultaneously published in the United States as *Flight and Rescue: Brichah,* 106–7. His footnotes (p. 335) make it clear that he followed the trail of the forged money in Europe through accounts of the principals themselves: Levi Argov, Moshe Ben David, and others, plus confidential informants in Israel.

190 They shipped out Viola van Harten first: Shalheveth Freier, interview by Nana Nusinow, July 17, 1966, Oral History 197.27, Haganah Archives, Tel Aviv, Bergman.

190 one of the members saw this world-class confidence man: Shmuel Osia, quoted by Bergman in "The Van Harten Affair."

191 the Mossad, or the Organization: The Hebrew word *mossad* comes from the verb meaning "to found." Hebrew not being as rich in synonyms as English, the derivative noun *mossad* can be variously translated as foundation, institute, or organization. I have chosen the last as the closest English equivalent.

191 No less than Goldie Myerson: Letter to Dr. M[ordecai] Eliash (later Israeli ambassador to London), 26 September 1947, S25/1247, Central Zionist Archives, Jerusalem.

192 This page of the Israeli record: Freier interview, quoted by Bergman.

192 Allied intelligence agents took him on "bird-dog" missions: Robert Wolfe, "Analysis of CIA Personality File of Friedrich Schwend"; Ruffner, "Shifting from Wartime to Peacetime Intelligence Operations." Kevin C. Ruffner is a CIA historian; this is the sanitized version of his article, from which all identifying sources and methods have been redacted. However, these redactions are readily identifiable through open sources at the National Archives in Washington.

192 buried 7,139 French and Italian gold coins: NARA, RG 226, Schwend Name File, Part 1, 20 and 28 July 1945 [LONDON X-2 PTS-13], also RG 226, E 210, box 42, folder 19377, Schwend.

192 Georg Spitz led his interrogators to stolen paintings: Wolfe; Ruffner.

192 named for its chief, the turncoat Nazi expert: In April 1956, the Gehlen Organization formed the nucleus of the BND (Bundesnachrichtendienst), the Federal Intelligence Service of the new Federal Republic of Germany. Reinhard Gehlen served as its chief until he retired in 1968.

193 Spitz bought up all copies of the first edition: CIA Chief of Base, Munich, Secret Dispatch to Chief, WLS, October 28, 1959, re: "American Interest in Banker Georg SPITZ, Mauerkircherstrasse 95/0, Munich," paragraph 1, NARA, RG 226, CIA Name File (Georg Spitz).

193 forwarded by his brother-in-law Hans Neuhold: CIA Name File, Friedrich Schwend, vol. 1, redacted CIA and Army Intelligence cables, January 27 and 30, 1948. The January 27 cable says the money was supplied by the Neuholds but actually sent by one Carl Flutterlieb of Geneva.

193 vicious Nazi escapees in Latin America: Linklater et al., *Fourth Reich,* 236ff. Schwend was also present at Barbie's hearing in Lima on currency-smuggling charges. *New York Times,* December 7, 1973.

193 The CIA shadowed Schwend for years: Schwend Interpol Circular (1963) No. 158/58/A3185.

193 attracted the notice of James Jesus Angleton: Marshall S. Carter, Acting Director [CIA], Action Memorandum No. 1-279, to Deputy Director (Plans) [Angleton], 1 August 1963, CIA Name File, Friedrich Schwend, Part 2.

193 jailed in 1976 for failing to pay: Arriving in Bonn on July 4, 1976, Schwend walked out on his hotel bill. After the Black Cat Hotel notified police, a routine check of records turned up his conviction in absentia thirty-two years earlier for killing Teofilio Kamber in 1944. *Times* of London, July 14, 1976, 5; *Washington Post,* July 14, 1976, A6, via Reuters.

194 Tried in Munich, Schwend received a suspended sentence: London *Daily Telegraph,* June 9, 1979, 3.

194 claiming poverty so he could receive legal aid: Linklater et al., 265.

194 walked out without paying his bill: Ralph Blumenthal, "The Secret of Schloss Labers," *New York Times,* June 22, 1986, quoting the current owner, Georg Stapf-Neubert.

194 He gave various versions of how he eluded: Krueger told Bloom (*American Weekly,* June 15, 1958) that his car was stolen, he obtained false papers from a German working as an interpreter for the Americans, and then he laid low for the summer for fear of execution, making his way home in September. In 1964 Krueger told John Fiehn of the Associated Press that he surrendered to the Americans on May 5, 1945, in Austria, remained in a POW camp for eight weeks, then drove off in his old staff car, a more unlikely story. *New York Times,* August 27, 1964.

194 British occupation authorities on November 25, 1946: Detention Report: B. Krüger, Records of the Judge Advocate General War Office, British Army of the Rhine [BAOR] War Crimes Group (North West Europe), PRO WO 309/1772. Arrested at Einbeck near Hannover, according to the French, Krueger was detained under "matriculation number" 208,449 at No. 2 Civilian Internment Camp of the BAOR British Zone, and then in 1948 at the Wittlich prison run by the French in Germany for war criminals. French Department of Defense, letter to author.

194 Krueger's card in the British file of wanted Nazis: 1942–48 Perpetrator & Witness card, PRO WO 354/26.

194 not even to George J. McNally or other U.S. Secret Service agents: As late as July 1952, McNally was writing in a *Reader's Digest* article, "The Great Nazi Counterfeit Plot," that Krueger "has never been heard of since, despite the efforts of half a dozen police forces to find him." (McNally also described Smolianoff as a "Gypsy.") There is no evidence that McNally thought he was writing anything but what he believed was the truth.

194 Captain S. C. Michel of French intelligence had accurately described: Report of Capt. S. [Serge] C. Michel, Military Mission, French Sécurité Militaire, Attached to U.S. Third Army. NARA, RG 260, box 451, Decimal File 950.31.

195 the French secret service offered him his old job: Krueger's French prison file (AJ 3627 p. 80 d. 3938) is lodged at the Archives de l'Occupation française en Allemagne et Autriche (Archives of the French Occupation of Germany and Austria) in Colmar, France, a city near the German border. The Krueger file is sealed for one hundred years, but at the author's request the French Foreign Ministry granted a dispensation (*dérogation*) on July 22, 2004, although permitted to see only a very small part of it: two pages concerning Krueger's release: Af. Ter. [*Affaire Terminé*] 3938, Krueger, Bernhard. This contains a printed form on which the Permanent Military Tribunal in Paris informed the French security services on November 17, 1948, that Krueger was being released. The form is filled in with Krueger's name, notes that an arrest warrant was issued for him on February 27, 1948, and adds that on November 17, charges of involuntary homicide and complicity in the deaths of four prisoners had been dismissed by one Captain Hardin, a military magistrate. The only other document in the part of the file opened to the author is a telegram to Paris from French occupation headquarters in Baden-Baden dated January 14, 1948, that "Krueger is accompanied by an arrest warrant." The telegram replies to a still secret letter dated January 8 and appears to be part of the legal justification for holding him. There is nothing in this tip-of-the-iceberg part of Krueger's file that confirms his statement

that he was asked to forge documents for the French — but there is nothing that contradicts it either. Krueger was held by two occupying powers in succession and released almost two years to the day after he turned himself in. That would provide ample time for the British to learn all they could about his wartime counterfeit operation, and for his French captors to bargain for the use of his services, their hand strengthened by the threat of a murder charge. Indications to the author about the secret section of the file are that it contains references to the 1948 currency reform that precipitated the formal division of Germany, a signal to the Allied occupation forces to clear out minor Nazis and prepare for the Cold War. By that time, the French were rebuilding their own secret services with homegrown talent and probably had lost interest in Krueger.

195 working as a storekeeper near Hannover: "'Pound-Note Factory' Director," *Times* of London, September 19, 1955, 7, a one-paragraph item at the bottom of the page datelined Berlin.

195 he made a fairly clean breast of his wartime counterfeiting: Signed statement by Krueger in Dassel, August 23, 1956, reprinted in Mader, 216; Burger (apparently a direct copy from Mader's book), 241. The text reads:

> In the function of technical consultant and director of a technical section in Office VI of the Foreign Intelligence Agency, I conducted, on orders from the Reichsfuehrer of the SS Heinrich Himmler, an operation for the counterfeiting of money with the code-name of Operation Bernhard, which served as an act of economic strategy against England.
>
> According to my orders, I was to carry out my mission with prisoners of Jewish heritage. For this reason, I first chose 39 prisoners from the concentration camp Sachsenhausen. I took more than 100 from other camps, mainly Auschwitz.
>
> I emphasize, that with only one exception, I employed no criminal elements, i.e., forgers or inmates of jails.
>
> It is true that all prisoners had been sent to the camps because of their race, and that they were classified as political prisoners. This is further proven by the fact that all these prisoners carried red identification marks on their prison garments, which showed the reason for their imprisonment.
>
> The prisoners had nothing to do with the production of the printing blocks. The printing plates were manufactured by members of the SS or by contractual employees in Friedenthal, approx. 2 to 3 kilometers from Sachsenhausen.
>
> B. Krüger

195 either testified or sent affidavits in his support: Bloom; Krakowski interview.

195 Shortly before Krueger's death in 1989: *Der Fluch des Toplitzsees,* German television documentary, 2003.

197 Cicero the Spy squandered everything: Wires, 180–82.

197 For five years, the British succeeded in hushing up: In April 2005, the British National Archives released additional material on the Cicero case: "Investigations

into leakage of information to the German Intelligence Service from British Embassy Ankara (Cicero case)," PRO KV 6/8; and "Safe keeping of documents at posts abroad 1944," FO, 850/128. See Christopher Baxter, "The Cicero Papers: Further releases concerning the security breach at HM Embassy, Ankara, in the Second World War, 1943–73," 2005, available via www.fco.gov.uk. Baxter is a historian at the Foreign & Commonwealth Office.

199 one real fiver for two fakes: Freier interview.

199 Private Allen Cramer of the U.S. Army was guarding a bridge: Unpublished memoir, Allen A. Cramer Collection, U.S. Holocaust Memorial Museum Archives (accessioned September 2005).

199 In Frankfurt, U.S. Secret Service agent George McNally was led: McNally, "The Great Nazi Counterfeit Plot"; McNally Report. Fakes with a face value of £1.5 million were found buried in a grave in Taxenbach, Austria, in October. NARA, RG 56, Department of the Treasury, International Statistical Division, Country Files: Germany 1921–1952, box 75, File: Germany: Currency — Counterfeit and Captured.

199 Reeves dryly reported that on Friday: P. [Patrick] J. Reeves, "Report on Bank of England Note Forgeries," 18 June 1945, classified Top Secret (hereafter cited as Reeves Report), PRO FO 1046/268 (#31A).

199 In McNally's somewhat more vivid description: McNally, "Great Nazi Counterfeit Plot," 26.

200 started asking the British uncomfortable questions: George McNally letter (Secret) to Lt. Col. Seligman of the Allied Control Commission for Germany (British Element), July 28, 1945, PRO FO 1046/268. McNally's questions summarized a longer list first raised by Frank Wilson, chief of the U.S. Secret Service, in a letter to McNally, June 18, 1945, NARA, RG 87, box 147.

200 Even bookies at the London dog tracks: Holland-Martin Correspondence, B/E ADM 24/5.

200 "I am sorry, as I do not want them to think us uncooperative": Lt. Col. Seligman to Brig. C. A. Gunston, re: Counterfeit Bank of England Notes, 8 September 1945, PRO FO 1046/268.

201 "Let sleeping dogs lie": Ibid. Gunston biographical background, Bank of England, *The Old Lady*, March 1985.

201 Even when the Allied Control Commission wanted to prosecute: Letter, 26 July 1946, expressing the hope that the Bank can "be prevailed upon to be retained for production at the Military Government Court where these individuals can be tried," PRO MEPO 3/2400.

201 Peppiatt wrote to Scotland Yard demanding: K. O. Peppiatt to Ronald Howe, deputy commissioner at New Scotland Yard, 25 March 1946, and Howe to Peppiatt, 27 March 1946; see also Metropolitan Police Report, "Forged Bank of England Notes," 23 April 1946, which details the investigation in France; all PRO MEPO 3/2766.

201 relieved to learn that the unfortunate Hans Adler: Ronald Howe, internal memo, "Production of Bank of England BB Notes 1945–64," 15 September 1945. This is Scotland Yard's file wrapping up its methodical investigation — more than two inches thick and declassified only in 2004. Its report summarizing the case, submitted 2 September 1949, contains only one glaring error: "The actual forger of the Bank of England notes was Solomon [*sic*] Smolianoff [citing his criminal record] . . . It is

known, however, that Smolianoff was released from prison in 1942 or 1943 and brought to the forgery camp, then in Sachsenhausen." PRO MEPO 3/2400.

202 "hypnotised by looking at their own beautiful notes": EWP (Edward W. Playfair), Minute Sheet [#52] to Ernest Rowe-Dutton, third secretary of the Treasury, PRO T 231/692.

202 "to meet the Bank of England's pride": Ibid.

202 a typically obscure British compromise: See "Repatriation (import and export) of sterling notes: Withdrawal of high denomination Bank of England notes 1945–47," in particular, memo from Bank of England [author's signature illegible] to C. G. Thorley of the Treasury, 22 November 1946, and undated Minute Sheet [#52], all PRO T 231/692.

202 Leo Strawczynski: Author interview in May 2005 with Strawczynski's son and daughter, now resident in Montevideo, Uruguay.

202 A regular trade developed in phony fivers: John Walker, British Embassy, Madrid, to K. S. Weston, Treasury, London, 27 November 1946. Traffic in Spain in forged Bank of England notes, PRO FO 371/60477.

203 From Stockholm, Harry Söderman: Letters and telegrams starting on 7 September 1946 and throughout the month to Scotland Yard, PRO MEPO 3/2400.

203 And a Hungarian refugee from Budapest: Letter, from the British consulate in Basel to the British legation in Bern, 26 October 1946. The file, "Alleged Circulation of Bank of England Notes in Switzerland, 1946," PRO FO 371/60518, also contains an article from *La Suisse* of that same date with a headline warning of false banknotes and concluding, "They are good imitations and are difficult for ordinary people [*au profane*] to distinguish from real ones."

203 inside the organ of the San Valentino church: "Cache Hidden in Organ Was WWII Nazi Counterfeit," Associated Press dispatch datelined Merano, Italy, in the Appleton (Wisconsin) *Post Crescent,* August 15, 1967.

203 Ricardo Coqueto, a carpenter, escaped execution: Quoted in "A Struggle With Memories of Torture Down the Street," *New York Times,* March 8, 2005.

203 "photographic copies and records": Memorandum [#11R], date-stamped 30 November 1949, B/E PW 17/5, Forgery.

204 His [Peppiatt's] obituary in the Bank's house organ: September 1983.

204 he continued believing that many of the Bank's own records: Sir Kit McMahon, former director of overseas finance and deputy governor of the Bank of England, e-mail message to the author, September 6, 2002.

204 Sir Eddie George, O'Brien's successor as governor: Sir Eddie George, communication directed to the author on December 10, 2001. George commented on a suggestion, made not entirely in jest, by a retired senior official of the British Treasury that the Bank had secreted the records of its most embarrassing counterfeit in some obscure warehouse that might remain inaccessible for many years. The governor denied this but was the first to use the word *conspiracy* in the correspondence, defensively.

204 the Foreign Office did have one and declassified it: Reeves Report.

204 John Keyworth, head of the Bank's museum: Quoted by Jonathan Glancey in the *Guardian* (London), September 24, 1998.

204 Yet the Bank's own promotional film: Viewed by the author (twice) in London, May 2001.

204 "found their way into circulation and were a constant headache": Fact Sheet: Bank Notes, http://www.bankofengland.co.uk/banknotes/factnote.pdf.

205 Smolianoff had filled his idle hours: Krakowski, 161.

205 so they arranged to meet at the Swiss border: Smolianoff, signed statement given to New Scotland Yard Criminal Investigation Department, September 11, 1947. Translation from German by Fiona Fleck. Swiss Federal Archives (SFA), E4323 (A) 1981, band 101 (Eugen Zotow); Bloom, *Money of Their Own*, 189–90.

205 The next year Miassojedoff/Zotow was convicted in Liechtenstein: Inspector Benz, report to Chief of Federal Police Service, Bern, September 17, 1948, SFA, ibid.; Interpol Notice 417/46.

205 Police Commission in Paris issued a wanted circular: Circular No. 1103, SFA, ibid.

206 weakened by Parkinson's disease, of which he died: Letter from S. Sondermann Espindola, Porto Alegre, Brazil, to Murray Teigh Bloom, March 31, 1986.

206 Oskar Stein, the meticulous bookkeeper: McNally Report.

206 Hirsche and Moshe Kosak, two brothers: Krakowski, 166.

206 Felix Cytrin, the chief engraver: NARA, RG 87, Index to General Correspondence. See entries for Counterfeiting Activities of Amt VI-F RSHA, Bernhard Krueger, and Salomon Smolianoff.

206 Norbert Levi adopted the name: Krueger, "I Was the World's Greatest Counterfeiter" (story signed by Krueger but source was Bloom).

206 a sworn deposition from Krueger: Reproduced in Burger, 241.

207 returned to work as a stereotyper: Nachtstern's daughter Sidsel, e-mails to the author, 2005.

207 publishing his memoirs in Czech and then in German: *Komando padelatel°u* (Prague, 1983); *Ďáblova dílna: V padělatelském komandu koncentračního tábora Sachsenhausen* (Prague, 1991), and *Unternehmen Bernhard: Die Fälscherwerkstatt im KZ Sachsenhausen* (Berlin, 1992). Burger republished the book under the title *Des Teufels Werkstatt* (Berlin, 2001).

207 knew him as "the rabbi": Krakowski interview.

207 Peter Edel became an author: *Wenn es ans Leben geht: Meine Geschichte* (1979).

207 "I knew the future. I'd be free": Groen interview.

207 his last wish was fulfilled: e-mail to the author, August 2, 2004, from Groen's former wife, Anne Makkinje.

207 complete with its own website: www.toplitzsee.at. It even has its own webcam, giving the day's temperature. The site also presents a short history titled "Treasures of the Toplitzsee," which beguilingly reports the discovery of many crates of gold, gold coins, diamonds, and, most intriguing of all, "3 crates of gold bullion from the Tatar Treasury." There is no such record, official or otherwise, of any of these discoveries (to say nothing of the Tatar Treasury, whatever that may have been).

207 the first catch was made innocently: Evelyn Irons, London *Evening Standard*, May 21, 1945, dispatch from Salzburg, Austria, B/E C 12/111: Note Issue Files (6 November 1862–25 November 1954), Press cuttings on forgeries, robberies, mutilated notes, etc.

207 U.S. Navy divers based in Cherbourg: McNally Report. They also tried the Traunsee and came up empty-handed. Photographs taken by McNally during the

dive were rushed by diplomatic pouch to the chief of the U.S. Secret Service, but were among the items apparently destroyed during the subsequent purge of Secret Service file CO 12,600.

207 In 1946, two former engineers: Hoettl, 158–59.

208 The most ambitious underwater expedition: See Löhde and Horbach, "Geld wie Heu" (Money Like Hay), *Der Stern*'s twelve-part report, published in 1959.

208 Their official report contains no hint: E. de M.R. [initials only], memorandum to Chief Cashier, Bank of England, with copies to Secretary, General Manager, Bank of England Printing Works, re: "Destruction of German Forgeries Salvaged from the Toplitzsee," December 1, 1959, B/E PW 17/5. They saved some for the Bank's museum, where a few are on display in a thick glass case, on which visitors are strictly enjoined from leaning too closely.

208 declared there was nothing more to be found: "Divers' Search of Austrian Lake Deflates Wild Tales of Nazi Gold," *New York Times,* December 8, 1963.

208 Again neither the Bank nor the Yard: Detective Sergeant A. E. Noble, report summarizing the report, dated 29 May 1964, of L. Cunnell of the Bank of England's Note Office, which said that 100,000 counterfeit notes had been destroyed, along with plated and numbering barrels. Noble added that "the forging equipment recovered from Lake Toplitzsee [*sic*] is now complete, these papers now can be 'put away.'" PRO MEPO 3/2400.

208 declared himself a Mossad operative: Hans Fricke, interview by *Geo* magazine (his sponsor), posted on Geo Explorer website as "Toplitzsee: The Myth That Will Eternally Live."

208 $600,000: Scott Pelley, "Hitler's Lake," transcript of segment on the CBS program *60 Minutes II,* originally broadcast November 21, 2000. http://www.cbsnews.com/stories/2000/11/21/60II/main251320.shtml.

209 beer caps: Luke Harding, "Last dive for Lake Toplitz's Nazi Gold," *Guardian* (London), April 6, 2005.

209 Norman Scott: Ibid.

BIBLIOGRAPHY

INTERVIEWS

Groen, Max. Interview by the author, October 12, 2002, Amsterdam.
Krakowski, Avraham. Interview by the author, November 10, 2002, Brooklyn, New York.
Landau, Paul. Telephone interview with Margaret Shannon, 2004, Tampa, Florida.
Soros, George. E-mail exchanges with the author, 2005.

UNPUBLISHED MANUSCRIPTS AND LETTERS

Krueger, Bernhard. Unpublished fragments, translated by Ingeborg Wolfe.
Nachtstern, Moritz. *Falskmynter i blokk 19*, unpublished English translation.

ARCHIVAL SOURCES

United States
NATIONAL ARCHIVES AND RECORDS ADMINISTRATION (NARA)
www.archives.gov

Records of the Department of the Treasury (RG 56)
Records of the Department of State (RG 59)
Records of the Federal Bureau of Investigation (RG 65)
Records of the Bureau of Aeronautics, U.S. Naval Technical Mission in Europe (RG 72)
Records of the Foreign Diplomatic Posts (RG 84)
Records of the United States Secret Service (RG 87)
Records of the Office of Strategic Services (RG 226)
Records of the Collection of Foreign Records Seized (RG 242)
Records of the United States Strategic Bombing Survey (RG 243)
Records of the Office of the Military Government, Germany (RG 260)
Records of the Central Intelligence Agency (RG 263)
Records of the Seventh Army, G-2 (RG 407)

FRANKLIN D. ROOSEVELT PRESIDENTIAL LIBRARY (FDRL), Hyde Park, New York
www.fdrlibrary.marist.edu

Papers of Henry Morgenthau Jr., *Morgenthau Diaries* (1938–1945)

UNITED STATES HOLOCAUST MEMORIAL MUSEUM ARCHIVES
www.ushmm.org

Allen A. Cramer Collection
Leo Haas Collection
Samuel Stammer Collection

France
ARCHIVES DE L'OCCUPATION FRANÇAISE EN ALLEMAGNE ET EN AUTRICHE, 1945–1955 (Colmar)
www.diplomatie.gouv.fr/archives/archives_modele/service/inventaires/colmar/colmar.html

Great Britian
BANK OF ENGLAND ARCHIVES (B/E)
www.bankofenglandarchives.co.uk

Administration Department (ADM)
Bank Note Office (BNO)
Chief Cashier's Department (C)
Governors and Secretary's Department (G)
Museum Holdings (M)
Printing Works (PW)

PUBLIC RECORD OFFICE (PRO) (The National Archives, since April 2003)
www.nationalarchives.gov.uk

Foreign Office Papers (FO)
Government Communications Headquarters Papers (HW)
Metropolitan Police Papers (MEPO)
Security Service Papers — MI5 (KV)
Treasury Papers (T)
War Office Papers (WO)

Israel
CENTRAL ZIONIST ARCHIVES — JERUSALEM
http://www.zionistarchives.org.il/ZA/pMainE.aspx

Yad Vashem
www.yadvashem.org/
The Central Database of Shoah Victims' Names

Switzerland
ARCHIVES DU COMITÉ INTERNATIONAL DE LA CROIX-ROUGE (ACICR), GENEVA
www.afz.ethz.ch/handbuch/nara/naraSchweizACICR.htm

Swiss Federal Archives (SFA)
www.bundesarchiv.ch
Swiss Bankers Association (SBA)
www.swissbanking.org/en/home/htm

BOOKS

Aga Rossi, Elena. *A Nation Collapses: The Italian Surrender of September 1943.* Translated by Harvey Fergusson II. Cambridge: Cambridge University Press, 2000.

Alford, Kenneth A., and Theodore P. Savas. *Nazi Millionaires: The Allied Search for Hidden SS Gold.* Havertown, Pa.: Casemate, 2002.

Auckland, Reginald George. *Air-dropped Propaganda Currency.* Stockton-on-Tees: John W. Baker, 1972.

Bauer, Yehuda. *Flight and Rescue: Brichah.* New York: Random House, 1970.

———. *Ha-Berihah.* Tel Aviv: Sifiria Ha'poalim, 1970. Hebrew translation of *Flight and Rescue.*

Blandford, Edmund L. *SS Intelligence: The Nazi Secret Service.* Shrewsbury, England: Airlife, 2000.

Bloom, Murray Teigh. *The Brotherhood of Money: The Secret World of Bank Note Printers.* Port Clinton, Ohio: BNR Press, 1983.

———. *Money of Their Own: The Great Counterfeiters.* New York: Scribner, 1957.

Blum, Howard. *The Brigade.* New York: HarperCollins, 2001.

Breitman, Richard, Norman J. W. Goda, Timothy Naftali, and Robert Wolfe. *U.S. Intelligence and the Nazis.* Washington, D.C.: National Archives Trust Fund Board, 2004.

Burger, Adolf. *Des Teufels Werkstatt: Die Geldfälscherwerkstatt im KZ Sachsenhausen.* Berlin: Neues Leben, 2001. Originally published as *Ďáblova dílna: V padělatelském komandu koncentračního tábora Sachsenhausen.* Prague: Svoboda, 1991.

———. *Unternehmen Bernhard: Die Fälscherwerkstatt im KZ Sachsenhausen.* Berlin: Hentrich, 1992.

Burke, Bryan. *Nazi Counterfeiting of British Currency During World War II: Operation Andrew and Operation Bernhard.* San Bernardino, Calif.: Franklin Press, 1987.

Byatt, Derrick. *Promises to Pay: The First Three Hundred Years of Bank of England Notes.* London: Spink, 1994.

Crankshaw, Edward. *Gestapo: Instrument of Tyranny.* New York: Viking, 1960.

De Fraine, Herbert G. *Servants of This House: Life in the Old Bank of England.* London: Constable [1960].

Dulles, Allen Welsh. *From Hitler's Doorstep: The Wartime Intelligence Reports of Allen Dulles, 1942–1945.* Edited with commentary by Neal H. Petersen. University Park: Pennsylvania State University Press, 1996.

Edel, Peter. *Wenn es ans Leben geht: Meine Geschichte* (When Life Is at Stake: My Story). Berlin: Verlag der Nation, 1979.

Eizenstat, Stuart. *Imperfect Justice: Looted Assets, Slave Labor, and the Unfinished Business of World War II.* New York: Public Affairs, 2003.

Elam, Shraga. *Hitlers Fälscher: Wie jüdische, amerikanische und Schweizer Agenten der SS beim Fälschgeldwaschen halfen.* Vienna: Überreuter, 2000.

Friedman, Towiah. *SS-Obergruppenführer Ernst Kaltenbrunner Chef des Reichs-Sicherheits-Hauptamtes RSHA in Berlin 1943–1945: Eine dokumentarische Sammlung von SS-Dokumenten.* Haifa: Institute of Documentation in Israel, 1995.

Garland, Albert N., and Howard McGaw Smyth, assisted by Martin Blumenson. *Sicily and the Surrender of Italy.* Washington, D.C.: Office of the Chief of Military History, 1965.

Georg, Enno. *Die wirtschaftlichen Unternehmungen der SS.* Stuttgart: Deutsche Verlags-Anstalt, 1963.

Gisevius, Hans Bernd. *Wo ist Nebe? Erinnerungen an Hitlers Reichskriminaldirektor.* Zurich: Droemer, 1966.

Goetz, Samuel. *I Never Saw My Face.* Danbury, Conn.: Rutledge, 2001.

Goñi, Uki. *The Real Odessa: Smuggling the Nazis to Perón's Argentina.* New York: Granta Books, 2002.

Hermann, Cornelia. *Ivan Miassojedoff / Eugen Zotow, 1881–1953. Spuren eines Exils.* Liechtensteinische Staatliche Kunstsammlung, Prof. Eugen Zotow-Ivan Miassojedoff-Stiftung Vaduz. Bern: Benteli, 1997.

Higham, Charles. *Trading with the Enemy: An Exposé of the Nazi-American Money Plot, 1933–1949.* New York: Dell, 1984.

Himmler, Heinrich. *Der Dienstkalender Heinrich Himmlers 1941/42 / im Auftrag der Forschungsstelle für Zeitgeschichte in Hamburg bearbeitet, kommentiert und eingeleitet von Peter Witte . . . [et al.]; mit einem Vorwort von Uwe Lohalm und Wolfgang Scheffler.* Hamburger Beiträge zur Sozial- und Zeitgeschichte 3. Hamburg: Christians, 1999.

Hoettl, Wilhelm. *Die geheime Front: Organisation, Personen und Aktionen des deutschen Geheimdienstes. [von] Walter Hagen.* Linz: Nibelungen, 1950.

———. *Hitler's Paper Weapon.* Translated by Basil Creighton. London: R. Hart-Davis, 1955. Published in Germany in 1955 under Hoettl's pen name, Walter Hagen.

———. *The Secret Front: The Story of Nazi Espionage.* Translated by R. H. Stevens. New York: Praeger, 1954.

———. *Unternehmen Bernhard: Ein historischer Tatsachenbericht über die grösste Geldfälschungsaktion aller Zeiten.* Wels Verlag, 1955.

Höhne, Heinz. *The Order of the Death's Head: The Story of Hitler's SS.* Translated by Richard Barry. London: Penguin, 2000. Published in Germany as *Der Orden unter dem Totenkopf,* Verlag der Spiegel, 1966.

Jörgensen, Christer. *Hitler's Espionage Machine: The True Story Behind One of the World's Most Ruthless Spy Networks.* Guilford, Conn.: Lyons Press, 2004.

Junz, Helen B. "How the Economics of the Holocaust Add" and Appendix S: Report on the Pre-War Wealth Position of the Jewish Population in Nazi-Occupied Countries, Germany and Austria." In *Report on Dormant Accounts of Victims of Nazi Persecution in Swiss Banks* by the Independent Committee of Eminent Persons ["Volcker Commission"]. Bern: Staempfli, 1999.

Kahn, David. *Hitler's Spies: German Military Intelligence in World War II*. New York: Macmillan, 1978.

Kaufman, Michael T. *Soros: The Life and Times of a Messianic Billionaire*. New York: Knopf, 2002.

Keegan, John. *The Second World War*. New York: Viking Penguin, 1990.

Kershaw, Ian. *Hitler: 1936–1945: Nemesis*. New York: Norton, 2000.

Kindleberger, Charles P. *A Financial History of Western Europe*. London: Allen & Unwin, 1984.

Köberl, Markus. *Der Toplitzsee: Wo Geschichte und Sage zusammentreffen*. Vienna: ÖBV, 1990.

Koch, Peter-Ferdinand. *Die Geldgeschäfte der SS: Wie deutsche Banken den schwarzen Terror finanzierten*. Hamburg: Hoffmann & Campe, 2000.

Kors, Ton. *De tocht opnieuw* (The Return Journey). Amsterdam: Van Gennep, 1990.

Krakowski, Avraham, with Avraham Yaakov Finkel. *Counterfeit Lives* (abridged edition). New York: C.I.S., 1995.

Krizental, Ivan Fedorovich. *Operatsiia "Bernhard."* Moscow: Mezhdunarodnye otnosheniia, 1964.

Lamb, Richard. *War in Italy, 1943–45: A Brutal Story*. New York: St. Martin, 1994.

Leith-Ross, Frederick. *Money Talks: Fifty Years of International Finance: The Autobiography of Sir Frederick Leith-Ross*. London: Hutchinson, 1968.

Linklater, Magnus, Isabel Hilton, Neal Ascherson et al. *The Fourth Reich: Klaus Barbie and the Neo-Fascist Connection*. London: Hodder & Stoughton, 1984.

Lovell, Stanley P. *Of Spies and Stratagems*. Englewood Cliffs, N.J.: Prentice-Hall, 1963.

Mader, Julius. *Der Banditenschatz: Ein Dokumentarbericht über Hitlers geheimen Gold- und Waffenschatz*. Berlin: Deutsche Militärverlag, 1965.

Malkin, Lawrence. "John Maynard Keynes." In *The Horizon Book of Makers of Modern Thought*. New York: American Heritage, 1972.

Matteson, Robert Eliot. *The Capture and the Last Days of SS General Ernst Kaltenbrunner: Chief of the Nazi Gestapo, Criminal Police, and Intelligence Services, by Robert E. Matteson, His Captor*. [St. Paul, Minn.: R. E. Matteson, 1993.]

McNally, George J. *"A Million Miles of Presidents": Narrative of Presidential Travels, Truman–Johnson*. Washington: 1600 Communications Association, 1982.

Moyzisch, Ludwig C. *Operation Cicero*. New York: Coward-McCann, 1950.

Nachtstern, Moritz, and Ragnar Arntzen. *Falskmynter i blokk 19*. Oslo: J. G. Tanum, 1949.

Nicholas, Lynn H. *The Rape of Europa: The Fate of Europe's Treasures in the Third Reich and the Second World War*. New York: Knopf, 1994.

Peis, Günter. *The Man Who Started the War*. London: Odhams Press, 1960.

Persico, Joseph E. *Roosevelt's Secret War*. New York: Random House, 2000.

Pirie, Anthony. *Operation Bernhard*. New York: Morrow, 1962.

Pomorin, Jürgen et al. *Blutige Spuren: Der zweite Aufstieg der SS*. Dortmund: Weltkreis-Verlag, 1980.

Pool, James, and Suzanne Pool. *Who Financed Hitler: The Secret Funding of Hitler's Rise to Power, 1919–1933*. New York: Dial, 1978.

Porch, Douglas. *The Path to Victory: The Mediterranean Theater in World War II*. New York: Farrar, Straus & Giroux, 2004.

Rathert, Ronald. *Verbrechen und Verschwörung: Arthur Nebe, der Kripochef des Dritten Reiches*. Münster: Lit, 2001.

Reitlinger, Gerald. *The SS, Alibi of a Nation, 1922–1945*. New York: Viking, 1968. First published 1956 by Heinemann.

Roskill, Stephen Wentworth. *Hankey: Man of Secrets*. 2 vols. London: Collins, 1970–74.

Schellenberg, Walter. *Invasion 1940: The Nazi Invasion Plan for Britain*. London: St. Ermin's Press, 2000.

———. *The Labyrinth: Memoirs*. Translated by Louis Hagen. New York: Harper, 1956. Reprint, New York: Perseus/Da Capo, 2000.

Schwarzwäller, Wulf C. *Hitlers Geld: Vom armen Kunstmaler zum millionenschweren Führer*. Vienna: Überreuter, 1998.

Sem, Julius, and Joseph Mayer. *Report on Forgery in Sachsenhausen Concentration Camp*. Czechoslovak Ministry of the Interior, Central Criminal Office, Secret Report No. U-395/45, December 15, 1945. Translated into English and published by Jørgen Sømod, Copenhagen, 1981.

Shirer, William L. *Berlin Diary: The Journal of a Foreign Correspondent, 1934–1941*. New York: Knopf, 1941.

Skidelsky, Robert. *John Maynard Keynes*. Vol. 2, *The Economist as Saviour, 1920–1937*. Vol. 3, *Fighting for Freedom, 1937–1946*. New York: Viking Penguin, 2000–2001.

Sofsky, Wolfgang. *The Order of Terror: The Concentration Camp*. Translated by William Templer. Princeton, N.J.: Princeton University Press, 1997.

Speer, Albert. *Inside the Third Reich: Memoirs*. New York: Macmillan, 1970.

Spier, Arthur, comp. *The Comparative Hebrew Calendar. Twentieth to Twenty-second Century, 5660–5860, 1900–2100*. New York and Jerusalem: Feldheim, 1986.

Steinbeck, John. *Steinbeck: A Life in Letters*. Edited by Elaine Steinbeck and Robert Wallsten. New York: Viking, 1975.

Taylor, James, and Warren Shaw. *The Penguin Dictionary of the Third Reich*. New York: Penguin, 1997.

Tenenbaum, Joseph E. *Legacy and Redemption: A Life Renewed*. Washington, D.C.: U.S. Holocaust Museum Holocaust Survivors' Memoirs Project, 2005.

Thyssen, Fritz. *I Paid Hitler*. New York: Farrar & Rinehart, 1941.

Weitz, John. *Hitler's Banker: Hjalmar Horace Greeley Schacht*. Boston: Little, Brown, 1997.

West, Nigel. *MI6: British Secret Intelligence Service Operations, 1909–1945*. New York: Random House, 1983.

Wiesenthal, Simon. *Justice, Not Vengeance*. Translated by Ewald Osers. New York: Grove Weidenfeld, 1989.

Wighton, Charles, and Günter Peis. *Hitler's Spies and Saboteurs: Based on the German Secret Service War Diary of General Lahousan*. New York: Holt, 1958.

Wires, Richard. *The Cicero Spy Affair: German Access to British Secrets in World War II*. Westport, Conn.: Praeger, 1999.

JOURNALS

Allen, Charles R., Jr. "The Vatican and the Nazis: Secret La Vista Report Reveals How Barbie and Other Nazi War Criminals Escaped Justice via 'Monastery Routes.'" *Reform Judaism* 11, no. 2 (1983): 4–5.

Bloom, Murray Teigh. "Uncle Sam: Bashful Counterfeiter." *International Journal of Intelligence and Counterintelligence* 2, no. 3 (1988): 345–58.

Bower, Peter. "Operation Bernhard: The German Forgery of British Paper Currency in World War II." *The Exeter Papers: Proceedings of the British Association of Paper Historians Fifth Annual Conference, Hope Hall, University of Exeter, 23–26 September 1994. Studies in British Paper History II* (1994): 43–64. Edited by Peter Bower. London: Plough Press, 2001.

Bradsher, Greg. "A Time to Act: The Beginning of the Fritz Kolbe Story, 1900–1943." *Prologue,* National Archives and Records Administration, 34, no. 1 (Spring 2002).

Braham, Randolph L. "The Nazi Collaborator with a Jewish Heart: The Strange Saga of Jaac van Harten." *East European Quarterly* 35, no. 4 (Winter 2001): 411–34.

[CIA History Staff]. "Wilhelm Hoettl: International Man of Mystery." *Bulletin,* Center for the Study of Intelligence, no. 12 (Fall 2001). www.cia.gov/csi/bulletin/csi12.html#toc8.

Deflem, Mathieu. "The Logic of Nazification: The Case of the International Criminal Police Commissions ('Interpol')." *International Journal of Comparative Sociology* 43, no. 1 (2002): 21–44. www.cas.sc.edu/socy/faculty/deflem/znazinterpol.htm.

Friedman, Herbert A. "British Espionage Forgeries of the First World War." *American Philatelist* 87, no. 9 (September 1973). www.psywarrior.com/BritishForgeriesWWI.html.

———. "Conversations with a Master Forger." *Scott's Monthly Stamp Journal* 61, no. 1 (1980). www.psywar.org/forger.php.

———. "A WW I British Forgery." *International Banknote Society Journal* 25, no. 4 (1986).

Groom, Nick. "Original Copies; Counterfeit Forgeries." *Critical Quarterly* 43, no. 2 (2001): 6–18.

Kallenborn, J. W. "An International Counterfeiting Champion." *International Criminal Police Review,* no. 133 (August–September 1957): 209–18.

———. "A Visit to the Interpol Counterfeits and Forgeries Museum." *International Criminal Police Review,* no. 39 (July 1950): 71–77.

Lengwiler, Yvan. "A Model of Money Counterfeits." *Journal of Economics (Zeitschrift für Nationalokonomie)* 65, no. 2 (1997): 123–32.

Ruffner, Kevin C. "Shifting from Wartime to Peacetime Intelligence Operations: On the Trail of Nazi Counterfeiters (Secret//X1)." Central Intelligence Agency *Studies in Intelligence* 48 (2002): 51–53.

PERIODICALS

Altig, David E. "Why Is Stable Money Such a Big Deal?" *Economic Commentary,* Federal Reserve Bank of Cleveland, May 1, 2002.

Bank of England. *Bank of England Quarterly Bulletin,* June 1967.

"Das Geheimnis um Prof. Zotow: Banknotenfälscher oder Erfinder eines physikalisch-chemischen Verfahrens zum Schutze der Banknoten gegen Fälschungen?" *Schweizer Illustrierte,* January 12, 1949.

Goldin, Milton. "Financing the SS: Nazi Industry, and Plunder of Jewish Assets, Led by Heinrich Himmler." *History Today,* June 1, 1998.

International Criminal Police Organization. *Contrefaçons et falsifications.* Paris, [195?].

———. *International Criminal Police Review.* Saint Cloud [France], September 1946.

Kempner, Robert M. W. "The Highest Paid Spy in History." *Reader's Digest,* June 1950, reprinted from *Saturday Evening Post,* January 28, 1950.

Kruger [*sic*], Bernhard, as told to Murray Teigh Bloom. "I Was the World's Greatest Counterfeiter," *American Weekly,* June 8 and 15, 1958.

Löhde, Wolfgang, and Michael Horbach. "Geld wie Heu." *Der Stern,* August 8, 1959, 18; August 15, 20; August 22, 18; August 29, 22; September 5, 34; September 12, 48; September 19, 46; September 26, 52; October 3, 64; October 10, 56; October 17, 72; October 24, 74; October 31, 64.

McNally, George J., with Frederic Sondern, Jr. "The Great Nazi Counterfeit Plot." *Reader's Digest,* July 1952, 25–31.

Steinbeck, John. "The Secret Weapon We Were AFRAID to Use." *Collier's,* January 10, 1953, 9–13.

DISSERTATION

Delgado, Arturo Raphael. "Counterfeit Reich: Operation Andrew, Operation Bernhard and SS-SD Finance." Master's thesis, Central Missouri State University, 2002.

NEWSPAPERS

England
Daily Express (London)
Daily Mail (London)
Daily Telegraph
Evening Standard (London)
Financial Times (London)
International Herald Tribune
The Sunday Times (London)
The Times (London)

Germany
Frankfurter Rundschau

Israel
Ha'aretz
Jerusalem Post

Switzerland
National Zeitung

United States
Boston Globe
New York Times
Seattle Times
Washington Evening Star
Washington Post
Washington Times-Herald

INTERNET SOURCES

Friedman, Herbert A. "British Forgeries of the Stamps and Banknotes of the Central Power." www.psywarrior.com/BritishForgeriesWWI.html
"The Greatest Theft in History." BBC News, December 1, 1997. news.bbc.co.uk/1/hi/special_report/1997/nazi_gold/35981.stm
Heller, Friedrich Paul. *Die Geschäfte von Friedrich Schwend und Klaus Barbie,* 2001. www.idgr.de/texte/geschichte/ns-taeter/barbie/schwend-barbie.php
Holocaust Through Art (forger Leo Haas). http://art.holocaust-education.net/
ODESSA: Organisation der ehemaligen (oder entlassenen) SS-Angehörigen. http://lexicon.idgr.de/o/o_d/odessa/odessa.php
Schloss Labers. www.labers.it/english/home.htm
Friedrich Schwend. http://lexikon.idgr.de/s/s_c/schwend-friedrich/schwend-friedrich.php

TELEVISION DOCUMENTARIES

The Great Nazi Cash Swindle. Channel 4, London, 2004.
"Hitler's Lake." Scott Pelley, *60 Minutes II,* CBS, 2000. http://www.cbsnews.com/stories/2000/11/21/60II/main251320.shtml
Tauchfahrt in die Vergangenheit: Der Fluch des Toplitzsees (Dive into the Past: The Curse of Lake Toplitz). ZDF, Germany, 2003. http://www.zdf.de/ZDFde/inhalt/16/0,1872,2061456,00.html

APPENDIX

THE FORGERS OF OPERATION BERNHARD

The prisoners of Operation Bernhard are usually listed by numbers copied from the Sachsenhausen Register because, even though the copies contain some duplications and omissions, the list gives the best approximation of the order of their arrival. The list in this appendix was created from the entries into the handwritten Mauthausen Register of Inmates as the surviving 137 men of Operation Bernhard were processed into Mauthausen on April 13, 1945. (NARA RG 242, A-3355 Mauthausen, roll 13, p. 841 et seq.). Insofar as it was possible, the names have been reconciled with the typed Mauthausen card index that can be accessed online via the Yad Vashem Central Database of Shoah Victims' Names (www.yadvashem.org). Most of the cards include the names of family members. Variant spellings, especially in Polish, are retained to facilitate online access and therefore may not match names as spelled in the text of this book, which have been taken mainly from memoirs and official Allied reports. Places of birth and residence as well as citizenship are spelled in this appendix as they are found in the Mauthausen Register. Litzmannstadt, for example, was not converted to Łodz; the citizenship is given, as in the Register, as DR *(Deutsches Reich)* rather than Poland.

The Register lists some prisoners from Austria, France, and the Baltic states as "DR" but when areas of these countries have been incorporated into Hitler's Reich, the original country appears in brackets. Men from Norway and Holland, for example, retain their country of origin. Czechoslovakia had ceased to exist as a nation and was split into the Nazis' Czech Protectorate and the puppet state of Slovakia, just as Yugoslavia was partly dismembered with a puppet regime of Croatia.

The names of five men do not appear in the Mauthausen Register because the men were executed after becoming ill while at Sachsenhausen. These men are believed to have been: (1) Pjotr/Isaak Sukenik/Sukiennik, a young man from Białystok who contracted tuberculosis and was murdered about February 15, 1945; (2) Jizchok Fingerut; (3) Abraham Kleinfeld of Vienna; (4) Ernest/Arnost Stastny of Brno; and (5) Heinrich Sonnenthal (b. 1920). A sixth man, Herman Gütig, was executed for burning pound notes in Block 18/19. The last prisoner to be executed for illness, Karl Sussman of Vienna, does appear in the Register because he was not murdered until May 1, 1945, two weeks after his registration. Most have calculated 144 as the total number of prisoners who passed through Block 19, but it is likely that Sussman was counted twice, which would make the total 143, although the precise number will probably never be known.

	Sachsenhausen number	Mauthausen number	Surname	First name	Birth year	Month/day	Place of birth/residence	Citizenship/nationality	Profession
1	14898	138410	Cytrin	Feiwel [Felix]	1894	5/6	Frankfurt / Leipzig	DR	toolmaker
2	23768	138526	Wilde	Samuel	1919	1/16	Warsaw	Poland	calligrapher
3	43811	138503	Speier	Walther	1893	4/27	Berlin	DR	electrician
4	46674	138480	Plapla [Papler]	Isaak [Jack]	1919	11/11	Grifte / Kassel	stateless	calligrapher
5	46674 [sic]	138481	Pick	Alfred	1906	10/12	Domazlice	Czech	dental technician
6	46675	138446	Kohn	Georg	1901	2/3	Reisen Lissa / Alt-Chemnitz	DR [Latvia]	merchant
7	46676	138426	Gottlieb	Ernst	1907	8/28	Wien	DR [Austria]	wallpaperer / upholsterer
8	46678	138482	Perkal	Chaim	1912	3/10	Lomza	Poland	printer
9	46680	138443	Kaufmann	Jaroslav	1901	1/19	Husova	Czech	dentist
10	46681	138450	Krebs	Leo	1910	11/17	Beuthen (Bytom)	DR [Austria]	printer / painter
11	46834	138461	Lewin	Arthur	1888	7/31	Berlin	DR	printer
12	46837	138469	Luka	Richard	1913	10/30	Milan (Italy) / Prague	Czech	architectural engineer
13	46840	138456	Lauber	Jakob	1906	9/1	Krakow	Poland	draftsman
14	46842	138524	Weissmann	Friedrich	1901	5/11	Plumacz	stateless	typesetter
15	46845	138424	Goldberg	Chias Aron	1909	1/8	Tarnoczeg / Berlin	stateless	bookbinder / printer
16	46848	138519	Tupler	Artur	1890	6/10	Nova Ves / Hodenova	Czech	bricklayer
17	46850	138462	Lewinski	Kurt	1908	3/17	Kulmsee / Berlin	DR	calligrapher
18	46852	138414	Ehrlich	Leib	1905	4/28	Osiek / Warsaw	Poland	printer
19	46853	138453	Kurzweil	Hans	1908	7/1	Wien	DR [Austria]	bookbinder
20	46855	138405	Bober	Hermann Max	1896	5/1	Berlin	DR	printer & typesetter
21	47140	136422	Gecht	Joszip	1918	9/1	Suchumi [Georgia] / Piatakowa	USSR	[unknown]
22	47148	138532	Zessarski[y]	Matej	1914	12/22	Owrutsch / Owrucz	USSR [Poland]	electrical machinist
23	47832	138513	Stein / Skala	Oskar	1902	8/5	Tabor / Klofacova	Czech	paper specialist
24	48854	138514	Steiner	Viktor Karl	1907	8/13	Wien	DR [Austria]	bookbinder
25	51110	138517	Tragholz	Felix	1908	12/1	Wien	DR [Austria]	offsetter / tinsmith

	Sachsenhausen number	Mauthausen number	Surname	First name	Birth year	Month/ day	Place of birth/ residence	Citizenship/ nationality	Profession
26	51316	138505	Springer	Artur	1888	3/4	Wien / Belgrade	DR[Austria]	industrialist / paper
27	61113	138402	Blaustein	Max	1904	5/6	Berlin	DR	printer
28	61117	138415	Epsztejn	Lejba	1903	6/18	Paris	Poland	writer / typographer
29	61120	138509	Schnapper	Friedrich [Fritz]	1893	12/18	Frankfurt am Main	DR	printer
30	61125	136423	Glanzer	Isaak / Israel	1899	8/22	Zborov / Nagyvarad	Czech	print shop owner
31	61127	138473	Nachtstern	Moritz	1902	11/11	Warsaw / Oslo	Norway	stereotypist
32	61129	138535	Zymerman	Persc	1919	4/5	Radom	Poland	printer
33	61136	138466	Libermann	Josef	1914	10/20	Piotrkow / Mlawa	Poland	printer
34	61138	138510	Schurek	Chaim	1915	3/10	Straygowo / Mlawa	Poland	[unknown]
35	67175	138530	Zakrzewski	Nachum [Nachim]	1926	1/19	Bialystok	USSR [Poland]	printer
36	67865	138516	Tiefenbach	Severin	1919	3/22	Leslaw / Litzmannstadt	Poland	engraver
37	67866	138436	Italiener	Leib	1915	7/27	Litzmannstadt	Poland	engraver
38	67867	138448	Kosak	Mojsche / Mosjek	1904	5/25	Bialystok	USSR [Poland]	typesetter
39	67868	138439	Jablocznik	Noach	1901	10/18	Litzmannstadt	Poland	printer
40	67869	138533	Zyberski	Leib	1892	7/5	Grajewo / Bialystok	USSR [Poland]	engraver
41	67870	138447	Kosak	Hirsch	1897	12/12	Bialystok	USSR [Poland]	typesetter
42	67871	138485	Rapoport	Towiec	1903	11/12	Litzmannstadt	Poland	printer
43	67873	138413	Edelsburg	Nuchim	1907	4/14	Minsk Mazowiecki / Litzmannstadt	Poland	printer
44	67874	138479	Plac	Chiel	1885	3/12	Belsk / Bialystok	USSR [Poland]	painter
45	68061	138476	Nieft	Horst	1920	5/23	Berlin	DR	decorator
46	68064	138475	Nieft	Gerhard	1917	7/7	Berlin	DR	retailer
47	72515	138425	Goldglas	Jakob	1911	1/22	Warsaw	Poland	lawyer / carpenter
48	73099	138435	Hoffgaard	Sven	1895	9/8	Copenhagen / Hellerup	Denmark	bank officer
49	73351	138463	Lewy [Leonard]	Norbert Wilhelm	1913	3/30	Berlin	DR	photographer

	Sachsenhausen number	Mauthausen number	Surname	First name	Birth year	Month/day	Place of birth/residence	Citizenship/nationality	Profession
50	75191	138489	Rozencwajg	Jakob	1898	12/22	Praszka / Bendsburg	Poland	office worker
51	75192	138417	Fajerman	Symcha	1915	1/20	Bendsburg	Poland	industrial technician
52	75192 [sic]	138432	Hirschweh [Edel]	Peter Hans	1921	7/12	Berlin	DR	painter
53	75193	138430	Hahn	Victor	1899	8/21	Prague	Czech	bank officer
54	75194	138434	Holländer	Feiwel	1908	8/19	Dombrowa / Sosnowitz	Poland	machine-builder
55	75195	138444	Klein	Arthur	1907	4/25	Königsberg / Lubisska	Czech	electrician
56	75196	138525	Werdigier	Szyia	1908	3/4	Sosnowitz	Poland	[unknown]
57	75197	138427	Gottlieb	Moric [Karel]	1917	5/24	Kaschau / Prague	Czech	carpenter
58	75198	138418	Fajman	Icek	1919	3/2	Warthenau / Bendsburg	Poland	tailor
59	75199	138520	Walter	Heinzel Hans	1921	12/14	Berlin	DR	laborer
60	75200	138438	Jakobsen	Abraham	1895	2/8	Amsterdam / Overseen	Netherlands	print shop manager
61	75204	138454	Landau	Paul	1922	8/5	Warsaw	France	carpenter
62	75205	138412	Drechsler	Georg	1913	4/8	Varazdin	Croatia	bookkeeper
63	75206	138399	Ajdels	Bernard	1911	12/26	Radom	Poland	office worker
64	75206 [sic]	138408	Burday	Josef	1904	12/21	Talnose	France	tailor
65	75207	138512	Stein	Max	1899	8/22	Wien / Prague	stateless	weaver
66	75208	138471	Markus	Mordke	1909	5/11	Slawkow	Poland	carver
67	75210	138452	Kühnauer	Rudolf Leopold	1906	4/4	Berlin	DR	lithographer
68	75211	138449	Krakowski	Abram	1918	9/9	Katowicz / Sosnowitz	Poland	bookkeeper
69	75212	138437	Iwanowicz	Rubin (Rywen)	1901	11/25	Lubraniec / Brzesc Kujawski	Poland	bookkeeper
70	75213	138406	Bosboom	Andries	1913	6/26	Amsterdam	Netherlands	lithographer
71	75214	138495	Salomon	Berek	1903	2/5	Bendsburg	Poland	bookkeeper
72	75216	138416	Fajerman	Heinrich	1905	3/29	Bendsburg	Poland	locksmith
73	75217	138428	Groen	Louis Mayer [Max]	1918	1/25	Amsterdam	Netherlands	newsreel cameraman

	Sachsenhausen number	Mauthausen number	Surname	First name	Birth year	Month/day	Place of birth/residence	Citizenship/nationality	Profession
74	75220	138431	Heitler	Chil	1911	5/6	Pinerow / Krakow	Poland	bookbinder / printer
75	75221	138401	Blass	Hans	1907	12/1	Wien / Fleurance	DR [Austria]	factory worker
76	75222	138534	Zylberberg	Chaim	1900	9/26	Janou / Bendsburg	Poland	laborer
77	75223	138483	Van Praag	Moses	1910	5/3	Amsterdam	Netherlands	[unknown]
78	75224	138445	Knock	Samuel / Overveen	1901	1/16	Amsterdam / Grandelaan	Netherlands	photographer
79	75225	138465	Lewkowicz	Szlama	1909	12/30	Wartheim / Zawiercie	Poland	bookkeeper / lithographer
80	75226	138457	Lehrhaft	Leon	1903	8/6	Krakow / Sosnowitz	Poland	bookbinder
81	75227	138433	Holländer	Chaim	1908	4/20	Dombrowa / Sosnowitz	Poland	painter / worker
82	75228	138487	Rojzen	Baruch [Boris]	1907	6/3	Ryzyszcze / Lemberg	Poland	physician
83	75229	138470	Marianka	David	1897	10/20	Sosnowitz	Poland	woodworker
84	75231	138518	Tuchmajer	Mordka	1914	5/14	Ilkenau / Sosnowitz	Poland	printer
85	75232	138458	Lehrhaft	Leonard	1924	10/23	Auschwitz / Sosnowitz	Poland	bookbinder
86	75233	138455	Laskier	Jakob	1900	8/7	Bendsburg	Poland	office worker
87	75233 [sic]	138486	Reis	Josef	1915	11/27	Krakow / Bochnia	Poland	painter / accountant
88	75234	138528	Wulfowicz	Max	1899	9/20	Kielce	stateless	locksmith
89	75235	138472	Milikowski	(Filip) Herman	1909	3/3	Den Haag / Amsterdam	stateless	teacher
90	75236	138484	Rajzner	Rafail	1904	1/15	Choroszcz / Bialystok	Poland	calligrapher
91	75238	138515	Stolowicz	Harry	1916	10/10	Warsaw / Belgium	Poland	truck driver
92	75239	138529	Zauberman	Fajwel (Felix)	1917	6/29	Radomsko / Bendsburg	Poland	[unknown]
93	75240	138400	Aron	Samuel	1902	6/28	Ulanow / Brussels	stateless	technician
94	75241	138459	Leibsohn	Chaim Karl	1919	8/6	Warsaw / Algiers	stateless	[unknown]
95	75242	138464	Lewkowicz	Simon	1917	3/19	Auschwitz	Poland	[unknown]
96	75243	138411	Domankiewicz	Wolf	1906	1/20	Litzmannstadt	Poland	carpenter
97	75244	138451	Krzepicki	Mosjek	1919	10/25	Krzepice / Litzmannstadt	Poland	[unknown]
98	75245	138507	Sussmann	Karl	1908	6/21	Wien	DR [Austria]	fashion artist

	Sachsenhausen number	Mauthausen number	Surname	First name	Birth year	Month/day	Place of birth/residence	Citizenship/nationality	Profession
99	75246	138504	Spenadl	Herbert Jarolim	1920	11/4	Wien	DR [Austria]	barber
100	75247	138478	Obler	Walter	1906	2/2	Berlin / Vienna III	DR	master machinist
101	75248	138511	Stammer	Samuel	1907	7/5	Dornfeld / Miedzyrzec	Poland	watchmaker
102	75249	138442	Jura	Wolf	1905	1/15	Bendsburg	Poland	bookbinder
103	75250	138488	Rozenberger	Mendel	1905	5/17	Bendsburg	Poland	bookbinder
104	76677	138531	Zeichmer	Chaim	1896	1/8	Kolomen / Vienna	stateless	carpenter
105	79100	138496	Salzer	Hermann	1912	11/16	Kiraly XB / Prague	Czech	engineer
106	79158	148508	Schipper	Ascher	1915	1/9	Jaroslau / Warsaw	Poland	printer
107	79159	136421	Gafne	Laib	1906	1/15	Bendsburg	Poland	printing machinist
108	79161	138409	Burger	Adolf/Adolph	1917	12/8	Bratislava / Velka Lomnica	Slovakia	printer
109	79163	138404	Bier	Eduard	1910	10/6	Bialowar / Zagreb	Croatia	chemical engineer
110	79165	138468	Lubetzki	David	1905	3/15	Wasiliski / Bendsburg	Poland	printer
111	79166	138521	Weill	Roger	1920	5/23	Bischheim / Drancy	France	photograveur
112	93594	138498	Smolianoff	Salomon	1887	3/26	Poltava / Berlin	stateless	painter / professional counterfeiter
113	102347	138477	Nyul	Ernö	1908	5/25	Bercttyc Reprod /	Hungary	canvas printer
114	102431	138492	Rubinstein	Ladislaus	1909	2/23	Grosswardein	Hungary	printer
115	102433	138490	Rubinstein	Alexander	1914	9/3	Grosswardein	Hungary	bookbinder
116	102434	138494	Rusznak	Henrik (Rezsö)	1891	7/7	Reprod / Lewa	Hungary	typographer
117	102438	138497	Selmann	Rudolf	1894	1/18	Temeszvar / Budapest	Hungary	[unknown]
118	102439	138419	Frenkel	David	1893	10/20	Marmaros-Sziget / Pesztujhely	Hungary	phototypist
119	102440	138523	Weisz	Henrik	1885	1/7	Budapest	Hungary	printer
120	102441	138420	Fried	Lejb	1902	12/24	Chelm / Litzmannstadt	Poland	engraver
121	102442	138506	Sugar	Izso	1886	9/5	Budapest	Hungary	printer

Sachsenhausen number	Mauthausen number	Surname	First name	Birth year	Month/day	Place of birth/residence	Citizenship/nationality	Profession
122 102443	138500	Sonnenfeld	Andreas	1896	11/18	Grosswardein	Hungary	lithographer
123 102444	138499	Somos	Stefan	1911	1/11	Budapest	Hungary	photographer
124 102445	138403	Bialer	David Israel	1908	1/1	Litzmannstadt	Poland	engraver
125 102446	138502	Sonnenfeld	Stephan	1924	12/23	Grosswardein	Hungary	lithographer
126 118029	138429	Haas	Leopold	1901	4/15	Opava / Ostrava	Czech	painter/graphic artist
127 ????	138474	Nejman	Max	1922	2/25	Brussels	Poland	draftsman
128 [102445]	138501	Sonnenfeld	Gustav	1895	12/21	Grosswardein / Nagyvarad	Hungary	lithographer
129 10243?	138491	Rubinstein	Zoltan	1913	3/28	Grosswardein	Hungary	printer
130 10243?	138522	Weisz	Bela	1891	11/29	Budapest	Hungary	printer
131 7521?	138467	Löwi	Mendel	1908	9/16	Zegocina / Bochnia	Poland	[unknown]
132	138407	Braschewitzki	Leon	1923	6/15	Paris	France	optician
133	138440	Jenöi	Lancz	1900	6/17	[unknown]	Hungary	printer
134	138441	Jilovsky	Georg	1884	3/15	Prague	Czech	painter
135	138460	Lenthal	Hans	1914	12/18	Wien / Paris	DR [Austria]	art restorer
136	138493	Rudoler	Jochim	1912	2/28	Bendsburg	Poland	printer
137	138527	Wajskop	Max	1909	1/18	Tomasjow	Poland	printer

A NOTE ON SOURCES

LAWRENCE MALKIN AND MARGARET SHANNON

The Nazi counterfeiting scheme has been public knowledge since newspaper accounts began appearing during the last months of World War II. Its enormity soon became evident as experts followed Allied troops to assess the danger to U.S. currency as well as the damage to British finance. Since then, the story has become as barnacled in myth as the sunken German warship *Bismarck*. Too many details descend from overheated, secondhand, and often self-promoting accounts circulated by officials who tracked the counterfeits, treasure hunters, imaginative journalists, East German propagandists, and even former Nazis peddling their own versions. Many have made their way onto the Internet as fact. One British writer claimed in 1961 that "most of the story's protagonists are dead," although they were not. He declared he had therefore "imaginatively reconstructed" some unrecorded events. Unfortunately, he neglected to distinguish between events that were fact and those that were imagination. This book represents our best efforts to scrape away the barnacles of such myths by telling a tale whose essential fascination is enhanced by being true.

The success of Operation Bernhard depended on secrecy, and that alone kept German records sparse. The SS also wanted all traces buried (or murdered). Our sources are primarily diplomatic cable traffic and contemporaneous documents of the investigations conducted by Allied intelligence officers, currency specialists, and officers of Scotland Yard's counterfeit division. Their reports were based heavily on interviews with the prisoners that were conducted within weeks or months of their escape. The prisoners' own drama unfolds mainly through memoirs, most of which were unknown or simply ignored by earlier writers. None was more valuable than *Falskmynter i blokk 19,* by Moritz Nachtstern and Ragnar Arntzen, published in Oslo in 1949. This virtually forgotten book was discovered on the Internet by Margaret Shannon with the help of the remnants of the Norwegian language she picked up during her childhood years in Oslo. We thank Anne Synnevaag of Norwegian Public Radio for obtaining permission from Nachtstern's son Jan to quote from an English translation. She also led us to his daughter Sidsel, who explained how he wrote the book, which is being published in Norwegian in 2006.

Another important source was the fragments of Bernhard Krueger's reminiscences, principally via interviews with Murray Teigh Bloom, whose own meticulous investigation was the first by an American writer. His fascination with our discoveries was undiminished by his age (approaching ninety), and his support and assistance for this project never wavered even when it disproved his own account of Salomon Smolianoff's role as Krueger's principal forger of sterling.

The author, Lawrence Malkin, has known the outlines of this story since he began reporting on finance from London in the 1960s. Margaret Shannon, senior research historian of Washington Historical Research, was the associate producer and principal researcher of an effort begun in the late 1990s to locate and return Nazi assets believed to have been looted and dumped in the Toplitzsee. It was financed by the Simon Wiesenthal Center and the Columbia Broadcasting System, and we are grateful to Rabbi Marvin Hier, dean and founder of the center, for permission to draw on Shannon's research. In 2002 Malkin was referred to her by Wayne deCesar, the U.S. National Archives specialist in the records of the U.S. Secret Service, which is the principal anticounterfeiting agency of the United States.

Thereupon followed three years of collaborative research, with Shannon principally uncovering official correspondence and reports, cables, intercepts, letters, diaries, film footage, captured documents, transcripts of interrogations, and photographs in various archives. Many of these documents have been available for thirty years to researchers willing to look for them. Others have been declassified only recently. Under the U.S. thirty-year rule, most OSS documents were not systematically reviewed for declassification until 1976, well after the first accounts of Operation Bernhard had been written. Only in the first years of this century did the CIA declassify its files on Wilhelm Hoettl, Friedrich Schwend, and Georg Spitz. The timing was fortunate for this book and is the direct result of the Nazi War Crimes Disclosure Act of 1998, which requires all U.S. federal agencies to identify and declassify records related to Nazi war crimes. More than 8 million pages of documents were declassified, some directly related to Operation Bernhard.

Missing from the U.S. Secret Service archives, however, is File CO 12,600, which contained the voluminous Secret Service master files on Operation Bernhard. Bloom was allowed to view the files privately at the U.S. Treasury and referred to them in his writing as "The Amstein Report" after André Amstein, the chief of Switzerland's anticounterfeit police and his country's representative to Interpol. According to the U.S. Secret Service archivist Michael Sampson, File CO 12,600 was "destroyed in a routine purge." Herr Amstein, a lawyer in private practice in Bern, wrote in 2002 refusing an interview on the grounds that he was an old man, remembered little, and had no documents from the period. This made it necessary to reconstruct the contents through archival research.

Among captured German records at the National Archives in Washington is one invaluable document: the 1942 and 1943 telephone directories of the RSHA, which helpfully list the division, building, and room number for its employees. By extrapolating from the names of those who worked in Amt VI F, we were able to confirm the identities of those who worked in the counterfeiting operation, its chain of command, and even who worked in what office. (Have you ever wondered why the Pentagon telephone book is classified?)

*　　*　　*

We have already singled out several people who contributed heavily to our research, but they are far from the only ones who have made this book possible. Our most essential guide was the historian and archivist Robert Wolfe, who for more than thirty years was chief of captured German records at the U.S. National Archives. Although officially retired in 1995, Wolfe remains actively engaged with documents covering German and Japanese war crimes. As a National Archives volunteer with Top Secret clearance, he has repeatedly given us wise and generous counsel about documents, and candid assessments of the credibility of many of the personalities, living and dead, who figure in this book.

At the Bank of England, the newly appointed archivist Sarah Millard and her staff helped breathe fresh air into this history by showing us files whose existence at the Bank had simply been denied by her predecessor. The British National Archives at Kew is a researcher's dream, computerized and efficient in delivery; we regret that its staff remained as anonymous as it was unfailingly helpful and courteous. Tim Hughes, a professional researcher based in nearby Twickenham, initiated us into the rules and procedures during a two-week research visit in 2003. Meanwhile, Professor Alan Milward, economic historian at the British Cabinet Office, helped point the author toward essential Treasury files.

At the U.S. National Archives, we are deeply grateful for the assistance in our search of intelligence and military records of Timothy K. Nenninger, Lawrence H. McDonald, and the legendary John E. Taylor. Among the archivists and historians overseeing civilian records, we thank Milton Gustafson, diplomatic historian, and Greg Bradsher, director of the Holocaust-Era Assets Records Project. Wayne deCesar cheerfully made repeated searches in the compressed shelving that houses the U.S. Secret Service records. In the microfilm reading room, we benefited enormously from the diligence of a former archivist, Neils Cordes, who unearthed Smolianoff's Mauthausen record and conclusively established the date of his transfer to Sachsenhausen. Edward Barnes, Elizabeth Lipford, and Louis "Smitty" Smith located records in places they were not supposed to be. John Fox, newly appointed historian of the Federal Bureau of Investigation, and Michael Sampson, archivist/historian of the U.S. Secret Service, went beyond the call of duty to assist us. At the Franklin D. Roosevelt Presidential Library, which is part of the National Archives, Robert Clarke took great pains to locate John Steinbeck's correspondence and to find pages in the voluminous *Morgenthau Diaries*. Susan Shillinglaw, director of the Steinbeck Center of San Jose State University, helped us find further traces of Steinbeck's encounters with FDR.

Fiona Fleck, an intrepid journalist based in Geneva and friend of the author's family, navigated the shoals of the Swiss bureaucracy with the invaluable help of Ruth Stalder of the Swiss Federal Archives in Bern and Claudia Wassmer, a lawyer for the Swiss police (Bundesamt für Polizei), who released in a most unbureaucratic manner some documents that might otherwise have remained sealed for several more years.

Batya Leshem of the Central Zionist Archives did research we could not do ourselves without a trip to Jerusalem. Hans Coppi of Berlin carefully conducted the author on a tour through the remains of the Sachsenhausen concentration camp, now a museum, and Winfried Meyer, then the museum's director, provided valuable leads.

The author also acknowledges — and can never sufficiently thank — the assistance of a number of friends and colleagues in breaking down inevitable bureaucratic barriers or providing advice and information when needed, often on short notice. Chief among them is Sir Derek Mitchell, formerly director of overseas finance for Her Majesty's Treasury, who has supported this project from its inception. So has David Kahn, dean of American cryptographic historians, whose invaluable assistance continued right through to a careful reading of the manuscript, which was also checked by Andrea Merrill. Others are Paul A. Volcker, Michael Bradfield, Stuart Eizenstat, Peter Jay, Yuval Elizur, Curtis Roosevelt, Shareen Brysac, Sanford Lieberson, William McCahill, Robert Wernick, the German writer Melissa Mueller, James Nason of the Swiss Bankers Association, Michael Rose of Interpol, Nathalie Moreau of the Colmar Archives, Nadine Coleman of Paris, Anne Makkinje of Amsterdam, Peter Bakstansky of the Federal Reserve Bank of New York, and Michael T. Kaufman and Michael Vachon, respectively the biographer and the spokesman of the financier George Soros. Ingeborg Wolfe, Jaakov Lind, Toby Molenaar, and Tina Vogel assisted with translations.

Finally, no book is ever realized without unseen hands that hold and shape it. Lianne Kolf of Munich, the author's European agent and summer neighbor, nurtured and stood by him when others had deserted the project; she staunchly continues to do so. The author's friends, his American agent, Thomas C. Wallace, and his lawyer Louis Atlas, defended this project against all who would stop it. The author's wife, Edith, closer to the subject of wartime survival than most, nobly endured her husband's entangling obsessions. Helmut Ettinger, the book's German translator, served as a meticulous guarantor of accuracy and quality, and the author thanks his German editor, Elmar Klupsch, for generously providing his services and much else. Likewise Peggy Freudenthal, Little, Brown's chief copyeditor, who saw this book and its complex scholarly impedimenta to press with meticulous skill and great charm. Geoff Shandler, editor in chief at Little, Brown, a colleague on several previous books, and a valued friend, offered imaginative structural advice and meticulous textual skill of a kind that has almost vanished from today's publishing world but, as long as he practices his craft, will continue to enrich the lives of authors and readers alike.

March 2006

INDEX

In his long career as a journalist, Lawrence Malkin was the European correspondent of *Time* magazine and New York correspondent for the *International Herald Tribune*. He has collaborated on the memoirs of Paul Volcker, Anatoly Dobrynin, Markus Wolf, and Stuart Eizenstat. His work has also appeared in the *Atlantic Monthly, Fortune, Connoisseur, The Times Literary Supplement,* and many other magazines. He lives in New York with his wife.

For more about *Krueger's Men* and to view the secret documents, please visit www.lawrencemalkin.com.